IDEALISM DEBASED

Idealism Debased

FROM *VÖLKISCH* IDEOLOGY
TO NATIONAL SOCIALISM

Roderick Stackelberg

The Kent State University Press

Library of Congress Cataloging in Publication Data
Stackelberg, Roderick.
  Idealism debased.

  Originally presented as the author's thesis, University of Massachusetts.
  Bibliography: p.
  Includes index.
  1. Germany—Intellectual life. 2. Idealism—History. 3. Nationalism—
Germany—History. 4. Racism—Germany—History. 5. National socialism
—History. 6. Germany—Politics and government—19th century. I. Title.
II. Title: From völkisch ideology to national socialism.
DD61.8.S72 1981   320.5′33   80-84663
ISBN 0-87338-252-8

For Trina and Nicky

CONTENTS

PREFACE

We have in this country seen at least two periods of, shall we say, "visionism" in German leaders—Kaiser Wilhelm II and the second one much worse. . . . Germans have an enormous capability for idealism and the perversion of it.

Chancellor Helmut Schmidt,
N.Y. Times Magazine, September 21, 1980

This study explores the insidious complex of traits that made *völkisch* ideology so seductive to generations of middle-class Germans.* This ideology, it is sometimes forgotten, was an outgrowth, albeit deformed, of the same venerable tradition of idealism that inspired some of Germany's greatest artistic and literary works. *Idealism* is used throughout this study not so much in its conventional meaning—the pursuit of a standard of perfection—but rather in its philosophical definition of the doctrine that gives primacy to spirit over matter and explains the world in spiritual terms. But even more importantly, idealism expressed the practical urge and obligation, so strong in the German tradition, to regenerate reality and transform humanity by infusing existence with timeless moral and spiritual ideals. This attitude, inherited from the glorious age of German letters in the eighteenth and nineteenth centuries and from a much older religious tradition, came to be vulgarized, wittingly and unwittingly, for political purposes. By dismissing material aspirations and rational self-interest as base, cowardly, and unworthy of human purpose, conservative publicists of neo-idealism gained popular acquiescence in the social and political status quo.

The biographical method used by Fritz Stern in *The Politics of Cultural Despair* served as the model for the present study. My interpretive emphasis is somewhat different, however. Stern's title implies that the ultimately pernicious quality in Germanic ideology lay in its destructive criticism of the Bismarckian and Wilhelmine regimes, both of which, for all their faults, tended to promote (or at least accommodate to) gradual modernization. My emphasis is less on the radicalism of *völkisch* thinkers than on their essential conservatism. If *The Politics of Cultural Despair* warns against

---

* The term *völkisch*, derived from *Volk*, the German word for a people, combines the meanings of populist, nationalist, and racialist.

prophets of doom, this book warns against the apologists of power. The lines are not so clearcut as this juxtaposition suggests, of course, for Stern is as critical of aristocratic conservatism as I am of utopian radicalism. But while Lagarde, Langbehn, and Möller van den Bruck emerge in Stern's treatment primarily as disgruntled outsiders, the three protagonists of this study—the Wagnerian Heinrich von Stein, the novelist Friedrich Lienhard, and the racialist Houston Stewart Chamberlain—seem more securely a part of the existing order, a social order they wished to make impervious to the democratizing and modernizing process of change.

This study is offered as a contribution to the continuing debate about the relationship of National Socialism to earlier German history. The link established in this book between the desire of *völkisch* thinkers to save the values and institutions of autocratic monarchism and their later receptivity to fascism or Nazism is dramatically illustrated by Chamberlain's close association with both William II and Hitler. Perhaps one reason that no biography of Chamberlain has been published since the war despite his acknowledged influence is because his career undercuts the assumption that there was little continuity between Wilhelmine imperialism and National Socialism.* Placing Nazism in the context of a more general defense against—even assault on—liberalism, socialism, and democracy, with roots in the nineteenth century, has a doubly unsettling effect: first, such an approach seems to tar nineteenth-century conservatives with the Nazi brush by relating their antidemocratic attitudes to the rise of twentieth-century fascism; and second, it may appear to exculpate Nazis to some degree, because they championed attitudes that respectable conservatives shared. These are hazards that cannot be avoided. The historian's task is to account for events without resort to demonology. It is my view that Nazism cannot be properly understood if its idealist component is overlooked. It is better to recognize the complex and dialectical nature of National Socialism, a movement that attracted high-minded people as well as criminals and brutes, than simply and conveniently to divide the world into villains and saints.

Although this study traces a connection between a major strand of Wilhelmine ideology and National Socialism, there is no attempt here to establish a causal link between *völkisch* thought and Nazism. Although it would not be difficult to show that Chamberlain, for instance, exercised

---

* There have been two dissertations on Chamberlain: Geoffrey G. Field, "Houston Stewart Chamberlain: Prophet of Bayreuth" (Ph.D. diss., Columbia University, 1972), and Donald E. Thomas, Jr., "Idealism, Romanticism, and Race: The *Weltanschauung* of Houston Stewart Chamberlain" (Ph.D. diss., University of Chicago, 1971). An expanded version of the Field dissertation, which traces Chamberlain's career up to 1914, will be published by Columbia University Press in 1981.

considerable influence upon important Nazis (a case inevitably much harder to make with Stein, who died in 1887, or Lienhard, who appealed to a more popular audience), it is not my intention to seek culprits to absorb the blame for the events that occurred in Germany between 1933 and 1945. Intellectual history can never explain historical causation, for ideas alone do not cause events. The problems of historical causation and the relationship of ideology to power are far too complex to be so easily solved. One reason the search for the "intellectual origins" of Nazism has fallen into a certain disrepute is because too often authors have posited a direct causal connection between nineteenth-century thinkers and Nazism and have seen proto-Nazis in every major German intellectual figure.

The usefulness of intellectual history, however, lies in helping later generations understand the mentality, the value systems, the ideologies of a particular age, society, or social group. A study of ideologies, themselves the product of social conditions, can in turn tell us something about the institutional organization, the social structure, and the political direction of a society. Since it is the business of intellectuals to articulate the concerns of their time (or to dissent from those dominant views), a study of their ideas can shed light on the meaning of events even if it cannot explain the causation of events. Intellectual history illuminates historical events by reconstructing the ideological climate in which these events occurred. Biographical details, while unimportant in themselves, can sometimes convey the temper of the times more effectively than generalized description.

I have treated the protagonists of this study not as proto-Nazis, then, but as children of their own age, representative publicists who articulated the world view of an important segment of Wilhelmine society. But their propagation of ideas and attitudes that would become official policy under Nazi rule *is* of historical significance, for it helps us to understand how and why ideas that today are discredited could gain acceptance under the conditions of an earlier age. Nazism was itself a belated and extreme manifestation of that widespread maladjustment to modernization for which there is so much evidence in the works of nineteenth-century European intellectuals. We understand Nazism better by examining the history of the ideas and attitudes it inherited.

Intellectual history is also instructive because the passage of time reveals hypocrisies and anomalies of which an earlier age may have been largely unaware. It is highly important to appreciate the damage that can be done in the name of high-sounding ideals and moral values. *Völkisch* idealism provides a classic example of the perversion of ideas that at one time seemed to epitomize respectability and virtue. As Edmund Burke said, the problem in history is to understand why *good* men do evil. Presenting *völkisch* ideas in caricature, as some earlier works on *völkisch* ideology tend to do, leaves the reader to wonder how any sane person could ever have adopted them. Yet in its own terms *völkisch* idealism did provide a plausible explanation of history and society. I have therefore tried to present *völkisch* ideas, if not sympathetically, at least seriously. They were taken seriously when they first appeared, and their very respectability generated widespread, uncritical support.

It is no easy task to present a discredited ideology credibly without at the same time making it seem creditable. One of the reasons I chose Stein as one of the subjects of my study is that he was a person of unquestionable moral standards, a "genuine" idealist. This choice proved fortunate insofar as his relations with Nietzsche, the great unmasker of hypocrisy and self-deception, offered a promising vehicle for exposing the self-deception and self-congratulation of *völkisch* thought. This does not mean that *völkisch* ideas caused Nazi crimes. But they served to conceal the nihilistic potential within German society (as well as its social inequities) in a way that later brought unfortunate consequences.

If this study offers any lesson, it is that idealism can harbor political dangers by obscuring social problems and inequities, which, because they remain unresolved, later rend the social fabric with explosive power. By denying or concealing the role of self-interest in human motivation, idealism (like religious fanaticism) can breed hypocrisy and lend itself to cynical manipulation for political purposes. Yet there is a dialectic operative here, too, which should caution us against the opposite extreme of condemning idealism per se. For throughout the ages idealism, in its original sense, has inspired creativity as well as service to others. When, however, it degenerates into anti-intellectualism or becomes a program designed, whether deliberately or not, to prevent the rational solution of social problems or the more equitable distribution of material benefits, then the consequences of idealism, if the German experience is any guide, are likely to be highly destructive.

This study originated as a dissertation written under the direction of Professor William M. Johnston, Jr., at the University of Massachusetts, Amherst. I would like to thank Professor Johnston for his many helpful suggestions and his constant encouragement, even when our views on specific questions did not coincide.

Preparation of the final manuscript was greatly facilitated by a grant from the Gonzaga University Research Council.

Portions of Chapter 5 and Chapters 9 and 13 were previously published as articles in *Nietzsche-Studien* and *The Wiener Library Bulletin*, respectively.

Finally, I would like to thank my wife, Steffi, for her patience and support.

Roderick Stackelberg
Spokane, Washington

1

INTRODUCTION:
THE GENESIS OF *VÖLKISCH* IDEALISM

> Kantians will make their appearance who know no piety in the world of phenomena either, who will mercilessly churn up the ground of European life with sword and axe, to extirpate the last roots of the past. Armed disciples of Fichte will appear, their fanaticism impervious to fear and egoism alike; for they walk in the spirit, they defy matter.
>
> Heinrich Heine, 1834

Within seventy-five years from the founding of the German Empire in 1871, the unified German state was destroyed as a result of the German drive for hegemony in Europe. In the wake of World War II, the *völkisch* ideology, which for decades had rationalized German expansionism and inspired patriotic fervor, was also swept away. National Socialism derived its strength in part because of the perception of many Germans that it was a movement of national regeneration, with roots deep in the German past. Regeneration in effect meant reversing the social consequences of the two major upheavals of modern times, the French Revolution and the Industrial Revolution. The democratic and acquisitive values associated with these revolutions came to be widely regarded in Germany as foreign in origin and incompatible with the tradition of German idealism. National Socialism was seen not as a repudiation of the German past but rather as a radical effort to revive the authentically German world view in the updated form required to guarantee its survival in a hostile and degenerate world.

The Nazis succeeded in giving their movement the aura of a spiritual crusade against materialistic values. In vowing to eliminate liberalism and Marxism, doctrines that emphasized the accumulation and distribution of worldly goods, the Nazis appealed to the self-interest of a lower-middle class squeezed by business and a growing labor movement. At the same time the Nazis also seemed to be fighting a battle for the spirit against earthbound forces. The soldierly ethos of self-sacrifice served the Nazi purpose of expansion well, but it also seemed to revive on a broad scale the heroic renunciation of the flesh of the martyr or the saint. The very term "Third Reich," besides putting the Nazis in the line of succession to the Holy Roman and Bismarckian empires, evoked mystical connotations of a spiritual realm in which the sordid conflicts of material existence would be overcome.[1] The Nazis stifled social criticism and dissent, but such anti-intellectualism could be disguised as a high-minded attack on the hubris of human reason. By suppressing "decadent" art the Nazis appeared to be striking a blow for morality against preoccupation with the degrading and animalistic aspects of the human condition. Even Nazi racial policies could be justified as a means of purging society of its materialistic elements.

The Holocaust and World War II revealed the full hypocrisy of National Socialism. The Nazis claimed to represent the venerable German idealist tradition with such success that some Western historians, in the heat of battle, could contend that the rise of National Socialism was inherent in the German intellectual tradition.[2] Hegel, Kant, Fichte, Herder, and even Goethe and Schiller have been variously portrayed as precursors of Nazism, thereby corroborating the Nazis' own version of their distinguished ancestry. Such a view not only distorts the subtlety and complexity of these intellectual giants, but it also fails to take into consideration the degree to which liberals and even socialists could appeal to the common idealist heritage. The retardation of Germany's political development and the weakness of German liberalism account for the fact that idealism came to be mobilized primarily for conservative and reactionary political purposes.

In a sense, of course, political conservatism *is* inherent in all idealist precepts, at least in their vulgarized form. In the broad sense in which it was derived from the philosophy of Plato, idealism stood for the view that the material world is merely the imperfect reflection of an underlying spiritual reality. Idealism implied a certain contempt for material existence, an attitude that perpetuated in more secular form the Christian renunciation of worldliness. German idealist ethics reaffirmed the Christian view that the pursuit of material happiness is unworthy of the human spirit. The proper goal of human endeavor is the moral perfection of the soul.

The conservative political implications of such attitudes emerged in the intellectual reaction in Germany to the French Revolution. Perhaps it was the hopelessness of revolutionary politics in eighteenth-century Germany that led so many reform-minded Germans to pin their hopes on moral improvement instead.[3] The Terror and the revolutionary wars reinforced the tendency of German idealists to view the French Revolution as inspired by basely materialistic motives. Moral freedom, the freedom from desire and temptation, came to be viewed as superior to the political freedoms espoused by the French.

There is an irony here, for idealism, too, reflected discontent with the political status quo. Hegel, for instance, sought to overcome the inadequacy of real conditions by subsuming them in a grandly rational historical process, the full meaning of which was not clear to mankind at any intermediate stage. This confidence in the ultimate beneficence of the world spirit enabled Hegel later in life to glorify the Prussian state. Nonetheless, *völkisch* ideologues tended to be suspicious of the progressive implications of the Hegelian dialectic. They appealed instead to the more safely apolitical idealism of Goethe or Schiller. This, too, is not without irony, for classical self-cultivation (and the Romantic flight into dream and fantasy) also reflected frustration in the face of stultifying social reality. Yet the effect of idealist attitudes was not to mobilize energies for social or institutional reform but instead to channel them into quiescent self-improvement.[4] Idealism represented a mode of adjustment to a stratified social order in which the aristocracy still enjoyed legally sanctioned privileges. This elitism was reflected in the idealist assumption that only the philosopher or poet could hope to cultivate the spirit in a manner leading to true self-fulfillment.

In the course of the nineteenth century, idealism permeated the educated stratum of German society in a vulgarized form.[5] Self-styled idealists professed opposition to the pursuit of wealth and material goods, as well as to the indulgence of bodily appetites and sensual pleasures. Most educated Germans embraced idealism as a superior German alternative to Western utilitarianism and liberalism, both of which stood condemned as egoistic, success-oriented doctrines. "Idealism is present," wrote Paul de Lagarde, one of the earliest exponents of *völkisch* thought, "wherever man acts out of inner needs against his own advantage, against his own comfort, against the world surrounding him."[6] Idealism was personified in the saintly, but martial hero who resists worldly temptation and overcomes evil. Idealists considered themselves the true heirs of the Lutheran tradition, whereas in Western Europe rational and materialistic values had triumphed. Idealists valued the underlying creative accomplishments of "culture" more highly than the ephemeral scientific and technological progress of "civilization."

In practice, to be sure, vulgarized idealism often served merely as a way of disguising or embellishing the very self-interest that self-styled idealists decried. Idealist attitudes reflected fear at the loss of the deference that protected traditional privileges. Idealism masked the interests of Germany's upper classes in maintaining social stratification and ethical norms in an Empire increasingly unsettled by rapid industrialization and the rise of organized labor. Idealism could be readily invoked to evade or deny such unpleasant realities as the inequitable distribution of wealth and power. Equalitarian reform could be discredited as the neglect of spiritual values in favor of materialistic aims.

Anti-Semitism was a frequent concomitant of the idealist world view in its vulgarized form, if only because *Vulgäridealismus* inherited from traditional Christian anti-Semitism the prejudice that Judaism was a materialistically oriented religion. Anti-Semites argued that the principal objective of Judaism was to strengthen the Jewish people in their quest for worldly power and prosperity. Yet it was the nonorthodox, progressive, and secular Jews that late nineteenth-century anti-Semites feared most. "It is not the religion of the Jews that threatens us," the Wagnerian publicist Hans von Wolzogen wrote in 1884, "but rather the irreligion, the modernization—which is at the same time the worst characteristic of Semitism: that egoistic and utilitarian self-deception, whose moral and ideal opposite is represented by the world-redeeming self-denial of the spirit of Christ."[7] Self-styled idealists proclaimed their opposition to the profit-oriented attitudes that Jews as a group were thought to represent. Anti-Semitism became a means of achieving a good conscience. It evoked an aura of virtuous renunciation all the more hypocritical in that it promoted the material interests of those who espoused it. "Principled anti-Semites" demanded the assimilation of Jews, by which they meant not only the conversion of Jews to Christianity but also their acceptance of the conservative consensus.[8]

Völkisch ideology represented a variant of vulgarized idealism in which the political motivation and hence also the anti-Semitic component became much more explicit. The emphasis in *völkisch* literature is no longer on idealism for its own sake, but rather on its usefulness as a unifying social creed to prevent liberalizing change. *Völkisch* ideology emerged as a major facet of the conservative reaction to democratic mass politics in the last quarter of the nineteenth century. Hermann Rauschning, a defector from National Socialism, recalled the sense of crisis which the "rise of the masses" provoked: "The current of destruction introduced by the great secular movement of human emancipation is going far beyond the natural rhythm of destruction and rebuilding. Here it is no longer a question of relative destruction and losses but of absolute and irrecoverable sacrifices of the very nature of man, of the human qualities formed by the untold thousands of years of man's social existence."[9]

Conservatives became obsessed with the "social question," the question of how to deal with the burgeoning labor movement in a rapidly industrializing society. In *völkisch* ideology the social question was transmuted into a question of race. The *Volk* stood for a unified people linked not merely by a common culture but by the mystical bonds of blood. Not classes but peoples and nations confronted each other in conflict. *Völkisch* politics were aimed toward the creation of a homogeneous national community in which the menacing urban masses were psychologically integrated.[10]

Völkisch ideology proposed to bridge the gulf between privileged and unprivileged without effecting any substantive change in class relations. The concept of *Volk* had exclusivist implications that belied its populist pretensions. The *Volk* by definition embraced only the healthy, undefiled members of the community, those whose devotion to the national good had not been corrupted by selfish materialism, the dominant motive behind liberalism and socialism. This fixation on ideological purity readily led, in an age that increasingly believed in the hereditary basis of human culture, to a definition of *Volk* in racial terms. Thus deviation from the *völkisch* consensus came to signify contamination by foreign—usually Semitic or Latin—blood.

As a movement to consolidate national consciousness and transcend class conflict, *völkisch* ideology inevitably incorporated many elements of the German intellectual reaction to the Enlightenment and the French Revolution. It was Herder who popularized the notion of the individuality of peoples and the mutual exclusiveness of national cultural traditions. But Herder's cultural nationalism was inspired by hatred of the rigidly absolutist regimes that kept Germany fragmented and backward; *völkisch* ideologues appropriated his ideas to bolster the absolutism of the German imperial state. Moreover, Herder delighted in cultural diversity, while the *völkisch* movement disdained foreign cultures as corrupt and inferior.[11]

In the literature of German Romanticism, too, the genuine instincts of the *Volk* were contrasted to the artificiality of contrived political institutions; but most Romantics subscribed to a cosmopolitan humanism that their *völkisch* epigones repudiated.[12] It is true that the wars of liberation against Napoleon generated doctrines of German superiority, the most famous of which was set forth by Fichte in his *Addresses to the German Nation* (1807-1808). Fichte portrayed the Germans as a "chosen people" whose mission it was to ennoble mankind: "To have character and to be German undoubtedly mean the same."[13] Of all the Germanic tribes only the Germans had remained uncorrupted by Roman institutions and Latin civilization. It must be borne in mind, however, that Fichte's addresses were held in Berlin when that city was occupied by Napoleon's troops. Fichte's purpose was to arouse patriotic feelings against the French invaders. His was a call for national liberation, not the subordination of one peoples to another. *Völkisch* messianism, on the other hand, was an aggressive doctrine that justified German expansion and domination.

Neither Fichte nor *Turnvater* Jahn, who sought to instill patriotic discipline and self-sacrifice in German youth through a rigorous gymnastic regimen, were sympathetic to autocratic government.[14] Though their writings had an anti-French and hence inevitably anti-Revolutionary thrust, both Fichte and Jahn still personified the alliance of nationalism and liberalism that characterized the movement for German unification in the first half of the nineteenth century. The failure of the Revolution of 1848 had momentous consequences, for it meant that Germany would not be unified under a liberal government. Instead unification was finally achieved by the force of Prussian arms.

The effect was inevitably to strengthen the Prussian monarchical system, the essential features of which were transferred to the new German Empire

in 1871. Bismarck effectively manipulated nationalist sentiments to undermine liberal goals.[15] By forcing liberals to choose between unification and
parliamentary government, Bismarck harnessed nationalism to the conservative cause. Henceforth allegiance to nation seemed to require the
abandonment of liberal demands. Erstwhile liberals or republicans like
Heinrich von Treitschke and Richard Wagner flocked to the national camp.
Nationalism, which originated as a democratic and anti-dynastic creed,
now became the vehicle of conservative demagoguery. Its populist over-
tones made nationalism especially useful as a means of mobilizing mass
support for illiberal objectives. Nationalism could be propagated as a form
of idealism (despite the cosmopolitanism of Goethe and Schiller) because it
demanded the subordination of self-interest and class-interest to the good
of the whole. Idealism signified the courage that gave a nation its strength,
materialism the cowardice that led to its decline.[16]

In *völkisch* ideology the marriage of idealism and nationalism was
consummated. *Völkisch* idealists glorified the state, both as the political
expression of a people's wholeness and as the bulwark of spiritual freedom
against materialistic self-seeking. To be sure, *völkisch* ideologues regarded
the early phase of the Bismarckian regime with considerable ambivalence.
They took their cues from conservatives like Konstantin Frantz (1817–
1891), who denounced Bismarck's *Realpolitik* and his concessions to
liberalism, especially in the economic sphere. Frantz, Lagarde, and
Wagner criticized Bismarck for failing to revive the spiritual traditions
(and the geographical frontiers) of the Holy Roman Empire and the
German past. They called for a national religion to overcome the divisions
that Bismarck's pragmatic policies failed to bridge.[17]

A later generation of *völkisch* writers would look back upon the 1870s
with mixed feelings, at once glorying in the grandeur of the newly founded
empire, while deploring the materialistic outlook of what they would call
the *Gründer- und Schwindlerjahre* ("years of founders and swindlers"). It
was in the wake of the financial crash of 1873 that the first manifestations of
völkisch extremism emerged.[18] Liberals and Jews became the scapegoats
for the economic slump. The imperial court chaplain Adolf Stoecker, who
founded the Christian Social Union in 1878, preached anti-Semitism in a
futile effort to undercut working-class support for social democracy.
Whereas Stoecker and Treitschke, who coined the slogan "The Jews are
our misfortune," continued to demand assimilation, publicists like Wilhelm Marr (1819–1904), Otto Glagau (1834–1892), and Eugen Dühring
(1833–1921) channeled economic discontents into an anti-Semitism defined in racial rather than confessional terms. The growth of racial anti-
Semitism reflected the fear that widespread assimilation of Jews would
only augment the liberal cause.[19]

Anti-liberal attitudes gained increasing respectability after the suppression of the newly organized Social Democratic Party (SPD), and the protective tariff campaign of 1878–1879 inaugurated the openly illiberal phase of Bismarckian rule.[20] While purging liberals from the civil service, Bismarck sponsored a comprehensive social insurance program designed to reduce the appeal of the SPD among workers. Protectionism further weakened the liberal movement while sealing the alliance between heavy industry and the Junkers that continued to dominate German society until the end of World War I. Fear of the labor movement helps to explain the fact that large segments of the *Besitz- und Bildungsbürgertum* ("the propertied and educated middle class") came to accept the conservative ideological consensus. In Germany the bourgeoisie became feudalized, as it were, neglecting democratization and uniting with agrarian interests to preserve the status quo.[21]

The 1890s proved to be a crucial decade in the growth of *völkisch* conservatism, as Bismarck's dismissal paved the way for a resurgence of the SPD and renewed pressures for democratic reforms. In a decade in which the absolute rural population in Germany declined for the first time, such conservative publicists as Otto Ammon (1842–1916) and Heinrich Sonrey (1859–1948) mobilized public opinion against the social and political consequences of urbanization.[22] They feared that *Landflucht* ("the flight from the countryside") would diminish the military capacities of German youth. At the same time conservatives propagated an aggressive foreign policy to deflect domestic pressures for reform.

Ironically, Bismarck now became a cult figure for the *völkisch* opposition to young Kaiser William II's efforts to conciliate the left and to gain working-class support. To be sure, after the dismissal of Bismarck's successor, Caprivi, in 1894, the imperial regime reverted to a repressive stance, while at the same time channeling popular enthusiasms into *Weltpolitik* and naval construction. For the far right, however, the Wilhelmine regime still remained too receptive to liberalizing change. Before 1914 *völkisch* authors typically remained monarchist in sentiment while increasingly criticizing the weakness of a regime that apparently could not prevent the steady gains of the SPD or the "Americanization" (i.e., commercialization) of German society. The classic statement of this kind was contained in the pamphlet *Wenn ich der Kaiser wär' (If I were the Kaiser)*, published in 1912 under a pseudonym by Heinrich Class (1868–1953), head of the Pan-German League. To keep the nation strong, Class wrote, "everything that strives for a transformation in a democratic direction must be ruthlessly fought."[23] Although under Hohenlohe, Bülow, and Bethmann-Hollweg, the last three prewar chancellors, the German government generally subscribed to this premise as well, their pragmatic efforts to placate progressives through compromise aroused the ire of the "German Opposition" on the right.[24]

The founding of the Pan-German League in 1891 was one symptom of growing reaction. It was followed in 1893 by the founding of the Agrarian League, a conservative pressure group that enjoyed remarkable success in recruiting peasant support for Junker interests. A rash of anti-Semitic parties made their appearance in various parts of Germany, catapulting to notoriety such demagogues as Hermann Ahlwardt (1846-1914), Max Liebermann von Sonnenberg (1848-1911), and Otto Böckel (1859-1923). The usefulness of anti-Semitism as a stratagem for deflecting anti-capitalist sentiment from revolutionary socialism into loyalist channels was not lost upon the Conservative Party, which officially adopted anti-Semitic provisions in its Tivoli Program of 1892. This helped to undercut the success of the radical anti-Semitic parties, whose rabble-rousing techniques contained a potential threat not only to social democracy, but to monarchical authority as well. It was not until the First World War and the Great Depression had fatally weakened traditional conservatism that right-wing radicalism came fully into its own.[25]

The decline of liberalism and the growth of aggressive nationalism were not limited to Germany, of course. The Czarist regime in Russia officially encouraged anti-Semitism, thereby stimulating Jewish immigration into Germany and Austria. In France, on the other hand, despite the founding of the Action Française in 1899, the democratic movement remained powerful largely as a result of popular revulsion against the miscarriage of justice in the Dreyfus Affair. In Austria ethnic rivalries exacerbated the radicalism of *völkisch* groups. Here the Pan-Germanism of Georg von Schönerer (1842-1921), founder of the *Los-von-Rom* movement, combined anti-Semitism with militant anti-Catholicism. The anti-Catholic current in *völkisch* thought in both Germany and Austria was fed by the fears of nationalists that allegiance to a supranational institution would weaken the emotional ties that bound the faithful to the nation. But for politicians dependent on mass support in countries with large Catholic populations, anti-Catholicism could only be self-defeating. Anti-Semitism offered a far more tempting vehicle for ambitious politicians, as the career of Karl Lueger (1844-1910), the popular mayor of Vienna from 1895 to 1910, attests. Whereas *völkisch* doctrinarians like Houston Stewart Chamberlain, who lived in Vienna from 1889 to 1908, remained hostile to Catholicism, Hitler and the Nazis were quite ready to sacrifice ideological consistency to practical politics by making their peace with the Church.[26]

Although the socialist threat was the crucial factor in provoking the upsurge of the radical right in the 1890s, the spread of *völkisch* idealism formed part of a much broader intellectual reaction to modernization in the nineteenth century. The tenacity of Germany's preindustrial inheritance and the weakness of the liberal movement help account for the fact that modernization created greater tensions and elicited more extreme reactions in Germany than in Western European countries. Idealism seemed a necessary guarantee of character and morality in an age of declining religious belief. In Germany in particular the trend toward a more secular, liberal, and rational society spurred diverse movements of cultural revitalization whose goal it was to eliminate foreign influence and revive traditional values.[27]

One of the most influential of such movements was founded by Richard Wagner. A onetime participant in the revolutions of 1848, Wagner later combined support for the monarchical state with criticism of its failure to promote art and culture more effectively. He insisted that the German victory over France in 1871 vindicated his own aesthetic doctrines and demonstrated Germany's cultural superiority. His first attacks on policies of the Imperial government came after the financial crisis had temporarily halted construction of his festival opera house at Bayreuth in 1873. Described by Fritz Stern as "the German anti-materialist materialist *par excellence*,"[28] Wagner accused the state of failing to provide adequate financial assistance for his endeavor to create a noncommercial national theater. The *Festspielhaus* was opened in 1876 to an audience that included Kaiser William I. Wagner made Bayreuth into a center both of pompously staged grand opera and social and cultural conservatism. Through his monthly journal *Bayreuther Blätter* and through propagandistic works, Wagner condemned the liberal tendencies of the age and proclaimed that art could redeem a debased society.[29]

In Wagner's view contemporary civilization was thoroughly corrupted by the worship of money and material possessions. According to him, the fashionable doctrine of material progress served only to conceal this process of degeneration by construing it as an advance. A religious reawakening was necessary to regenerate the purely human (*reinmenschlich*) and eternally natural (*ewig natürlich*) qualities of mankind. Only when self-seeking utilitarian values had been replaced by truly Christian ideals could a harmonious society emerge in which each individual (as well as the people as a whole) would realize his inner potential.

Art was the instrument by which regeneration would be achieved, for art was nothing, in Wagner's words, but "religion represented in living form."[30] Influenced by Schopenhauer, Wagner held that the artist's gaze could illuminate what was inaccessible or unclear to logical comprehension. This intuitive faculty gave the artist his social mission; his task was to reveal the goals and ideals toward which the populace (*Volkheit*) was unconsciously moving. The function of art was to advance the moral education of society, as Schiller had advocated in his *Letters on Aesthetic Education* (1795). The artist who is responsive to the spirit of his people serves as their moral guide. Although art does not teach directly, it awakens in those who experience it a sense of their own inner potentialities and makes them want to change their lives. Wagner considered his *Gesamtkunstwerk* particularly suited to the task of regeneration. By combining music with poetry and drama it conveyed the moral essence of human behavior—the aspect that is entirely free of external conventions—more directly and more effectively than could any single art form by itself.[31]

Wagner's active participation on the Dresden barricades in the Revolution of 1848 later embarrassed his followers, who sought to minimize his former republican sympathies. Chamberlain explained this lapse on the grounds that Wagner had admired the moral imperative of the revolutionary movement without sharing its political objectives. In any case a political revolution meant only that power changed hands while the whole edifice of modern civilization remained untouched. Wagner's ultimate ideal was a society united by religion, in which political activity, with all its conflict and compromise, would become unnecessary. As Carl Schorske has pointed out, Wagner's repudiation of the Revolution of 1848 paralleled the response of disappointed idealists to the French Revolution. Frustrated revolutionary idealism became internalized in the exhortation that man must perfect himself. In psychological metaphysics Wagner found refuge from social politics.[32]

Wagner insisted that the German character was uniquely suited to religious regeneration, if Germans only would follow their true nature. To his own query, "What is German?" (the title of a pamphlet he published in 1878), Wagner answered: to do something for its own sake rather than for pleasure or reward. Wagner idealized a mythical past in which Germany had not yet fallen prey to the forces of degeneration. In a classic example of projection and *ressentiment*, he attributed the rise of calculating rationalism to the influence of Jews on German culture. According to this view, so widespread in late nineteenth-century Germany, the purely functional intelligence, personified by Jews pursuing their own interests, obstructed the creative imagination of the German artist who disregarded personal advantage in the pursuit of an ideal.

In 1881, two years before his death, Wagner befriended the French racial theorist Arthur Comte de Gobineau, whose four-volume *Essai sur l'inégalité des races humaines* had appeared between 1853 and 1855. He did not question Gobineau's explanation for the degeneration of modern culture: the purity of the three original races (white, yellow, and black) had been gradually destroyed by intermixing, through which the strongest races lost proportionately more in quality than the weaker race gained.[33] He also wholeheartedly endorsed the Frenchman's postulate that the Indo-

Germanic white race was innately superior to all others. Wagner did not, however, share Gobineau's relentless pessimism, but clung instead to the conviction that a reversal of historic trends could be accomplished by moral regeneration. In this Jews, too, could participate, if they adopted Christian values.

Wagner's followers gave his doctrine of regeneration an increasingly racist and reactionary coloration. Ludwig Schemann (1852–1938), founder of the Gobineau Society in 1896, was largely responsible for the popularity that Gobineau's ideas enjoyed in Germany. The work of another Wagnerian, Chamberlain's *Foundations of the Nineteenth Century* (1899), was to become the bible of *völkisch* thought. No single publication was more instrumental in legitimating racial anti-Semitism among educated people.[34]

The growing cult of Wagnerism and racialism was an extreme manifestation of the sense of crisis that gripped segments of the educated stratum of Wilhelmine society in the years before World War I. On the highest intellectual levels this crisis formed part of the widespread revolt against positivism and scientism in European thought at the turn of the century.[35] Positivism appeared to undermine the autonomous status of mind and will by explaining the causation of all phenomena in material terms. A world view that dispensed with any supernatural agency was not only psychologically dissatisfying, but posed a threat to authority and absolute moral standards as well. Neo-idealists sought to defend eternally valid ideals against the relativizing environmentalism of monist philosophies. At the same time social Darwinism, eugenics, and racialism appealed to conservatives as means of making science useful to reactionary rather than progressive causes.

The ultimate source of the psychosocial malaise that afflicted so many segments of European society at the turn of the century lay in the widening gulf between traditional values—particularly the liberal, humanist faith in the independent individual—and the actual conditions of a rapidly industrializing society. Though critics of liberalism, *völkisch* ideologues reflected the psychological instability and unease of a society in which liberal ideals no longer commanded the confidence they had in earlier decades. Their hostility to contemporary society paralleled the threatened extrusion of the upper and middle classes from power in an age of incipient mass politics.

A letter received by the popular *völkisch* writer Friedrich Lienhard in 1900 from one of his readers illustrates the cultural despair that gripped many Germans in a time of unparalleled economic growth:

We are making no headway against the plebeian mob, against the current of democratization which disintegrates everything and everybody and which acknowledges only one thing: success and the golden calf. I do not know how the leaf of culture is to turn. I think a lot about this, perhaps too much, and I can find no conceivable ways and means. Has prosperity, the cultural blessing, as it is called, ennobled England or America? Have the achievements of the 1870's, the immense increase in prosperity, been a blessing for us?[36]

Ironically, Lienhard, Chamberlain, and other *völkisch* authors advocated aristocratic ideals to restore the stable society that had emerged from the struggle against aristocratic privilege earlier in the century, but that now found itself threatened by the political aspirations of the liberated masses. In the "degenerate" liberal ideology of material progress they saw the source of the present-day malaise. By legitimating the pursuit of selfish material interests and by sponsoring liberalizing political reforms, liberals had opened the floodgates to the egalitarian movements that now threatened to rend the social fabric. Hence *völkisch* publicists rejected parliamentary politics and pinned their hopes on monarchical autocracy and an idealist ethos that would put primary emphasis on cultivating mind and soul rather than on pursuing material goals.

As the growth of technology and mass democracy progressively eroded the traditional order and as the classical liberal ideal of the autonomous individual in a stable social order grew ever more inconsistent with reality, *völkisch* idealists sought to buttress individuality, authority, and hierarchy by reviving the Goethean ideals of inner freedom and aristocratic self-cultivation. They regarded with disdain, even horror, the changes that the Industrial Revolution had wrought in the nineteenth century. "Toward the end of the eighteenth century," Chamberlain wrote, "the great transformation took place which will probably one day be recognized as the most terrible catastrophe ever to have befallen mankind, so that one may ask oneself whether the dignity of man can still be saved; I am speaking of the mechanization and the resulting industrialization of life."[37] Like their Romantic predecessors, *völkisch* idealists blamed this catastrophe on rationalism and secularism, though their opposition to industrialization rested more on political than aesthetic grounds. It was the leveling impact of industrialization, the rise of working-class and middle-class movements for liberalizing reforms, that conservatives most deplored.

In a time of economic and social dislocations, *völkisch* idealism catered to a widespread yearning for a preindustrial and prerevolutionary age. *Völkisch* idealists equated preindustrial Germany with the realm of the spirit as they sought to give substance to the poet Emanuel Geibel's oft-quoted couplet: "Und es mag am deutschen Wesen / Einmal noch die Welt genesen" ("And the world may yet be healed through German character").

The German Youth Movement, founded in 1896, helped to spread *völkisch* ideas to alienated members of the middle class who had lost faith in liberalism, who feared socialism, and yearned for a return to a simpler life.[38] Inspired by a book that spearheaded the neo-Romantic revolt against modernity, Julius Langbehn's best-selling *Rembrandt als Erzieher* (1890), middle-class German youth fled the industrial cities to cultivate the sturdy virtues of rural life. Lienhard, too, became one of their favorite authors. In the early 1900s he championed the patriotic values of *Heimatkunst* ("regional art") against the social criticism of urban naturalism. The same period witnessed a surge of popular enthusiasm for various forms of evangelism, mysticism, occultism, and Oriental religions, which provided an escape from the social realities of an industrializing society.

It is hardly surprising that the outbreak of war in 1914 was widely greeted as the salutary challenge that would finally free the body politic of its festering malaise. Juxtaposed to the revolutionary divisiveness of 1789, the "ideas of 1914" became a symbol for the unity and common purpose that had evaded the nation for so long.[39] For the German elite, the war had a dual aim: victory would stifle revolution at home and establish German dominance abroad.[40] Defeat and the revolutions of 1918–1919, such as they were, only temporarily aborted these aims. In the *völkisch* movement between the wars, swelled by revulsion against Weimar and Versailles, conservatives carried on the struggle against democracy that eventually culminated in the Nazi triumph in 1933.

The three writers discussed in this book were each members of a generation that spanned the years of the disintegration of the old order. With varying degrees of desperation they sought to salvage a culture that would buttress authoritarian politics in a traditional social order. In their works—representative manifestations of Germany's social crisis—we can see the evolution of idealism into a defense against the disruptive consequences of modernization and industrialization in the late nineteenth century. These were transitional figures who represented various facets of the *völkisch* struggle against democratizing change.

In the works of the short lived Wagnerian publicist Heinrich von Stein the origins of the *völkisch* perversion of idealism may be seen. One of the most persuasive advocates of Wagner's doctrine of regeneration through art and religion, Stein juxtaposed German idealism to the commercialism and materialism of modern industrial society. His works, which include some important contributions to the literature of aesthetics, reflect alienation and disorientation more than conscious political motive. For later *völkisch* writers he came to serve as a model of Germanic rectitude. A critique of *völkisch* idealism must begin with a critique of the cast of mind that Stein typified. As an intermediary between Nietzsche and Wagner, Stein may inadvertently have played a key role in provoking the vehement anti-Wagnerian tirades in Nietzsche's later works.

If Stein was more a victim of illusion than its perpetrator, Friedrich

Lienhard and Houston Stewart Chamberlain consciously pursued political goals. Lienhard waged the struggle for idealism on a more popular level. His works exemplify *Vulgäridealismus*, the term Fritz Stern has given to the idealization of events and conditions in order to deny social and economic realities. Lienhard reduced idealism to little more than a set of slogans to rally support for his campaign against secularism, liberalism, and democracy. In an effort to stem the tide of reform, he counseled his readers to avoid political participation. More escapist than activist in temperament, Lienhard shared the ambivalence of conservative idealists toward the tactics of Nazis and other right-wing extremists after World War I.

Houston Stewart Chamberlain played the most important role in the formulation and dissemination of *völkisch* idealism. In his works the ideological transition from Wilhelmine imperialism to National Socialism was clearly delineated. The expatriate offspring of an aristocratic English family, Chamberlain embraced German culture with all the passion of a convert. Writing in excellent German, he evolved from a publicist of Wagnerian idealism into an eloquent prophet of Nordic racial and cultural superiority. What made him one of the most controversial and influential authors of the era of imperialism was his readiness to do battle for *völkisch* ideas on a far more sophisticated level than most of his ideological colleagues. In the final stages of his career, however, Chamberlain encouraged the counterrevolutionary violence of the Nazis.

If this study is to offer a convincing critique of *völkisch* idealism, it must also evoke the aura and appeal of a mental idiom that is quite foreign to us today. While such an approach runs the risk of appearing to give to discredited ideas an importance they do not deserve, it does enable us to understand how *völkisch* idealism could provide not only a rationale but also a source of great (albeit destructive) strength for Germany during two world wars. Most educated Germans came to regard idealism as the distinctively German world view. Idealism could be both a heroic vision and a hypocritical pose. For some it represented an intensely personal experience, for others it stood for a program of social or cultural regeneration. Idealism provided both an escapist creed and an exhortation to action. Even as some political leaders became inured to idealism while others hypocritically exploited its rhetoric, millions of soldiers on the battlefield had absorbed its ethos of noble self-sacrifice. However bizarre and outlandish *völkisch* idealism may seem to us today, it did not seem so to its many adherents at the time. As Nietzsche had anticipated in his critique of Wagner, *völkisch* idealism generated destructive potential even though (or perhaps because) it seemed to epitomize virtue and respectability. No historical example shows more clearly how an ethos of self-denial could in fact merely justify self-aggrandizement. By identifying German culture with the pinnacle of human achievement, *völkisch* idealists succeeded in giving a high-sounding moral purpose to megalomaniac political aspirations.

Heinrich von Stein with Wagner and friends, House Wahnfried, 1882. Top row, left to right: Blandine v. Bülow, Heinrich v. Stein, Cosima and Richard Wagner, Paul v. Jukovsky. Bottom row, Isolde and Daniela v. Bülow, Eva Wagner, Siegfried Wagner. (*Courtesy Richard-Wagner-Gedenkstätte, Bayreuth.*)

PART ONE

Heinrich von Stein
and Wagnerian Idealism

All idealists imagine that the causes they serve are intrinsically better than the other causes in the world, and they don't want to believe that if their cause is to prosper at all, it requires the same ill-smelling compost as all other human enterprises.

NIETZSCHE, Human, All-too-Human

long aristocratic tradition. His father and both his younger brothers pursued military careers, his brother Otto achieving the rank of lieutenant general before his death in 1916. Heinrich's deeply religious mother died when he was only eleven years old. Her pietist upbringing had a lasting effect on her son. Young Stein's earliest ambition was to become a pastor. "I have one life," he wrote in his diary at the age of sixteen, "and a short human lifetime is not too long to apply fully to the knowledge of true religion."[3] Long before his exposure to Wagner's ideas, Stein was convinced that a new Reformation was needed to return Christianity to its basic principles. Yet he chastized theologians who disparaged Plato and Socrates because they had not been Christians. Stein's own earliest literary efforts included five poems in Greek.

Stein's precociousness rivaled that of another Wagnerian, Nietzsche, who would eventually turn his intellectual gifts to quite different ends. Stein so excelled at school that he was excused from the oral portion of his *Abitur*, the graduation exam. Selected to deliver a public address in 1873, the sixteen-year-old chose a theme appropriate to Germany's recent unification. He denied that Goethe's and Schiller's indifference to the wars against Napoleon implied a lack of patriotism, for these poets had created ideals that Germans still heeded. The year 1848 had been an important date despite its revolutionary turmoil, for it had demonstrated to Germany that her salvation lay with Prussia. Stein closed with an admonition to his classmates to maintain and strengthen the glorious German Empire.[4]

Those who knew him were impressed by two outstanding traits in Stein's character: his earnestness and his sense of duty. His aunt remarked that he was a person one could not help but tease. Another relative, Adelheid von Schorn (1841–1916), author of a two-volume work on post-classical Weimar, could not imagine that Stein had ever indulged in the customary pleasures of young men of his age. Some years later, Nietzsche would take pride in the fact that he had gotten Stein to laugh. Others remarked on Stein's diffidence and formality. When a fellow Wagnerian of his own age, the Russian emigré artist Paul von Jukovsky, offered him the use of the familiar form of address, Stein blushed and declined.[5]

At the University of Heidelberg, where he enrolled in 1874, Stein soon became disenchanted with the study of theology. In an academic setting it appeared a hopelessly relativistic field in which each professor expounded his own particular point of view. In the conflict between orthodox and liberal theologians, Stein preferred the former, despite their narrow dogmatism; the liberal efforts to synthesize religion and science could only lead to a diluted religion. True to the Protestant tradition, he viewed the dogmas of institutionalized religion as more a product of history than a legacy of Christ.

Under the guidance of Kuno Fischer, professor of philosophy at

2

NEO-ROMANTIC ALIENATION: THE LIFE OF HEINRICH VON STEIN

I not only loved Stein but worshipped him as an Archangel Michael wandering on our planet.

Cosima Wagner to Chamberlain, 1900

The career of Heinrich von Stein (1857–1887), an early and intensely loyal member of Wagner's Bayreuth Circle, offers a striking example of the disaffection of traditionalists in the newly founded Reich.[1] Although Stein personified the alienated genius whose early death seems like Romantic wish-fulfillment, his significance derives from the orthodoxy, not the originality, of his views. Stein's life and works epitomized the troubled relationship of members of the German intelligentsia to the social realities of an industrial age. This is why, despite his aristocratic background and his proclaimed indifference to politics, his works can be read as documents of liberal demoralization in late nineteenth-century Germany. His attitudes were typical of the wishful thinking and self-deception that eventually drew so many middle- and upper-class Germans to *völkisch* ideology and National Socialism.

Yet there is something undeniably attractive about Stein. The fervid tributes of his contemporaries testify to the esteem in which he was held. His works exemplify the most admirable side of the *völkisch* mentality. Stein was that rare person, the genuine idealist who seemed to practice what he preached. His early death gave his renunciation of worldliness the added force of total sincerity; here was the selflessness his *völkisch* successors extolled but grotesquely lacked. In the words of a commemorative speaker in 1932, forty-five years after Stein's death, here was "the eternal German youth with a glowing heart and a high mind, who takes risks and sacrifices himself, who rises again and again, no matter on how many battlefields he already lies buried."[2] The ethos of self-sacrifice and the suicidal impulse that Stein embodied would exercise its force long after the cause he stood for had been thoroughly corrupted.

Karl Heinrich Freiherr von Stein zu Nord- und Ostheim was born in 1857, in Franconia, a province in northern Bavaria, into a family with a

Heidelberg, Stein read Schopenhauer, Kant, Spinoza, and David Friedrich Strauss. Stein dreamed of devoting his life to creating his own philosophy. "If only, in Heaven's name," he wrote a friend in 1874, "a so-called agreeable life is not the dominant factor in choosing a career." He disdained the economic materialism of the burgeoning German Empire. "The struggle is between idealism and materialism," Stein wrote in his diary in 1874. "There is a God. . . . There are things that are lofty, eternal, great. May mankind believe in these." His reflections were prompted by concern about incipient social conflict. Young Stein thought that only a large-scale effort by the state to promote education and religion could prevent a revolution by the "brutalized" masses. Although he hoped such a revolution could be stifled, Stein sympathized with the victims of self-seeking factory owners. He might even have become a Social Democrat, he claimed, if this party had not been so infuriatingly anti-national.[6]

Young Stein's religious crisis reflected the challenge of positivism and science to traditional theological assumptions in the nineteenth century. Stein found fault with the pessimistic Christian conception of man's condition in the world; beneficent developments were everywhere in evidence. He yearned for a theology based on knowledge and demonstration. "My understanding rebels against believing what it does not know."[7] Stein changed his field of study to philosophy and science the following year. But in rejecting theology he felt he was being true to religion.

Stein's new interests brought him into contact with one of the most idiosyncratic and prolific intellectual figures of his time. Transferring to the University of Berlin in 1875, Stein completed his studies under Eugen Dühring (1833–1921), an eccentric economist and philosophical naturalist who increasingly expressed his personal and professional resentments in strident anti-Semitism.[8] Under Dühring, a critic of religion and of philosophical idealism, Stein published in 1877, at the precocious age of twenty, his doctoral dissertation, *Über Wahrnehmung* (*On Perception*). Stein redefined Kant's conception of inaccessible noumena to conform to the positivist axiom that direct perception of reality was possible. Dühring's influence was also evident in Stein's first book, *Die Ideale des Materialismus* (*Ideals of Materialism*), which appeared under the pseudonym Armand Pensier in 1878. The book had been commissioned as a popular explication of Dühring's positivist philosophy, as will be discussed later. But instead of providing a systematic philosophical exposition, Stein extolled materialism in a series of prose poems. His purpose was to demonstrate that Dühring's rejection of supernatural religion was not at odds with the traditional Christian ideals of sainthood and heroism.

It was this book that first attracted Nietzsche's attention to Stein.[9] Otherwise, however, it was not well received. The Nobel Prize-winning poet and novelist Paul Heyse spoke deprecatingly of immature writers who rushed into print too soon. Stein's espousal of philosophical materialism apparently caused some consternation among family and friends. Malvida von Meysenbug, a confidante of Mazzini, Wagner, and Nietzsche, was amused by the religious enthusiasm she discerned in the young Stein, even as he defended Dühring's positivist doctrines. Another friend of the family's, Caroline von Sayn-Wittgenstein, was less amused. A lack of religion, she feared, would always lead to French communes and to assassination attempts in Berlin.[10]

After a year of military service in 1878–1879, Stein obtained through Malvida von Meysenbug a position as tutor to Richard Wagner's eleven-year-old son, Siegfried. It proved to be the crucial experience of his life. Through Wagner, Stein found his way back to religion, though he did not cease in his efforts to reconcile Dühring's thought with Wagnerian idealism. In hoping for the moral regeneration of Germany, and through Germany of mankind, both men shared a similar aspiration.

Put off at first by what he regarded as a flight from reality, Stein soon found in Bayreuth the kind of community he came to value as the supreme good. He called it a *Gemeinsamkeit der Gesinnung*, a mutuality of conviction, a sense of community far deeper than mere congruence of thoughts and opinions. *Gesinnung*—a word that suggests both character and conviction—involved, in Stein's view, the total personality in a way that mere thoughts and opinions could not. In his essay on Stein, Chamberlain stressed *Gesinnung* as the key to Stein's personality. The absence of an adequate equivalent for *Gesinnung* in either French or English reflected, according to Chamberlain, a genuine difference in national character. *Gesinnung* was typically German, in the same way that *esprit*, a word for which there is no exact equivalent in German, was a typically French characteristic. Just as Wagnerians felt that only Germans could fully appreciate Wagner's art, so Chamberlain despaired of making Stein's personality fully comprehensible to non-Germans.[11]

The Wagnerian circle exercised a profound effect on the impressionable young man. Stein felt the capacity for sympathy to be more highly refined among Wagnerians than among anyone else he had ever met. This capacity arose from veneration for Richard Wagner—for his person as well as for his art—for such veneration developed the kind of "receptivity" that is a precondition of community. Stein elevated hero-worship to a moral principle. The human spirit must lose itself in something higher in order to realize its full potential. Art, not science, shows the way to knowledge and salvation, for art reconciles man to a higher order of things in which the death of the individual is no longer tragic. No deeper understanding of the world is possible to man on earth than through the flow of tears evoked by music.[12]

At Bayreuth and at Wagner's winter residence in Naples, Stein began work on a series of dramatic episodes, a number of which were published in 1883 under the title *Helden und Welt* (*Heroes and the World*). Wagner's lengthy introduction to *Helden und Welt* was his last published work before his death in 1883. *Helden und Welt* was modeled after a similar work by Gobineau, whose collection of historical portraits, *La Renaissance: Scènes historiques* (1877), was praised by Stein in *Bayreuther Blätter* in 1881.

Stein's Bayreuth idyll came to an end in 1881. At his father's behest, Stein returned home to pursue an academic career at the University of Halle. Although he had previously advised Stein against a university career, Wagner urged the irresolute young man to respect his father's wishes. Stein acquiesced, seizing the chance to do battle for Wagnerian ideas in the outside world. But in the few years left to him he never again found the happiness he had enjoyed at Bayreuth. In a letter to Hans von Wolzogen (1848–1938) in 1883, Stein wondered whether his fellow Wagnerian, who spent a lifetime at Bayreuth as editor of *Bayreuther Blätter*, had not chosen the better course.[13]

Bayreuth scarcely offered adequate preparation for a scholarly career. Stein's habilitation dissertation on Giordano Bruno, whom Dühring considered the greatest philosopher because of Bruno's belief in a single universal principle combining matter and soul, was rejected three times before a thoroughly revised version was finally accepted. The original version, entitled *Der Wahn eines Helden* (*The Vision of a Hero*), contained more rhapsody than scholarship. The use of the term *Wahn* reflected the influence of Wagner, who named his home in Bayreuth *Wahnfried* (combining the concepts of "visionary" and "peaceful"). The final version of Stein's dissertation received the more suitably academic title, *Über die Bedeutung des dichterischen Elements in der Philosophie des Giordano Bruno* (*On the Significance of the Poetic Element in the Philosophy of Giordano Bruno*), but its scholarly method still left a great deal to be desired.[14]

Although he himself considered proselytizing Wagnerian ideas his true vocation, Stein blamed his repeated failures in academic scholarship in part on Jewish opposition to Wagner and Dühring. "The Jews appeared in full numbers," he wrote Cosima Wagner's daughter, Daniela von Bülow, after defending his dissertation in 1881, "and agitated against me in front of everybody; an experience that is worth something."[15] This outburst notwithstanding, Stein was never obsessed with the "Jewish question" as Chamberlain would be, nor did his occasional anti-Semitic remarks ever remotely approach the virulence of Dühring's language. But like both Dühring and Wagner, Stein channeled personal frustrations into anti-Semitism and unthinkingly equated Jewishness with the materialistic temper of the times.

Stein's decision to offer a course on Wagner at Halle met with the objections of many of his colleagues and little student response. His words *ver-Hallen* ("fade away"), Stein punned, with an uncharacteristic touch of humor. His letters of this period bear witness to the frustrations of a teacher who could not reach his students. Students lost interest, Stein complained, because his lectures were not of a kind they could take notes on. Yet his efforts were not in vain, Stein felt, if he could minister to those students who expected more from their education than an arid scholarly approach. Scholarship was timebound, while the wisdom emanating from inner experience remained valid for all time. Scholars would never acknowledge his work, Stein lamented, unless they recognized emotions not just as incidental traits but as a genuine source of knowledge. Yet he envied the contentment of scholars who had managed to carve out and to take full possession of a narrow specialty.[16]

His failure to attract students at Halle induced Stein to seek a position at the University of Berlin, where he taught from 1883 until the premature end of his life four years later. Once again he had difficulties with the habilitation process. His dissertation on the relationship of language to philosophic knowledge was rejected as an exercise in mysticism rather than scholarship. Stein argued that language, particularly German, contains the key to wisdom, for words and expressions reflect metaphysical truths. Mankind can fathom these truths by becoming conscious of the original meaning of words. Stein went beyond this relatively moderate thesis to argue that the common root of *Liebe* and *Leben* ("love" and "life") conveys an important message for mankind. For Stein the link between these two words provided a philosophic foundation for the moral regeneration that Wagner demanded. To fulfill their cultural mission, Germans needed above all to heed properly the wisdom contained in their own language.[17]

Stein's essay was not a total failure, however. Wilhelm Dilthey (1833–1911), the pioneer of intellectual history, was sufficiently impressed by Stein's gifts to recommend a second chance. Under Dilthey's sympathetic guidance, Stein now completed a work of genuine scholarship. His dissertation, *Über den Zusammenhang Boileau's mit Descartes* (*On the Relationship of Boileau to Descartes*), a topic suggested by Dilthey, was accepted with special commendation for its exemplary method in the summer of 1884. It was published in the *Zeitschrift für Philosophie und philosophische Kritik* in 1885 and became the first chapter of Stein's major work, *Die Entstehung der neueren Ästhetik* (*The Development of Modern Aesthetic Theory*). In this four-hundred-page volume, published in 1886, Stein applied Dilthey's principles of *Geisteswissenschaft* (human studies as opposed to natural science) to the history of aesthetic theory from French classicism to the idealism of Johann Joachim Winckelmann.

At the University of Berlin, Stein not only attracted several devoted seminar students, including Arthur Seidl (1863–1928), author of works on Wagner, Nietzsche, and Richard Strauss, and Robert Sommer (1864–1937), author of works on psychology and aesthetics, but to his own surprise he found himself for a brief time one of the most popular lecturers as well. His lectures on Goethe and Schiller in the summer of 1886 had to be moved into the *auditorium maximum*, otherwise occupied only by such luminaries as Heinrich von Treitschke. Subsequently published in the inexpensive paperbound series of publisher Philipp Reclam, these lectures received the widest circulation of any of Stein's works.

Stein concentrated an extraordinary volume of work into the last years of his short life. His chief interest, however, remained in the Wagnerian cause. In collaboration with Karl Friedrich von Glasenapp (1847–1915), the author of a six-volume adulatory biography of Wagner, Stein published the *Wagner-Lexikon* in 1883, an encyclopedia of Wagner's cultural and political views. Stein's contributions to *Bayreuther Blätter* between 1881 and 1887 included lengthy studies of Schopenhauer, Shakespeare, Luther, Rousseau, Kant, Goethe, and Jean Paul, as well as numerous book reviews and articles on such Wagnerian concerns as vivisection and vegetarianism.[18] A future of great promise was cut tragically short by Stein's unexpected death, due to heart failure after a severe bout of influenza, at the age of thirty in June, 1887.

In spite of his increasing success, the last years of Stein's life had not been happy. "No person near or far who understands me," he wrote in his diary a few months before his death, "no woman who will ever love me."[19] It seemed to Stein that he had a special faculty for sadness. He felt out of place at the cold and indifferent university in a hostile urban setting. His brooding temperament aggravated physical infirmity. Like his Romantic predecessors, he often sought solace in the thought of death. "Living is harder than dying," he wrote to Daniela von Bülow.[20] His early death became an important component in a cult, nurtured by Lienhard, Chamberlain, and members of the Bayreuth Circle, that depicted Stein as a martyr to idealism in a hostile materialistic world. "This dream of his life," Chamberlain wrote in 1896, shortly before beginning work on *The Foundations of the Nineteenth Century*, "to have an educational effect on others, Stein will not have dreamed in vain with me."[21] To those who knew him personally, Stein's death meant a profound loss. Cosima Wagner felt that she would never get over it. And Nietzsche, who had hoped in vain to find in Stein a kindred spirit, wrote to Franz Overbeck: "Why was I not called in his place—it would have made more sense."[22]

Stein became a model of integrity for writers who preached idealist precepts during an era in which such precepts seemed increasingly incompatible with the tenor of modern life. Nostalgic idealists esteemed Stein as the transmitter of traditional attitudes in undefiled form. To conservatives who opposed the relentless modernization of society, Stein became a paragon of lost inwardness and purity. "In Stein," the Austrian novelist Hermann Bahr wrote after World War I, "who under tremendous inner stress strove to bring into congruence such powerful opposites as Dühring, Wagner, and Nietzsche, there was already that third Germany, upon which lay only the curse of having remained ineffectual—right up to the present."[23] Unlike other members of his generation Stein was not confronted by the necessity of making political choices in the period of deepening social conflict after 1890. As the quintessential Romantic genius who died young, Stein was not forced to compromise his ideals with the realities of a world he condemned. Hence Stein could come to be regarded as the incorruptible conscience of an incipient *völkisch* movement, whose excesses he would hardly have sanctioned.

3

THE CULT OF THE *VOLK* AND THE HERO

We seek the purely human [*Reinmenschliche*] as Germans, and we regard others as equal to us only insofar as they do the same from their own standpoint.

Stein to Hans von Wolzogen, 1884

Heinrich von Stein's works provide fascinating evidence of how the lineaments of *völkisch* doctrine emerged from efforts to revive aristocratic ideals in an age of mass consumption. His neo-Romantic fixation on the heroic personality mirrored both admiration for Bismarck's achievements and estrangement from a mass society in which institutions increasingly represented the needs and interests of groups and collectivities rather than individuals. The rebirth of aristocratic ideals was one manifestation of the decline of nineteenth-century liberalism as industrialization and urbanization increasingly rendered faith in the autonomous personality irrelevant to the actual conditions of life. In its early formulations, *völkisch* doctrine reiterated monarchist values, including hierarchy, martialism, and deference, while providing secular equivalents for the religious norms of the past.

Stein's close association with four of the most influential personalities of his age, Dühring, Wagner, Dilthey, and Nietzsche, give his works a fascination beyond their limited subject matter. Stein succumbed to the influence of his mentors as he in turn embraced Dühring's positivism, Wagner's idealism, and Dilthey's historicism. He failed to follow Nietzsche, however, the most uncompromising thinker of his time. When put to the test by the dispute between Nietzsche and Wagner, Stein clung to Wagnerism, a choice that epitomized the eventual surrender of so many talented Germans to the seductions of *völkisch* thought.

Dühring and Wagner had their differences, too, of course, for Dühring rejected religion and art as "Asiatic" corruptions. Dühring was in fact for a time the most important exponent of positivism in Germany. Nonetheless, the differences between Dühring and Wagner proved far easier to bridge than the differences between Nietzsche and Wagner. In their search for an ideology worthy of the newly founded empire, both Dühring and Wagner arrived at a nationalistic creed. In *völkisch* ideology there was room for the philosophical monism of Dühring or the Darwinism of Ernst Haeckel as well as for the metaphysical dualism of Wagner or Chamberlain.

Of the important figures of nineteenth-century German intellectual history, Dühring's reputation has suffered most. The strident nationalism and anti-Semitism of his later years (he lived to the age of eighty-nine) have tended to obscure the more constructive works of his academic phase. Forced to give up a career in law by blindness at the age of twenty-eight, Dühring became a professor of economics and philosophy at the University of Berlin in 1863. Here he established his reputation with a wide range of works in which he set forth an idiosyncratic brand of positivism.[1]

Dühring's bellicose and egocentric temperament impeded his scholarly career and marred his later works. A feud with his colleagues led to Dühring's forced resignation in 1877, the same year that Stein completed his dissertation. Dühring is remembered today chiefly for having provoked Friedrich Engels's *Anti-Dühring* (1878), one of the classics of Marxist literature.[2] Engels's polemic undercut the support that Dühring's proposal for the creation of state-supported worker cooperatives in a competitive free-market economy had previously attracted in the Social Democratic Party. Dühring's economic theories owed their inspiration in part to the optimistic positivism of the American economist Henry Carey (1793–1879). Dühring's affirmation of the sanctity of private property (when acquired through labor and not by force) and his assumption that harmony could be attained between the interests of labor, capital, and land-ownership, once the propertyless segment of society had been strengthened through collective action, differentiated Dühring's "German" socialism from its Marxist counterpart. Even during the brief socialist phase of his career Dühring's objective was not egalitarian social revolution but rather the conciliation of rival sectors of the economy through equalization of their competitive potential and through the development of an ethos of national solidarity. He propagated a tough-minded realism that would free man of religious superstition, corrosive skepticism, economic egotism, and sentimental humanitarianism, all of which he perversely came to attribute to Jewish influence.

Dühring's dismissal from the University of Berlin and his feud with the Marxists marked the turning point in his career. Thereafter he abandoned even such moderate social reform proposals as the establishment of cooperatives, and instead propagated nationalism and anti-Semitism as solutions to Germany's social problems. As in the case of Treitschke, Wagner, and so many other former liberals in Germany, this shift paralleled the increasingly illiberal tenor of Bismarck's domestic policies. Jews and Marxists became the targets of Dühring's most intense hatred. From his home in Leipzig he churned out polemics of increasing virulence and bitterness. His talent for invective found expression in derisive puns:

his epithet for Nietzsche, for instance, was *Nichtske* (*nichts*, meaning
"nothing"). Dühring's contribution to the new wave of anti-Semitism that
swept through Germany in the late 1870s and early 1880s was his emphasis
on race, derived from his positivist assumption that all existence was
susceptible to a material explanation. His most radical proposal for handling the "Jewish problem" ominously foreshadowed the Nazis' "final solution."[3]

This vicious streak had not yet surfaced at the time that Stein came under
Dühring's tutelage. Disappointed by theology, yet thirsting for comprehensive knowledge, the twenty-year-old Stein readily absorbed Dühring's
"philosophy of reality." Dühring rejected the notion of infinity, arguing
that, since the universe and all its parts are finite, man will eventually be
able to discover the entire mechanism of the world. All human resources
should be put into this effort. Dühring stridently opposed Christianity,
which he condemned as an oriental importation, as well as metaphysical
speculation and even art, for these served only to veil reality and corrupt
natural instincts.[4]

Like Auguste Comte, whom he regarded as the only significant philosopher of the nineteenth century, Dühring considered philosophy capable
of answering all meaningful questions about life. In embracing ethics and
epistemology in a materialist doctrine, Dühring differed radically from em-
piricists in the British tradition as well as from such influential materialists
as Karl Vogt (1817–1895) and Ludwig Büchner (1824–1899). Although he
rejected Comte's altruism as necessarily hypocritical, Dühring shared
Comte's conviction that moral laws are contained in nature; the ultimate
purpose of studying nature is to learn how to act in a moral fashion.

This practical appeal (as well as Dühring's racialism and ethnocentrism)
would commend Dühring's work to such philosophical idealists as Chamberlain, who thoroughly disagreed with him on epistemological grounds.[5]
Dühring's rejection of philosophizing for its own sake helps to explain how
Stein was able to absorb Dühring's influence without giving up his own religious and reformatory goals. Although he decried Wagnerian art as Romantic and reactionary, Dühring preached the necessity of Germanic regeneration with equal zeal. Dühring, too, celebrated the allegedly Nordic
virtues of loyalty, integrity, trust, firmness, and inner freedom. The avowed
goal of his philosophy was to "internalize these ideals in flesh and blood."[6]
Even his attack on supernatural religion was made not solely on epistemological grounds, but on the grounds that religion, by too easily absolving
man of his sense of guilt, did not provide an adequate basis for morality. As
a substitute for religion Dühring preached a *völkisch* creed very similar to
Wagner's.

In Stein Dühring and Wagner found an apt and fervent disciple determined to bridge the differences between them. "No book appearing now,"

Stein wrote to Bayreuth after the appearance of Dühring's autobiography in 1881, "will bring as much that is related to us in the deepest sense."[7] Whatever other influences Stein may have absorbed, however, he did not adopt Dühring's straightforward style. Stein's early works so abound in circumlocutions that Chamberlain deemed Stein's dissertation on Kant far more abstruse than the *Critique of Pure Reason* itself.[8]

Calling his method *kritischer Positivismus*, Stein attempted in his dissertation to reconcile Dühring's monism with Kant's dualism. The basis of all fruitful philosophizing, Stein argued, is to assume the unconditional reality of all external objects. Kant's analysis of experience—our relationship to the world around us—represented for Stein a return to this assumption, in contrast to the dogmatic rationalism of Descartes and his followers, who recognized reality only in pure thought. Yet Kant erred in denying that man can have knowledge of the unconditional reality of nature—the "thing-in-itself." This error had led to the unrestrained subjectivism of Fichte as well as to the reduction of the world of experience to mere phenomenality, developments that continued to plague the nineteenth century. Knowledge of reality is indeed possible, Stein argued, through a return to Kant's method of gaining deeper insight into our relationship to the objective world. "By recognizing in the perceiving subject the highest expression of world laws, but no supernatural element, a deductive construction and subjective discovery of a comprehensive natural law becomes possible."[9] Stein's contention that one can best learn about the world by looking into oneself echoed a similar argument of Dühring's. Its source was the fundamental assumption of Comtean positivism that the phenomena of human thought and social life are continuous with the phenomena of nature and therefore susceptible to analogy.[10] However, Stein's "critical positivism," as he called it, tended far more toward solipsism than toward scientism.

One year after completing his dissertation, Stein published *Die Ideale des Materialismus*, a much less systematic work. Here Stein sought to popularize Dühring's "philosophy of reality" as an inspirational doctrine. The exuberant but often bombastic style betrays its author's youth. "At fifteen I believed in Jesus," the opening sentences read. "At eighteen I was an atheist, at twenty a materialist. A lie at first, then a conversion, and then a religion."[11] There would have been no need for this book, Stein wrote, if Dühring's philosophy had become more widely known. Except for an occasional anti-clerical remark, however, Stein did not attack Christianity; he instead insisted that Dühring's brand of philosophical materialism reinforced Christian ideals.

The book juxtaposes idealized portraits of historical figures with utopian visions of a perfect society and fictional episodes of personal heroism. Its impulse was largely autobiographical, and it gives the picture of an impressionable young man with a high moral purpose. His praise of friendship as the highest good on earth foreshadows the sense of fulfillment that Stein would find as a member of Wagner's intimate circle. But Stein's bombast and hyperbole put off many readers and the book had little impact.

Dühring steered Stein's interest to the intellectual figures he admired most: Giordano Bruno and Jean-Jacques Rousseau. Rousseau was also a favorite among Wagnerians, not for his egalitarian doctrines, but for his rejection of the shams of civilization and his revival of emotionalism as an acceptable style. Stein's essay on Rousseau in *Bayreuther Blätter* in 1881 stands out as one of his most explicit statements of *völkisch* values. Like Dühring before him and Chamberlain after him, Stein deprecates *The Social Contract* as Rousseau's weakest work. The notion of the General Will, so often cited as a source of modern totalitarianism, found little endorsement among *völkisch* writers. Stein holds that Rousseau's postulate of human equality had been effectively refuted by Gobineau in his *Essai sur l'inégalité des races humaines*, a work Stein greatly admired. But Rousseau was right in recognizing man's natural motives as sympathy for his fellow man and desire to reduce human suffering. Chamberlain would later claim that such sympathy derived from the natural inclination of all people to share the interior lives of great men. Stein concludes that Rousseau's ideas had fallen on infertile soil in France, for otherwise they could never have led to the revolutionary despotism of Robespierre and Napoleon. As a foreigner of Swiss and probably German descent, Rousseau was bound to be misunderstood by the French. Following Gobineau, Stein attributes Rousseau's unhappiness to the hostility that his "Aryan-Germanic" personality aroused in a "Semitic-Latin" civilization.[12]

Would Rousseau have found a home in Germany? No, Stein concludes, because in Rousseau's day the German *Gemüt* (the mind conceived as the seat of emotion) had not yet emerged to consciousness. It was soon to do so, however, in the form of German idealism in art and philosophy. While probably not directly influenced by Rousseau, Goethe's *Werther* (1774) and Schiller's *Die Räuber* (1781) reflected a similar way of viewing the world. Stein stresses Rousseau's influence on Kant, though Kant's efforts to deduce moral laws entirely from reason also represented a reaction against Rousseau. By denying to Kant his claim of having arrived at the moral law through logic, Schopenhauer revalidated Rousseau's basic insight that morality was founded in *Gemüt*.

The ease with which Dühring's and Wagner's predilections could be subsumed under the principle of German uniqueness and superiority offers an early demonstration of the usefulness of *völkisch* doctrine as a unifying myth. Stein used the concept of race to denote little more than national character, a usage not uncommon in the nineteenth century. Yet the logic of his arguments points toward biological determinism. It was left for Chamberlain, a later convert to Bayreuth, to transform this hypothesis into dogma. In Stein's major writings on aesthetics, he did not use race as a category of explanation or analysis. Yet Stein's article on Rousseau remains a striking example of Gobineau's influence in Germany, as racialism increasingly provided a rationale for nationalist and conservative prejudices.

Like Stein's earlier work on Dühring's philosophy, his essay on the Italian Renaissance philosopher Giordano Bruno, *Der Wahn eines Helden*, tells the reader more about its author than about the philosopher it purports to discuss. Stein's interest in Bruno had been aroused by Dühring, who apparently admired Bruno's pantheistic philosophy for its exclusion of a divine mediator from a universe in which God and nature are one. Dühring's confidence in the capacity of man to solve the riddles of the universe bears some resemblance to Bruno's ecstatic vision of man as capable of penetrating the secrets of nature, albeit by magical means. For both philosophers the ultimate identity of matter and spirit made knowledge of the universe both possible and imperative.

Stein's exposition of Bruno's thought recalls the main thesis of his doctoral dissertation. Because the internal world of the mind corresponds to the external world of nature, man can learn directly about the world through contemplation and introspection. Of course, Kant was right that one can never comprehend reality through theoretical reason. But one can obtain such comprehension through art, philosophy, and religion.[13]

Bruno's poetic effusions gave Stein the opportunity to extol the importance of art as a vehicle to knowledge. Here Wagner—and Schopenhauer—supplanted Dühring as Stein's mentors. The artist espies the ideal content (*Gehalt*) of objects, Stein wrote, quite apart from their causal origin or other time-bound conditions. To the extent that feelings (*Empfindungen*) are fully involved in these intuitive visions, one must attribute full reality to them. In this highly subjective sense Stein contends that Plato's ideas were absolutely real. Art seeks to portray the ideas of things, while philosophy communicates ideas in conceptual form. Religion reproduces the artistic process in the ethical realm.

Like Gobineau, Stein viewed the Renaissance with considerable ambivalence. While it provided the setting for individual excellence, this era did not prove equal to the great cultural tasks proclaimed by its leading figures. Stein's indictment of an age that condemned Bruno to martyrdom implicitly censures the present for its indifference to Dühring and Wagner:

> It is a terrible responsibility to be the contemporary of a man who has something to say to his times: if we do not hear him, this single individual will transmit the memory of his contemporaries into posterity burdened with a curse. Rightly so. The inner worthlessness of an era expresses itself—solely and precisely—in its inability to nurture those impulses which point to the distant future because their content is eternal.[14]

In the final paragraph of *Der Wahn eines Helden*, Stein challenges his readers to emulate Bruno's unyielding faith: "Do you believe that there is something in the hard reality of things which is intimately related to the melodies inside us, and that the secret of our soul—love—is at once happiness, power, and life? Do you believe it? Is it a faith for which you can die?"[15] The Bruno whom Dühring admired—however spuriously—as the martyr for a monistic world view became for Stein the personification of martyrdom itself.

Under the influence of Wagner's dualism, however, Stein treats Bruno quite differently in his volume of dramatic dialogues, *Helden und Welt*. Here Stein's portrait is as outspokenly critical as Chamberlain's treatment of Bruno's thought would later be.[16] In an episode entitled "Thinker and Poet," Stein imagines a confrontation between Bruno and Shakespeare in a London inn. Only moments before, the English poet had saved the apostate Italian monk from a mob aroused to fury by Bruno's heretical utterances. Shakespeare, a man closer to the people, is able to communicate effectively with aristocrats and workers alike. Shakespeare berates Bruno for chasing abstract phantoms: "You see a realm of abstract designs [*Schemen*] before you, for which you strive in vain; you struggle for shadows of thoughts, and want to conjure up the divine day in an instant."[17] The path to regeneration, Stein's Shakespeare continues, leads through art and not intellect. A symbol (*Gleichnis*)—the picture of an inner vision—contains more truth than does conceptual thought. "That which would enrich your inner life as a symbol, will lead you to your death through a thousand tortures."[18] Here Stein's passage from Dühring's systematic positivism to Wagner's aesthetic idealism seems complete. As a brief against intellectualism (and revolution), however, the selection would probably have gained Dühring's approval.

This dialogue is typical of the dramatic method Stein employs in his book. Despite its assertion of the superiority of art over abstract philosophy, *Helden und Welt* derives whatever force it has from the interplay of ideas rather than from the interaction of persons. The clash of ideas reflects the social and ideological conflicts of Imperial Germany. In sections on "Greece," "Rome," "Christianity," and "The Modern Age," Stein propagates Wagnerian ideas. Not surprisingly he finds few heroes in the modern age. The leveling and brutalizing effects of industrialization destroyed the ground for heroism: only a moral regeneration could bring back an heroic age. Nevertheless, in an appendix in which he predictably condemns the French Revolution, Stein praises Saint-Just for his commitment to an idealistic vision.

Each section of the book consists of three episodes, in most of which historical figures reach heroic decisions contrary to conventional values. Thus Solon, the Athenian lawmaker, rejects King Croesus's tempting offer of power and wealth, admonishing him to change his life, "so that after all the glamor and pleasures of your life you do not have to find out in the hour of your death that you have cheated yourself out of true salvation."[19] Here Solon speaks the passage that Wagner cites in his introduction as best expressing the theme of the book: "However the powerful dark background of things may in truth be constituted, access thereto is open to us solely in this our poor life, and hence our transitory acts also embrace a serious, deep, and ineluctable significance."[20] Fifteen years later, Chamberlain would use this same passage in *The Foundations of the Nineteenth Century* to emphasize the importance of man's "transitory" physical and racial characteristics.[21]

The historical episodes of *Helden und Welt* gave Stein a vehicle for addressing present-day issues. An episode from the Roman period, entitled "The Curse of Hannibal," for instance, contains an attack on party politics, an alien system introduced to the kingdom of Bithynia by the Roman invaders. In protest against the peace the king had made with Rome—a peace that had brought material welfare while destroying native customs—Hannibal commits suicide. This denigration of partisan politics reflected a bias widely shared by educated people in Imperial Germany. Often this bias was coupled with anti-Semitism, as in the case of Wagner, whose views Stein paraphrased in his introduction to the *Wagner-Lexikon*: "It is a superior trait of the German that he never was skilled in political expediency; this trait, however, threatens to lead to his complete ruin since an alien element has gained esteem, behind the mask of education, in the parties, the press, yes, in art: Jewry, the bad conscience of our civilization."[22] *Helden und Welt* is entirely free of such anti-Semitic utterances, however, a noteworthy fact in view of its otherwise emphatic affirmation of *völkisch* values.

Stein's treatment of the Reformation reflected the continuing strength of Pietist tradition. His Luther regrets in old age that his teachings had been converted into rigid doctrine: "I want a community of believers who are one in love, and therefore find themselves united in the rules and forms of worship, and perform these with faith and a full heart: and no word more, no concordias, no doctrine."[23] In Stein's view the Reformation had achieved only partial reforms. A change in the spirit of the Ten Commandments was needed. Dühring, too, had criticized the Ten Commandments for supposedly revealing a Jewish proclivity to sin.[24] Stein's strictures are far more positive. "Thou shalt not steal" ought to read "Thou shalt not value possessions," and "Thou shalt not covet thy neighbor's house" ought to contain the more positive command "Thou shalt help thy neighbor."[25] The idealistic ingredient in Protestantism has rarely been more vividly stated.

Stein has Luther also regretting his failure to back the peasants in their revolt against the princes. Yet in an article in *Bayreuther Blätter* Stein defended Luther for saving the spirit of the Reformation, which might well have been destroyed by a victory of the peasants. True, Luther's attacks on the peasants had meant that the Reformation was not to become a truly popular movement. Thus it was left to Bayreuth to complete the unfinished task of uniting the spirit of the Reformation with former aspirations.[26]

Stein's defense of the peasants in *Helden und Welt* was not based on any sympathy for social revolution, but rather on his respect for peasant virtues and agrarian pursuits. An appeal for the establishment of a foundation to assist the peasantry was discovered among Stein's papers after his death. His counsel to the educated sons of middle-class families to go into farming and rural handicrafts (a goal that Stein said could only be achieved if these vocations were accorded higher status) reflected the growing concern among conservatives in Germany about the social consequences of rapid urbanization.[27]

This concern is also evident in an episode from the contemporary period, entitled "Homeless." Based on an actual occurrence in the city of Bayreuth, this selection harshly indicts the callousness of industrial society. An indigent worker, the victim of an accident that occurred while he was trying to rectify an oversight caused by the factory owner's negligence, is refused admission to local hospitals because he has no money. Even the workers' hospital turns him away because he had arrived in town too recently to be registered properly. The last words the dying worker speaks are "Flee, flee!" His death induces the family that had taken him in out of pity for his plight to emigrate to America. The motif of flight from a corrupt civilization would recur in Stein's choice of "Fugitives" as the projected title of a similar collection of dramatic dialogues which he did not live to complete.[28]

Through the harangues of his victimized protagonist, Stein attacked the advocates of industrialization in characteristically figurative language: "As long as what you call your industry does not sprout from field and forest and fresh nature like a flower, I consider the sap of this plant as all the more poisonous the more abundantly it grows."[29] Yet Stein offered no concrete proposals for the alleviation of industrial abuses, even to the limited extent that Dühring had done. For Stein, as later for Lienhard, the most deplorable effects of industrialization lay not in impoverishing workers but in corrupting ideal values and deprecating art. Like Wagner, Stein expected improved social conditions to follow from a moral regeneration in which love of fellow man would become the dominant social value.

The call for a changed social ethos was sounded again in the selection "Karl Ludwig Sand," published posthumously in the collection *Dramatische Bilder und Erzählungen*. Sand's assassination of the reactionary writer August von Kotzebue in 1819 provoked Metternich's repression of the universities and their nationalistic student fraternities, the *Burschenschaften*. As portrayed by Stein, Sand acted not out of a concern for political liberties but out of aversion to the weakness and subservience that Kotzebue's values bred. Because the values to which a society subscribes determine the quality of individual growth and of individual relationships, Sand's desperate deed was justified:

> For the sympathy of a being with a soul is the air in which we breathe; such a meeting of souls should, where it appears, be supported by general approbation and respect so as to facilitate the emergence of such relationships. Where, however, heartlessness is the general law, this feeling between individuals will never grow to the courageous joy of freedom, but will remain weak and fitful; and so from youth onward we are cheated of our life.[30]

Sand's deed, then, was not a narrowly political act to liberate German society from autocratic oppression, but an act designed to effect a total cultural transformation—the kind of transformation Wagnerians advocated. Sand's inspiration, according to Stein, came from art, not politics. This became the most popular of Stein's dramatic dialogues, partly no doubt because the *völkisch* creed it set forth was vague enough to appeal to moderates and extremists alike. Performed in 1922 at a convention of the German Youth Movement in Meiningen, it was the only belletristic work of Stein's to be reissued after World War II—a token of the revulsion against politics that the Nazi experience bred among disappointed nationalists.[31]

Most of the religious episodes in *Dramatische Bilder und Erzählungen* had been intended by Stein for a volume to be entitled *Die Heiligen* (*The Saints*), a project Stein had been working on at the time of his death. Stein's interest in the Christian saints resulted in part from his preoccupation with Schopenhauer, for whom sainthood and artistic genius represented the ultimate human efforts to surmount the world. In the saint, Stein wrote, the world becomes conscious of its meaning. Only saints and artists experience the unconditional necessity in their personal lives that makes them witnesses to higher truths.

Contrary to Chamberlain's judgment, who considered them Stein's masterpieces, the religious episodes represent the weakest of Stein's dramatic efforts. The moralism so characteristic of the Wagnerian mentality weaken the dramatic effectiveness of his work. Too often the protagonists are made to proclaim their own virtuous motives. In some measure this form of self-congratulation obtained in all his dramatic dialogues, but in none was the effect so unrelievedly self-righteous. Stein failed to solve the problem of how to convey religious feeling in dialogue form. It is hard to accept the humility of a person solely on the basis of his own asseverations. Nor was the effect any more convincing when, in an episode from *Helden und Welt*, Saint Katherine and her father confessor extol each other's piety. Here, as so often in this book, Stein's characters appear excessively sanctimonious. For Chamberlain and other Wagnerians, to be sure, didacticism was precisely what they valued most highly in Stein's work.

With *Helden und Welt* Stein professed his faith in Wagnerian idealism. Its publication coincided with the appearance of the first two parts of Nietzsche's *Also Sprach Zarathustra*. In celebrating a nobler type of man both works reflected disenchantment with the leveling and dispiriting forces of modern society. Their preoccupation with monumental tasks and personalities was not untypical of an era bedazzled by the achievements of Bismarck and other *Gründer*.[32] Both works formed part of a literary culture that included such diverse products as Conrad Ferdinand Meyer's novels of aristocratic heroism, Ernst von Wildenbruch's dramas of the Hohenzollern dynasty, and Treitschke's calls for an heroic literature to inspire Germany's youth. But their respective conceptions of heroism differs markedly. If Stein glorified the traditional Christian saint who renounced worldliness for the sake of his ideal, Nietzsche rejected such self-denial as hypocritical and unhealthy. The debasement of idealism into messianic nationalism would bear out Nietzsche's misgivings. Yet its nostalgic Romanticism and humanitarianism set *Helden und Welt* apart from the more strident *völkisch* literature spawned in the crisis atmosphere of the 1890s and 1900s. The cult of the *Volk* and the hero increasingly was to become the literary genre of writers determined to divert populist sentiments into conservative channels.

4

TOWARD A GERMAN RELIGION OF ART

> Certain aspects of organized religion help to conceal the higher self, be-
> cause even though Christianity does address itself to what is lofty in man,
> Church doctrine did not learn to appreciate the truly better and more no-
> ble self in man.
>
> Stein, *Die Entstehung der neueren Ästhetik*

In his major work, *Die Entstehung der neueren Ästhetik*, Heinrich von
Stein traced the evolution of aesthetic theory from seventeenth-century
French classicism to the eighteenth-century idealism of Johann Joachim
Winckelmann, a pioneer of art history and archaeology. Covering the aesthetic writings of French, English, Italian, Swiss, and German literary figures of the period, this book is a work of formidable erudition. In style it represents a considerable improvement over Stein's earlier writings. A work
of genuine scholarship, it proved less amenable to exploitation by nationalists than Stein's other writings. Its tone of impartiality led Chamberlain to
impute to the book a veneer of coldness, through which the glow of Stein's
German disposition (*nationale deutsche Gesinnung*) could only rarely be
discerned. Lienhard, too, deemed the book too academic to be of great use
in popularizing the values of German idealism.[1] Today these criticisms read
like compliments. Stein did, however, clearly differentiate between the
French and German aesthetic traditions, leaving no doubt as to his judgment that the latter represented a higher level of truth and creativity. His
book reaffirmed the unique superiority of the German idealist faith and its
metaphysical foundations. But at the same time his work provided a splendid example of Dilthey's historical method of sympathetic reconstruction.
Stein's treatment of the French classicists—indeed, of all the writers he
considers—is appreciative, for in Stein's view each of them contributed elements to the aesthetic doctrine that culminated in Winckelmann's idealism.
Successive generations of writers and critics imbued with new meaning and
content the aesthetic formula first enunciated by Nicholas Boileau-
Despréaux (1636–1711): "Rien n'est beau que le vrai."

Boileau held that a natural object is capable of producing an aesthetical-
ly pleasing effect if it is reproduced simply, clearly, and in accordance with
the rules of reason. In common with Descartes, Boileau trusted rational

thought more than sense perception or imagination. Descartes had found in man's capacity for abstract, dispassionate thinking the uniquely human trait, the trait that raises man above the animals. Stein, and Chamberlain after him, esteemed Descartes as an innovator of philosophical dualism, despite their disdain for Cartesian rationalism. In considering a faculty of the inner self superior to the changeable outside world, Descartes and Boileau had gone beyond the formalism of their predecessors and pointed the way to idealism.[2]

Stein went on to point out that eighteenth-century French thinkers modified the primacy of reason by again focusing attention on nature. Bernard de Fontenelle (1657–1757) challenged the Aristotelian canon of unity of time and place in drama by calling for the unity of action. Antoine de La Motte (1672–1731) extended the range of the drama even further by proposing the unity of interest as an aesthetic standard. The Jesuit critic Dominique Bonhours (1632–1702) proclaimed the importance of *delicatesse* ("refined taste") as a category of aesthetic judgment equal in importance to reason. Montesquieu theorized that aesthetic pleasure derives not solely from the application of aesthetic rules, but from exceptions admitted by the organ of taste. *Esprit*, with its suggestion of the unexpected and unusual, gradually supplanted systematic reason as the criterion of aesthetic judgment and enjoyment. No longer did the Cartesian disdain for emotions and feelings hold undisputed sway. Stein's treatment of *esprit* as a stage in the maturation of aesthetic theory gave no hint of the scorn that Chamberlain would express for a trait so typically French (*Ästhetik*, pp. 82ff.).

Stein used Taine's *Histoire de la littérature anglaise* (1864) as the source for his segment on English aesthetic theory. In French classicism the academic tradition of the Renaissance had been maintained relatively intact. In England, on the other hand, an independent aesthetic tradition deriving from the Reformation attached greater value to the imagination. Joseph Addison (1672–1719), for instance, considered imagination a necessary precondition for art and aesthetic enjoyment. Stein extols him as among the first to realize that what one sees in nature depends on how one looks at it, an insight Stein expresses as, "Soul is necessary to see nature" (*Ästhetik*, p. 142). No one extolled the imagination more vigorously than the English poet Edward Young (1683–1765), whose work received wider recognition in Germany than in France. Stein stresses the superiority of Young's conception of an artistic originality that exceeds normal comprehension over the rationalism of Boileau, who denied the label "beautiful" to anything that could not be understood. In England and in Germany the term "genius" came to have a dimension beyond its connotation in French, where the meaning of *génie* remained roughly equivalent to "talent" (*Ästhetik*, pp. 128ff.).

The longest section of *Die Entstehung der neueren Ästhetik* was devoted to Lord Shaftesbury (1670–1713), to whose aesthetic doctrine Stein attached great significance. Shaftesbury's fusion of man's aesthetic and ethical senses in a single faculty provided a rationale, so dear to Wagnerians, for the artist as a moral agent in society. The harmony perceived by this faculty as beauty is also perceived as virtue, and thus the purpose of art is to ennoble life. To be sure, Shaftesbury called for a faithful representation of nature, by which he meant both man's inner nature and external reality. The artist must not remain passive in the struggle for virtue. He must not be content simply to copy nature (an impossibility in any case in view of the infinite multiplicity of objects in nature), but must select those elements that will lead to the desired goal: the representation of a perfected character. Since nature in its entirety cannot be included in a work of art, and objects in nature are not of equal value, the artist must perforce choose and evaluate: "He must fill himself with the meaning of the whole; when he then proceeds to represent the individual object, he imparts to it meaning out of his own spirit. He creates out of the Idea" (*Ästhetik*, p. 180).

This form of naturalism, defined by Stein as present whenever an artist conveys the fullness of nature, leads to idealism. Stein's definition implicitly rejects the doctrine of naturalism expounded by Émile Zola during Stein's own lifetime. Accurate representation of detail alone is insufficient to satisfy aesthetic standards; the artist must illuminate the slice of life with a sense of the whole. Stein's citation of Rembrandt as the foremost practitioner of naturalism anticipated the use of Rembrandt as a paragon of creativity in Julius Langbehn's anti-modernist tract *Rembrandt als Erzieher* four years later.[3]

Stein acknowledges that, as in Rembrandt's case, artistic creation often precedes the articulation of theory. Stein denies a cause-and-effect relationship between practice and theory of art, however, for both arise from a common source. The aesthetic doctrines of both Shaftesbury and Alexander Pope, for instance, originated in opposition to the libertinage of the Stuart reaction. For both of them art was to help create a culture worthy of the Glorious Revolution. Here the allusion to Wagner's similar mission in the German Empire seems only barely disguised (*Ästhetik*, pp. 144ff.).

Stein attributes Shaftesbury's greatness to his reinvigoration of Boileau's axiom that beauty is truth. Wherever a classical tradition is formed, Stein writes, be it in France, England, or Germany, this principle has been infused with new vitality. In each instance the call has been sounded to take art seriously and to act on its imperatives. Like Descartes, Shaftesbury sought a guide to knowledge and life through reflection upon the self (*Besinnung auf sich selber*). But where Descartes resorted to abstract reasoning, Shaftesbury found a view of life (*Lebensanschauung*) in Ideas. There exists a higher self superior to the one that changes daily. The object of the artist's contemplation must be the inner law that man obeys in his best moments. Art thus inspired influences life far more deeply than merely providing enjoyment (*Ästhetik*, pp. 160ff.).

After treating the descriptive aesthetics of eighteenth-century British writers, Stein turns his attention back to the epoch of Rousseau in France. The Cartesian distrust of emotions as disruptions of pure intellect came under attack in the writings of the French historian Jean-Baptiste Dubos (1670–1742), who claimed that life would not be worth living without the passions. Diderot's discovery of beauty in the relationship (*rapport*) of objects to each other and to the viewer had the effect of opening up the richness of nature for art. Earlier, Charles Batteaux (1713–1780) had elevated nature to the status of man's teacher. For Rousseau, who opposed the supremacy of the intellect and of *esprit*, nature became an ideal in which man could find the conditions of true humanity. Stein discovers a congruence between Rousseau and his German contemporary Winckelmann: "One of them calls his ideal nature; the other finds it in works of art. Yet both share the same conviction [*Gesinnung*], the enthusiasm for an ideal not yet seen by others—an enthusiasm that fulfills them and that determines an entire future age" (*Ästhetik*, p. 268).

In the aesthetic writings of the Swiss critics Johann Jacob Bodmer (1698–1783), Johann Jakob Breitinger (1701–1776), and Johann Georg Sulzer (1720–1797), affective judgment or sensibility (*Empfindung*, as opposed to mere *Gefühl*) came into its own for the first time. No longer is the body viewed as simply a machine, thereby rejecting the Cartesian view. For the first time it became possible to say that there is no disputing about tastes. Aesthetic judgment and enjoyment contain a subjective element of "je ne sais quois." In their efforts to establish aesthetic norms based on the whole range of feelings as well as of thought, the Swiss aestheticians paved the way for German classicism (*Ästhetik*, pp. 271ff.).

The Swiss critics refused to recognize mere beautification as the primary function of art. Beautification is only a social function, as Kant suggested when he said that a man on a desert island would not clean house. Breitinger insisted, however, that a man on a desert island would still be stimulated by reading Milton. Breitinger demanded that art portray what is possible, not merely what exists. While English writers had called for an element of novelty in art, Breitinger pleaded for inclusion of the extraordinary. Sulzer formulated the expressive rather than imitative function of art even more explicitly. In Stein's exposition of Sulzer's ideas a theme of later aesthetic controversies is sounded. Sulzer's emphasis on expression (*Ausdruck*) as the primary function of art recurred in the later nineteenth-century attack—in the name of *Ausdruckskultur*—both on formalism and on a naturalism that superficially imitated life. *Ausdruckskultur*, a favorite Wagnerian catchword, attained its apotheosis through music, the least imitative of the arts.[4]

Parallels among artists who rebelled against the rigidity of French classicism led Stein to conclusions about the emergence of genius that Cosima Wagner selected as constituting the heart of the book: "There is analogy in the appearance of such genius. Here the life of the mind seems to be regulated according to a deeply concealed law which controls even superior personalities and makes them into its mouthpieces and executing organs. The same force guides Jupiter and Saturn in paths separated by worlds but identical in form" (*Ästhetik*, p. 321). The existence of such laws gave assurance of the purposefulness of life. Stein's idealism rested on the faith that a metaphysical reality lay beyond the historical world; individuals and temporal phenomena reflect aspects of eternity. Thus the history of aesthetics reflects divine purpose as ineluctably as the law of gravity, however much the laws governing the mind might differ in operation from mechanical laws. Stein no longer shared Dühring's confidence in man's ability eventually to comprehend the mysteries of the cosmos. No causal analysis of the conditions of race or power in the world could suffice to explain reality to man. But through art man might gain insight into the ideals which provide moral direction (*Ästhetik*, p. 321).

The German philosopher Alexander Gottlieb Baumgarten's (1714–1762) great contribution to aesthetic theory was to recognize art as constituting in itself a vehicle to knowledge. Conceiving of aesthetics as the science of feeling, Baumgarten finally gave to contemplative intuition (*Anschauung*) its due importance as a cognitive faculty. With his student G. F. Meier (1718–1777), Baumgarten stressed the necessity of seeing every object as a whole. A beautiful face may look repellent when part of it is seen under a microscope. However indistinct it might be, the beautiful is always a whole and as such contains the seeds of what may later come to be known distinctly. Even Kant, Stein pointed out, recognized in aesthetic beauty a form of knowledge that cannot be translated into concepts. The artist depicts what he has come to see in nature through the faculty of *Anschauung*, which Stein defined as the ability to see more deeply into an object than one can in a normal workaday fashion: "Human art creates beauty as an ever-renewed attempt to represent the conciliatory power in things in order to make this power our own. The creative artist carries this conciliatory power in himself. He reveals it as a no less compelling fact of nature" (*Ästhetik*, p. 356).

Modern aesthetic theory culminated in the idealism of Johann Joachim Winckelmann. Winckelmann used the term "ideal" in various senses: in its meaning of "imaginary" or "speculative" (in contrast to "real"), the concept "ideal" has a somewhat negative connotation. As the *beau idéal* of French classicism, on the other hand, "ideal" designated the end-product of judicious selection and arrangement in art. In the sense that Winckelmann used the term most frequently, "ideal" designates the quality of wholeness that distinguishes a type from its individual manifestations. "Ideal" describes that element of a work of art in which the artist perfects nature. Of course, naturalistic art, as defined by Stein, contains such an idealist motif insofar as it seeks to recapture the wholeness of nature. Stein formulated sweeping definitions of idealism in art:

> We call idealist in principle an aesthetic doctrine which emphasizes the fact that an artistic design originating within the artist is the determinant in artistic creation. . . . The seed of idealism exists wherever one speaks of the form and not the material content [*Stoff*], of the subject and not of the object, of artistic originality [*Eigenart*] and not of the imitation of nature. The full impulse of idealism, however, appears where one speaks of the extraordinary element in the human soul as the origin of art, where one assumes the existence of something suprahuman in man which corresponds to the "supra-natural" element in art. [*Ästhetik*, pp. 371, 374]

Although no art is possible without faithful observation of nature, each man possesses in his own soul a divine element, an ideal standard that is not derived from nature. Winckelmann expressed this ideal as "noble simplicity, serene grandeur" (*edle Einfalt, stille Grösse*), an ideal, originating in his own mind, which he found expressed both in the great art of antiquity and in such modern works as Raphael's *Sixtina*.

> With this inward definition of the ideal we mark a first great achievement of true aestheticism. For this definition is derived solely from consciousness of the content of the affective faculty and not from concepts; hence it is completely immanent. It is capable in turn of decisively influencing conceptualization, so that it gives the so-called transcendental, which as a concept is problematical, a definite content: at least for Winckelmann and spirits congenial to his. [*Ästhetik*, pp. 402–3]

Despite numerous nebulous passages, *Die Entstehung der neueren Ästhetik* remains a useful reference work in aesthetic history as well as an interesting document of the aesthetic and moral attitudes subsumed under the rubric of idealism. Too often, however, Stein failed to recognize that his definitions of idealism applied not to any particular school of art but to the creative process itself. The antimodernism implicit in Stein's book would be explicitly developed by later *völkisch* authors.

The many ways in which idealist attitudes could be harnessed to conservative political causes can be illustrated by the following example. According to Stein, Winckelmann despised French art and *modernité* because of the constraints placed on aesthetic standards in France by social norms. Although he shared the French love of moderation, Winckelmann's discipline derived from the fullness of his inner life, not from external conditioning. In the external world the definition and destiny (both meanings are suggested by the German term *Bestimmung*) of objects and beings are determined by their given boundaries; in the inner world definitions and destinies grow out of what is put into them from the potentially limitless reservoir of the affect. Inner limits develop from the strength of inner feelings. He who lacks such inner strength will also lack personal standards of judgment or conduct. Chamberlain would later pervert Stein's distinction between inner and outer limits to rationalize the separation of races. Extending this distinction into the political realm, Chamberlain attacked Catholicism, British Imperialism, socialism, humanitarianism, and cosmopolitanism on the grounds that universal movements fail to respect the unique qualities and destinies of individual peoples. Such movements are tyrannical, for they violate organic boundaries and seek to impose a common destiny on all peoples.[5]

Stein's own proclivity to cultural nationalism emerged more forcibly in his brief volume on Goethe and Schiller, based on his popular lectures at the University of Berlin in the summer of 1886.[6] In this most widely circulated of his works, Stein excelled at enlivening a potentially tedious academic subject. His now crisp and sure-handed style radiates enthusiasm. Like *Die Entstehung der neueren Ästhetik*, *Goethe und Schiller* does more than reflect the idiosyncracies of its author: it may be read with profit for the information it contains. However eulogistic his approach, Stein aimed at genuine understanding. In this respect the book contrasts favorably with so many tendentious works on Goethe and Schiller by later *völkisch* publicists, including Lienhard and Chamberlain, who tried to make of German classicism a platform for their own ultraconservative social and political views.[7]

The human personality is in an ultimate sense free and independent of the mechanism of nature—thus Stein summarized the distinctive doctrine of German idealism, reiterated in the works of Kant, Goethe, and Schiller. In an idealist work of art, the artist shapes his material in accordance with the higher laws of the personality, which are distinct from those of nature. Yet according to Stein idealist art is also realistic, for by its idealizing method the true meaning and essential character of things becomes manifest. It cannot be the task of art merely to imitate nature, for if this were true, the artist would do better to plant flowers than to paint them. Idealism represents man's triumph over nature—not in the sense of technological mastery, but in the sense of human autonomy: "The great power of the soul to take possession of things for the mind [*Gemüt*] and to express itself clearly in the representation of objects—this original sign of the dominance of man over nature is the artistic capacity, from which all the individual arts emanate, like the functions of an organ."[8]

Stein cited Schiller's preface to *Die Braut von Messina* (1803) to support his contention that art does not just induce a dream or illusion of freedom in man. Art actually sets man free by awakening in man the strength to gain objective distance from the sensual world and thus to dominate the material world through ideas. Since aesthetic beauty distills the qualities of humanity in their purest form, it follows that the primary function of a work of art is to educate mankind. It was Wagner who had fallen heir to the legacy of German idealism and who brought to culmination that program for the regeneration of mankind through art first voiced in Schiller's *Briefe über die ästhetische Erziehung der Menschheit* (1793). Stein's exposition stressed the need to maintain art as a realm insulated from politics. The reform of mankind will not come through immediate practical changes. The mood that will create future reality must first be fostered and refined in a world apart: "Probably many a person, affected by sincere sympathy for the very real sufferings of contemporary mankind, was rightly astonished to learn that high-minded idealists expected much of the 'make-believe' world of art [*Scheinwelt der Kunst*] and were preparing to put this 'make-believe' into practice."[9]

Schiller had envisioned his program of aesthetic education as a genuine alternative to the excesses of the French Revolution. German idealists had originally welcomed the revolution, and Kant, who rudely broke off conversation with anyone who disputed the importance of this event, never entirely lost this feeling of sympathy. The radical course of the revolution, however, disenchanted its former supporters. Not humans, Stein wrote, but tigers and hyenas had done their will in Paris. Schiller's program of reform through art represented an effort to achieve by a different route the goals that had not been reached in France. When another such opportunity presented itself, mankind would need to be better prepared. "Only the artist [*Dichter*] is the true and genuine human," Stein concluded. "Only from him is anything serious and therapeutic for the cause of mankind to be expected."[10] Upon Bayreuth the task of preparing mankind had devolved.

For Stein, "the idealist *par excellence*,"[11] the walks that Goethe and Schiller shared along the banks of the Ilm and the Saale seemed more important than all the battles waged by Napoleon. In contrasting Weimar and Paris as antipodes, Stein followed a model that Lienhard, Chamberlain, and other *völkisch* publicists would adapt to political purposes. To annul the pernicious consequences of the egalitarian and materialistic French Revolution, subsequent ideologists would increasingly advocate a "conservative revolution" in which the absolute values of the ideal realm would at last be implemented in social reality.[12]

Stein, however, was freer from ulterior motive than his successors, for whom advocacy of idealism served as a disguised plea for social conservatism. That is why Stein's work—however nostalgic or derivative it might have been—is still useful as a guide to Wagnerian aesthetic doctrine, the most systematic exposition of which may be found in Stein's posthumously published *Vorlesungen über Ästhetik* (*Lectures on Aesthetics*). A beautiful work of art contains four indispensable elements: first, exaltation (*Erhebung*), by which Stein meant the overcoming through form of the resistances imposed by man's body, whether they be pain, appetites, or passions. Works of art (or natural events) which evoke in us a feeling of exaltation we call sublime (*erhaben*). No matter how powerless our physical existence, our inner life remains unimpaired and conscious of its superiority to the natural forces that assail it. "Every inner condition," Stein wrote, "which impels man to despise his own life and to apply all his strength to the attainment of a high objective is heroic."[13] The metaphysical equivalent of this feeling of exaltation is expressed in the immortality of the soul.

The second component of aesthetic beauty, conciliation (*Versöhnung*), represents the healing power that reconciles man to the existence of evil and unhappiness in life. Vision of the beautiful bestows upon the viewer the conviction that there is a friendly essence in things. Art shows man how to overcome guilt by purely spiritual means, the metaphysical equivalent of which is faith. Art teaches us that providence may choose to implement good through evil by testing the power of the soul to expiate guilt. Ideally, self-imposed penitence would eliminate the need for punishment; thus Stein held the death penalty to be justified only if the criminal himself desired it.

A beautiful work of art also conveys a special mood (*Stimmung*), defined by Stein as the inner principle of form. We describe natural surroundings as having a special mood or atmosphere if they correspond to emotions within us. Just as a deep breath expands the chest, a new work of art expands the soul. If an artist portrayed a terrible event just the way it occurred in reality, it would paralyze man rather than setting his inner life into motion. Hence the material content of a work of art must be extirpated (*vertilgt*) by its form, as the German classicists demanded. In metaphysical terms *Stimmung* expresses the concept of nature as a whole, the principle by which unity is imposed on what would otherwise be a mass of chaotic detail.

No work of art is complete, however, unless it can be communicated. *Mitteilung*, the fourth major aesthetic principle, is as important to the artist as the work of art itself. Art gives an idea of what human beings can mean to each other. The highest works of art have always originated in a communal setting, whether it be Athens, the London of the Globe Theater, Weimar, or Bayreuth. The artist and his public share an aspiration to give themselves up to something higher, something purer, something unknown. It was for his art that Bach sacrificed his eyesight, and Schiller his life. In metaphysical terms this principle expresses a higher order of things in man, the transcendental element (*Überpersönliche*) that goes beyond individual existence.

These components of beauty in art—exaltation, conciliation, mood, and communication—express functions of the human soul: "The same traits that make up the characteristic elements of the human soul become elements of beauty when seen in their sensual appearance. This may be summarized in the proposition: 'Beauty is soul, and soul is beauty.' "[14] It follows that through art we may obtain a more definite conception of the makeup of the human soul. Art likewise provides the means by which the soul penetrates and permeates reality—the only means by which reality itself becomes more soulful.

Stein's aesthetic metaphysics provided an elaborate and sophisticated rationale for the primacy of art—a tenet central to the world views of both Schopenhauer and Wagner. In affirming the metaphysical link between art and religion, again in conformity with Wagner's views, Stein unconsciously reflected the need to find a viable substitute for religion in the increasingly secular atmosphere of the nineteenth century. The spirit of Christianity, Stein argued, is better expressed through art than through dogma. The dogma of Christ's death as a sacrifice—a residue of more ancient religions—has obscured the principle of redemption. Art has inherited the mission of expressing once again the living content of Christianity. Art supersedes dogma by giving direct and undisguised expression to the depth of man's feelings and the strength of inwardness. The connection between aesthetic and religious principles is necessary and not merely accidental, for the same basic characteristics of the soul contain the impulse to both. Man's ability to transcend suffering by the ascendancy of his inner nature over outer reality constitutes the basis of both art and religion.[15]

Stein reaffirmed the Christian doctrine of renunciation in Schopenhauerian terms. According to Stein, Schopenhauer realized in the realm of philosophy the German classicists' presentiment of a higher reality. Schopenhauer went beyond Kant in asserting that man's knowledge is not restricted to the world of appearances. Man can gain knowledge of the essence of things by viewing the world in purely aesthetic fashion, free of all interest or willfulness. The aesthetic mode of viewing—pure *Anschauung*—asks not "Why?" or "For what?" or "Where?" or "When?" but only "What?" of objects. Aesthetic contemplation of a still-life, for example, does not raise our appetite, no matter how delectable its contents. Through the disinterested absorption of an object into our consciousness we perceive its essential nature—its idea. As he is both more receptive and more creative than persons who view objects as means to satisfy their interests, the artist is able to express ideas. Yet even persons who have no special talent are capable of viewing the world in an aesthetic fashion. Everyone can learn from the ingenuousness of children how to view the world with astonishment and awe. These were the traits that conservatives sought to cultivate in society at large, at least in those whose role it was to observe and respect rather than to shape the rules that society lived by.[16]

Unlike Nietzsche, who repudiated pessimism, Stein embraced Schopenhauerian renunciation as a source of great moral strength. Stein admired Schopenhauer for recognizing the unavoidably tragic nature of life, in which the higher orders of being constantly strive to liberate themselves from the baser expressions of the will that suffuses all reality. All suffering results from this conflict between higher and lower orders, arising from a "hungry will that feeds on itself": "All pain originates in the collision between matter, which forever follows its mechanical and chemical laws, and consciousness which has other inner laws."[17] Bodily pain necessarily awakens compassion (*Mitleid*) in others, for it represents to all the struggle of consciousness against corporeal forces. A great suffering, even if borne invisibly to others, has a mysteriously palliative effect and eases the suffering of others. The greater a person's capacity to suffer, the more there are transcendent powers striving within him to realize a higher order of being. Stein emphasized the necessity of struggle and criticized Thomas Carlyle for accepting eternal laws of the good too much as given. Eternal laws are not self-evident, but must be discovered through experience (*Erlebnis*).

Stein's bleak vision of the world served as the backdrop for moral heroism. If we assume an indifferent world, a world in which the will is not operative in all things at all times, then human heroism, the inner conquest of the will, becomes no longer possible. Schopenhauer's philosophy demonstrates that all greatness is necessarily tragic and necessarily involves suffering. Only in the supreme moment of death is man freed from the tyranny of the will; then will and idea become one. Only in the awareness of necessity can there be any consolation.[18]

In devoting his literary epitaph to an exposition of Schopenhauer's philosophy, Stein remained a loyal Wagnerian to the end. Stein's tragic view of life echoed the neo-Romantic esteem of inner heroism faced with a hostile outer world, a theme characteristic of the "culture of rejection" that emerged as a protest against rapid modernization in the Second Empire.[19] It is a view that involves a distrust of worldly activity as ultimately pointless and futile. Such a view entailed social and political conservatism. Stein differed from later *völkisch* publicists, however, in his genuine commitment to idealism. He drew no social or political conclusions from Schopenhauerian doctrine other than to attribute to Germans a predisposition to inwardness and to claim for such inwardness a superior wisdom. It remained for later *völkisch* publicists—in particular, Chamberlain—to apply these aesthetic principles to propagating social and political goals. Since Schopenhauer's radical rejection of the world could hardly serve as a spur to action, Chamberlain looked to more affirmative sources as well to buttress his nationalistic and imperialistic doctrines. What makes Stein a more admirable intellectual figure than Chamberlain is that he did not deliberately subordinate art and religion to political ends. That Wagnerian idealism involved a degree of intellectual capitulation, however, was quite clear to perceptive critics. Such a critic was Friedrich Nietzsche, who overcame his own addiction to Wagnerism, but failed in his efforts to induce a similar change in Stein.

5

STEIN'S ROLE IN NIETZSCHE'S EMERGENCE AS A CRITIC OF WAGNERIAN IDEALISM AND NATIONALISM

Will anyone look a little into—right into—the mystery of how *ideals* are *manufactured* in this world? Who has the courage to do it? Come!
Nietzsche, *The Genealogy of Morals*

Stein's talent for conciliation, already demonstrated in his synthesis of Dühring's and Wagner's thought, was put to its greatest test by the apostate Wagnerian, Friedrich Nietzsche. The abortive relationship between Nietzsche and Stein paralleled in miniature the earlier break between Nietzsche and Wagner himself. Although thirteen years apart in age, the personal affinities between Nietzsche and Stein seemed to augur well for friendship and mutual understanding. Walter Kaufmann has described Stein as the only serious candidate, aside from Lou Andreas-Salomé and Peter Gast, for the role of Nietzsche's disciple.[1] Both Nietzsche and Stein came from a staunchly Lutheran background. Both men had enjoyed a thorough academic training, yet both regarded academic scholarship as an excessively confining vocation. Both combined philosophy and poetry in their work, and both disdained the materialistic ethos and shallow mass culture of their day. Both chafed under a sense of isolation and felt themselves misunderstood and ignored. Most importantly, both belonged to the same conscientious and introspective category of human beings who cannot avoid raising questions concerning the fundamental character and significance of life. In the search for values to live by, both men sacrificed health and happiness.

Various explanations have been offered for the rupture of the initially promising relationship between Stein and Nietzsche. For Chamberlain and other members of the Bayreuth Circle the explanation was simple: Nietzsche's mental health had already begun to deteriorate in the late 1870s, when he first challenged the assumptions of Wagnerian idealism. Chamberlain argued that Stein was a more original thinker than Nietzsche, for the latter had not shown strength enough to retain his individuality in the shadow of the great composer, but had had to rebel. Lienhard attributed the fault to Nietzsche's excessive intellectuality and incapacity for love. Nietzsche admittedly possessed a greater sense of humor than Stein, but Stein was right not to have adopted Nietzsche's cynical and compulsive way of laughing at the world.[2]

Elisabeth Förster-Nietzsche, on the other hand, blamed their rupture on Stein's efforts, under pressure from Bayreuth, to win Nietzsche back to the Wagnerian cause. Failing to grasp (or unwilling to accept) the full import of her brother's philosophy, Förster-Nietzsche attributed their misunderstanding not to philosophical or temperamental differences, but rather to Stein's well-meaning ineptitude as an intermediary. Förster-Nietzsche's efforts to palliate her brother's thought are reflected in the following astonishing description of the two men: "Both of them personified the highest and finest morality that the Christian and chivalrous ideal has ever brought forth."[3] This view was to serve as a model for writers intent on incorporating both the Nietzschean and Wagnerian legacies into völkisch ideology after World War I. Although he attributed their estrangement to Nietzsche's stubborn pride, Stein's biographer, Gustav Wahnes, also minimized the differences between Nietzsche and Stein (as well as between Nietzsche and Wagner himself).[4] Yet the differences between Nietzsche and Stein were fundamental and important, and an understanding of them enhances our insight into the relationship of Nietzschean thought to Wagnerian idealism and later völkisch ideology.

Although Nietzsche first heard about Stein through Paul Rée in 1876, they did not meet until 1884.[5] Their correspondence dated from 1882 when Stein went to see Nietzsche in Leipzig at the latter's invitation, only to find that he was not at home.[6] Nietzsche responded with a note regretting his absence. He did not regard Stein's attachment to Wagner as a barrier to friendship: "I have been told that you, perhaps more than anyone else, have embraced Schopenhauer and Wagner with heart and mind. This is of inestimable value, provided it is only for a time."[7] The later breach between them would have its source in Nietzsche's disappointment that Wagnerism did not constitute merely a stage in Stein's maturation.

Nietzsche sent Stein a copy of *The Gay Science* to which Stein responded with the proofs of *Helden und Welt*. Nietzsche's reaction was mixed: while acknowledging Stein's promise as a poet, he criticized his sententious language. "You still *read* too many books," he wrote, "particularly German books! How can one read a German book!"[8] Nietzsche could not resist deflating Stein's hero worship: "As for 'the hero': I don't think as well of him as you do. Nevertheless: it is the most acceptable form of human existence, especially if one has no other choice."[9]

With characteristic aplomb, Nietzsche unmasked Stein's treatment of heroism as a preoccupation with cruelty. No sooner have we to come to love something, when the tyrant in us (whom we like to call "our higher self") forces us to give it up. "I tell you frankly," Nietzsche went on, in a passage that provides insight into the purpose of his philosophical work, "that I myself have too much of this 'tragic' complexion in my body not to frequently curse it. . . . I would like to take from human existence some of its heartbreaking and cruel character."[10] Nietzsche concluded his letter with a remark designed to arouse Stein's interest and curiosity: "To be able to continue here I would have to reveal to you what I have not yet revealed to anyone—the task before which I stand, the task of my life."[11] Here Nietzsche's hopes of eventually provoking in Stein a conversion similar to his own seem barely disguised. This is borne out by a reference to Stein as his "successor" in a letter to Ida Overbeck, whom Nietzsche sent an extract from *Helden und Welt*. Nietzsche's remark was occasioned at least in part by the romantic feelings which he suspected Stein of harboring for the talented and vivacious Lou von Salomé, whom Stein had met at Bayreuth. Although Nietzsche appears to have exaggerated this liaison, his readiness to project his own feelings onto Stein reinforces the impression that he viewed Stein as his alter ego—a replica of his former self.[12]

Nietzsche sent Stein a copy of *Zarathustra* with the request that he withhold criticism and allow the book to act upon him. Stein's reaction was as mixed as Nietzsche's had been to *Helden und Welt*. In a letter to Hans von Wolzogen, the editor of *Bayreuther Blätter*, Stein criticized the "affected pathos" and linguistic virtuosity of Nietzsche's work, but he welcomed its trumpet call to "Remain true to the earth." Stein thought this exhortation equivalent to Wagner's demand to put timeless aesthetic and moral ideals into practice in the world: "In a very broad sense Nietzsche surely belongs with us."[13] Yet he advised against the publication of a review of *Zarathustra* in *Bayreuther Blätter*. Nietzsche later claimed to be pleased that Stein had understood only about twelve sentences of his book. It proved to Nietzsche the novelty and importance of his thought, to the elucidation of which he now planned to spend the rest of his life.[14]

Stein struck exactly the right note when, in the spring of 1884, he sent Nietzsche his translations of several poems by Giordano Bruno. Nietzsche was exuberantly grateful: "If you only knew how rarely anything strengthening still comes to me from outside!"[15] Nor was he in the least put off by Stein's well-meaning invitation to attend a performance of *Parsifal* at Bayreuth that summer. Declining because his work did not permit a prolonged interruption, Nietzsche invited the younger man—calling him one of his "great hopes"—to visit him at Sils-Maria.[16]

This three-day visit, in late August, 1884, turned out to be the high point of their relationship. Nietzsche was flattered that Stein made a point of having come specifically to see him and not the sights of the Engadine valley—"A way of accentuating a visit that impressed me."[17] For Nietzsche,

Stein's visit was the event of the summer. "This is a splendid human being," he wrote to Overbeck,

and because of his heroic frame of mind thoroughly understandable and congenial to me. At last, at last a new man who belongs to me and instinctively respects me! To be sure, for the time being still *trop wagnerisé*, yet quite prepared for me through the rational discipline he received in the proximity of Dühring. In his company I felt very sharply what practical task my life's work includes once I have enough young people of a very certain quality![18]

To Stein, Nietzsche wrote that from now on they shared a common lot.[19]

Four years later, in his autobiographical *Ecce Homo*, written a year after Stein's death, Nietzsche recalled Stein's visit in the light of the disappointments of the intervening years:

This excellent human being, who had walked into the Wagnerian morass with all the impetuous simplicity of a Prussian Junker (and, in addition, even into that of Dühring!), acted during these three days like one transformed by a tempest of freedom, like one who has suddenly been lifted to his own height and acquired wings. I always said to him that this was due to the good air up here, that this happened to everybody, that one was not for nothing six thousand feet above Bayreuth—but he would not believe me.[20]

Stein left an equally enthusiastic record of his visit, during which at one point he apparently had even spoken of moving to Nice after his father's death to be close to Nietzsche.[21] Stein wrote to Wagner's stepdaughter, Daniela von Bülow, of Nietzsche's vitality (*Lebensgefühl*), despite the obviously pitiable state of his health.[22] Stein had been struck by the vivid metaphors in Nietzsche's conversation. Describing his feelings toward Germany, Nietzsche had conjured up the image of a man in a dark room who is uncomfortably aware of the ceiling beams directly above his head. Stein had apparently interpreted this feeling as similar to his own sense of alienation in the urban environment of Berlin. The full import of this metaphor seems to have been lost on Stein, however, for he reassured Hans von Wolzogen that on his visit he had sought and found the author of *The Birth of Tragedy*, a work from Nietzsche's Wagnerian period. Alluding to Nietzsche's defection from Bayreuth, Stein doubted whether Nietzsche would ever again find happiness, "now that he had been untrue to that highest community."[23]

Nietzsche's radical independence exercised an unmistakable fascination for Stein, however, and put him on the defensive about his own life-style. His letter to Nietzsche shortly after his visit contained an apologia for his commitment to an academic career: "This may be good or bad—I myself, as I used to be, would call it bad—for the moment it determines my life. In the depths an infinite yearning for real, free life lies and waits. But I no longer want to give in to it—until I can put it into practice. That is why you now see me moving from library to library."[24]

Nietzsche responded with a poem, *Einsiedlers Sehnsucht* (*Hermit's Longing*), which he later entitled *Aus hohen Bergen* (*From High Mountains*) and appended to *Beyond Good and Evil*. It expressed his great longing for friends and followers who would understand the purpose and significance of his attack on conventional morality:

> O noon of life! O time to celebrate!
>   O summer garden!
> Restlessly happy and expectant, standing,
> Watching all day and night, for friends I wait:
> Where are you friends? Come! It is time! It's late![25]

The key line in the poem—"Only he who changes, remains akin to me!" (Nur wer sich wandelt, bleibt mit mir verwandt!)—expressed both Nietzsche's disappointment with his friends of earlier days and his hopes for his young admirer.

Stein, harrassed by the daily demands of his profession, no longer knew how to respond to such importunities. His oversolicitous response, designed to placate Nietzsche rather than to entertain seriously his appeals, struck Nietzsche as demeaning. Stein invited Nietzsche to participate by letter in a weekly discussion group with two friends on topics drawn from the *Wagner-Lexicon*, writing

> these discussions take on an ever higher and freer significance. Recently we called artistry the transition from the fullness of the personality to the transpersonal [*Überpersönliche*]. Here I thought of you and thought you might have enjoyed this discussion. And now it occurred to me: what if I could now produce a letter from Nietzsche which added a few sentences to the theme of our discussion? Would this be a form in which you would care to communicate? Would you consider something like this as a preliminary stage, a preparatory school for the ideal cloister?[26]

It is unlikely that the suggestion of participating in a discussion group, even with Wagner as a topic, would in itself have affronted Nietzsche. Stein's description, however, must have struck Nietzsche as epitomizing the kind of pretentiousness he had been assailing ever since his break with Wagner in the late 1870s. Nor could he have been pleased with Stein's coy reiteration of his loyalty to Wagner's cause. Referring to an earlier remark of Nietzsche's in which he had compared himself to Philoctetes on his island (without whose poisoned arrows Troy could not be conquered), Stein wrote that he still believed the "dead hero" (a reference to Achilles—and Wagner) bore the greatest share in the conquest of Troy.[27]

Nietzsche did not answer this letter. He gave vent to his indignation in a letter to his sister: "What an obscure letter Stein has written to me! And that in answer to such a poem!"[28] Two drafts of a response to Stein were later found among Nietzsche's papers. He was wise not to have sent them, for their sarcastic tone could only have pained him later. "In reading your last worthy letter I was overcome by such malice," he wrote, "that I laughed for a long time and enjoyed myself at your expense."[29] Nietzsche advised Stein not to become a philosopher. "My worthy friend," the second draft began, "you do not know who I am nor what I want." "Poor Stein!" Nietzsche wrote to Malvida von Meysenbug. "He even considers Wagner a philosopher!"[30] Nietzsche's reference to Wagner as "the great actor," both in his drafted response to Stein and in his letter to Meysenbug, anticipated the phrase he was to use in his polemical pamphlet of 1888, *Der Fall Wagner* (*The Case of Wagner*). To his sister, who attempted to mediate in behalf of Stein, Nietzsche wrote an indignant letter in March, 1885: "Do you really think that Stein's works, which I would not have written even at the time of my worst infatuation with Wagner and Schopenhauer, are of equal importance to the immense task which lies before me?"[31]

Stein was puzzled not only by Nietzsche's silence but also by the expectations which Nietzsche placed upon him. He confided his qualms to Malvida von Meysenbug a month and a half after his unanswered letter to Nietzsche: "As yet I do not know how Nietzsche conceives of our future relationship. He wants disciples—to comprehend a great, as yet unexpressed, idea. The mental energy involved in nurturing such an unexpressed, disciple-seeking idea is like a fraternal greeting from out of the chaos of an age proud of its non-philosophy."[32] Nietzsche remained an enigma to the younger man, a fact of greater significance in their relations than any question of personal loyalty to Bayreuth. Stein's visit to Sils-Maria may have enhanced his admiration for Nietzsche, but hardly his understanding of Nietzsche's point of view. This was, in the last analysis, the source of Nietzsche's frustration.

Stein and Nietzsche met only once more, on the road between Naumburg and Kösen in September, 1885, when by a curious coincidence each was on his way to visit the other. Stein recorded fragments of their conversation in his journal. They discussed a tropical fig tree whose trunk is too weak to carry its massive branches. The tree develops tentacles by which it supports itself on an oak tree, but the oak tree dies in the process. Transferring this allegory into the moral sphere, Stein said he had learned from Schopenhauer that man can free himself of devouring nature by growing beyond himself. Nietzsche replied that man can grow beyond himself—beyond his reflective consciousness—only if he acts like the fig tree. Stein expressed doubts that in this way man could become free. Nietzsche did not answer.[33]

This cryptic exchange illustrates the fundamental, indeed irreconcilable, difference between the two men. It reveals Nietzsche as fundamentally opposed to the Manichean aspect of German idealism, which pitted man against nature, spirit against matter, mind against body, the eternal against the temporal, and good against evil. To Nietzsche the idealist frame of mind represented wishful thinking, a form of vanity as well as cowardice in the face of truth and reality. In its denial of man's true nature, its self-seeking piety duplicated the vices of supernatural religion.

A note of resigned acceptance of their differences pervaded the last letters that Stein and Nietzsche exchanged in October, 1885. Stein, always a model of decorum, adopted a suitably deferential tone, but in expressing his disappointment at not having had more time to listen to Nietzsche's ideas he implied that he had not understood them.[34] Yet Stein confessed to feeling a sense of liberation in conversation with Nietzsche—the courage to voice ideas otherwise repressed. This was a compliment the older man greatly valued.

In his reply, apparently the last letter extant between them, Nietzsche criticized a book by Paul Rée for its shallow content. But his praise of Rée's lucid style represented an indirect criticism of Stein: "Among Germans it cannot be respected enough when someone . . . foreswears the real German devil, the genius or demon of unclarity—The Germans consider themselves deep."[35] His letter concluded, however, on a conciliatory note: "Let's all bravely remain at our posts, with some consideration for each other: for one thing will not do at all for two."[36]

Nietzsche's hopes that Stein's development might eventually have paralleled his own were expressed in a letter to Malvida von Meysenbug a month after Stein's premature death in 1887: "I actually never doubted that this noble creature was in a sense saved for me for later life, when his rich and deep nature should really have come to light: for he was still terribly young, far younger than his age, as is appropriate for trees which have a long and powerful destiny."[37]

Nietzsche's animus against Wagnerism, culminating in the passionate denunciations of 1888, was undoubtedly aggravated by the disappointment he suffered in his relations with Stein. Nietzsche bitterly accused Wagner of having seduced the best of Germany's youth—not by his music so much as by his idealism. "The youth becomes a mooncalf—an 'idealist.' He is beyond science, hereby attaining the level of his master. Instead, he acts the philosopher."[38] Nietzsche rejected the claims of an absolute morality. How do you test, he asked, the eternal content of ideals? Absolute beauty, like absolute ideas, is but a phantom of the mind. Yet the only thing Germans take seriously is the "idea," which Nietzsche described as the obscure, the uncertain, the presentient.[39] Nietzsche's method of psychological analysis differed radically from Stein's preference for metaphysical synthesis and conciliation. Hope, which Stein once called the highest of virtues, was for

Nietzsche only a means for the prolongation of suffering, and faith, the ultimate Christian value, meant only unwillingness to face the truth. For Stein, on the other hand, Christian morality was not subject to question. If God was indeed dead, as Zarathustra claimed, then it was up to man to resurrect Him. Christian moral values were to be professed and practiced, not examined or dissected.

Nietzsche's philosophical method was to pierce the superficial aspect of human thought and behavior—the layer of self-deception—and to lay bare the unacknowledged motives beneath. His great contribution to ethics is to have shown how human "virtue," by cloaking the will to power in respectable dress, can serve as a mask for evil. Although his premonition of the dangers inherent in nationalism made Nietzsche overstate his case against German idealism, his unequivocal condemnation of an incipient *völkisch* ideology was vindicated by the course of German history in the twentieth century. In *Ecce Homo*, Nietzsche made clear that his target in *Der Fall Wagner* was not Wagner alone:

> Ultimately, an attack on a subtler "unknown one," whom nobody else is likely to guess, is part of the meaning and way of my task—oh, I can uncover "unknown ones" who are in an altogether different category from a Cagliostro of music— even more, to be sure, an attack on the German nation which is becoming ever lazier and more impoverished in its instincts, ever more *honest*, and which continues with an enviable appetite to feed on opposites, gobbling down without any digestive troubles "faith" as well as scientific manners, "Christian love" as well as anti-Semitism, the will to power (to the *Reich*) as well as the *évangile des humbles*.[40]

Could Nietzsche have been thinking of Stein in his cryptic reference to an unknown person, whose identity could not readily be guessed?

Certainly Stein's works were not free of the cultural nationalism espoused by so many of Wagner's followers. Moreover, in striking contrast to Nietzsche, Stein shared the generalized anti-Semitism so typical of his generation of idealists in Germany.[41] In his assessment of political anti-Semitism—a movement thoroughly despised by Nietzsche—Stein displayed a characteristic ambivalence. While he considered anti-Semitism an ineffective way of mobilizing national sentiments, he nonetheless felt that the movement contained the healthy forces on which a renewal of German social and cultural life would eventually have to be based. In a review in 1882 of *Die Weltpolitik unter besonderer Bezugnahme auf Deutschland* (*World Politics with Special Reference to Germany*) by Konstantin Frantz, a critic both of liberalism and of Bismarck's "smaller Germany," Stein endorsed Frantz's proposal for Germans to colonize South America to create the "humane culture" (*menschliche Kultur*) that was lacking in North America. Nietzsche's sister and her virulently anti-Semitic husband, Bernhard Förster, sought to put such a plan into effect in Paraguay—a project Nietzsche viewed with considerable distaste. Stein's view of anti-Semitism was far more sanguine than Nietzsche's: "From anti-Semitism we learned what the forces must be like in which we can place our trust. Certainly the magic word has not yet been found which can form of these forces a peaceable German world power; nevertheless, the most minute trace of genuine, instinctive impulses among the people is more important than the ever so dexterous distinctions of politicians."[42]

Stein's failure to heed or understand Nietzsche's precepts anticipated his country's later enthrallment to nationalistic ideology. In purveying idealism as a doctrine for the betterment of the world, Stein, like his mentor Wagner, anticipated the cultural messianism of Lienhard, Chamberlain, and later *völkisch* ideologists. Where Western ideologues of imperialism sought to export liberalism to free the individual and society from institutional despotism, German ideologues extolled idealism to free the individual and society from personal egotism. Against the libertarian ideals of democracy, Germanic ideologists advocated an inner freedom from the restraints imposed by human frailty. Their concern was not with the external autocracy of despots, but with the internal tyranny of sinfulness.

In the light of the *völkisch* exploitation of idealism as a rationale for imperialism, the vehemence of Nietzsche's assault on Wagnerian idealism and German cultural nationalism appears less indefensible than it might otherwise seem. Like Heine before him, Nietzsche foresaw the destructive potential that idealism could generate, even though (or precisely because) it seemed to epitomize virtue and respectability. With the same exaggeration with which Wagnerians idealized the German past, Nietzsche cast Germany in the role of historical villain. His charge in *Ecce Homo* (written in 1888, but withheld from publication by his sister until 1908) that Germans had all the great cultural crimes of the past four centuries on their conscience is the ultimate antithesis of Chamberlain's version of history in *The Foundations of the Nineteenth Century* (1899), published a decade later. Unlike Stein or Chamberlain, who considered the Reformation the greatest achievement of the Renaissance, Nietzsche blamed the Germans for having defrauded Europe of the harvest of this last great historical epoch. Their wars of liberation had likewise deprived Europe of the benefits of Napoleon's existence, giving rise to nationalism, "this most *anti-cultural* sickness and unreason there is."[43] As against Stein's panegyrics of German inwardness, Nietzsche defined the "German spirit" as "the by now instinctive uncleanliness *in psychologicis* which every word, every facial expression of a German betrays."[44] In spite of Förster-Nietzsche's efforts to make his philosophy serviceable to German nationalism, Chamberlain and later *völkisch* ideologists knew full well that Nietzsche was their antagonist, not their ally.[45]

Stein did not alone precipitate Nietzsche's frontal attack on German idealism and national self-glorification; the roots of Nietzsche's disenchantment with the idealist mind-set lay well in the past. But Nietzsche's failure to make a dent in Stein's outlook, despite his impression of initial success, must have confirmed the bitter apprehensions which found such drastic expression in his late works. Stein's unmistakably benevolent intentions and genuine moral zeal gave a sense of urgency and immediacy to Nietzsche's chosen task of unmasking a mentality he regarded as benighted. Nietzsche clearly apprehended a danger in this way of thinking, though he could not, of course, foresee the actual form this danger would take. No one has warned more fervently—in the words of George Bernard Shaw which he derived from reading Nietzsche—that "the road to Hell is paved with good intentions."

Friedrich Lienhard during World War One. (*Courtesy Deutsche Staatsbibliothek, Berlin/DDR.*)

PART TWO

Friedrich Lienhard
and Vulgarized Idealism

Our educated people of today, our "good people," do not tell lies—
that is true; but that is *not* to their credit. . . . All they are
capable of is a *dishonest* lie; whoever accounts himself today a
"good man" is utterly incapable of confronting any matter except
with dishonest mendaciousness—a mendaciousness that is
abysmal but innocent, truehearted, blue-eyed, and virtuous.

NIETZSCHE, *The Genealogy of Morals*

6

FRIEDRICH LIENHARD'S CAREER AS A PUBLICIST OF *VÖLKISCH* IDEALISM

> I stand closer to Parsifal than to Zarathustra. . . . I do not number myself among those who investigate the grail [*Gralforscher*], but among those who seek the grail [*Gralsucher*].
>
> Lienhard, *Parsifal und Zarathustra*

Three months after Heinrich von Stein's death in June, 1887, a young student of similar disposition arrived in Berlin. He would look back nostalgically at the 1880s as the decade in which the last great generation of idealists—among whom he numbered Carlyle and Emerson, as well as Wagner, Gobineau, and their disciple Heinrich von Stein—had died. His name was Friedrich Lienhard (1865–1929), and he would devote his literary career to popularizing and disseminating the values that Stein and other transcendental idealists had stood for.[1] Through dramas of heroic legend, historical novels, and publicistic tracts Lienhard would seek to perpetuate a bygone literary culture in a rapidly changing society.

Lienhard sought to maintain the social basis on which such an idealist culture could flourish. Addressing himself primarily to an educated middle class of teachers, ministers, civil servants, rural doctors and lawyers, and their families, he gave comfort to those who felt threatened or confused by the cultural and social changes accompanying modernization.[2] He became one of the most popular authors of the German Youth Movement. After World War I excerpts from his works were widely used in readers for German schools. Reducing philosophical concepts to inspirational slogans for household consumption, Lienhard lacked the intellectual rigor and creativity both of the great predecessors in whose footsteps he thought he was following and of the major literary figures of his own day whose fame and influence he fought. His works remain of historical interest, however, because they shed light on the attitudes and values of an important segment of German society during the declining years of the German Empire and the Weimar Republic.

Lienhard's literary career mirrored the growing desperation of an embattled social order. From 1887 to 1903 Lienhard lived in Berlin, assailing the social and cultural currents of change in the German capital. In articles, books, and such influential pamphlets as *Die Vorherrschaft Berlins* (*The Predominance of Berlin*), which popularized the catchphrase *los von Berlin* ("away from Berlin"), he attacked materialism, secularism, and social democracy. After 1903, when he settled in Weimar, the tone of his work became less polemical and more escapist. In the works of the German classicists he found the values that would redeem a decadent age. As he grew ever more out of touch with the progressive forces of his time, the evolution of his thought reflects the degeneration of one strand of *völkisch* idealism into moral evangelism and vulgarized mysticism. Although nationalistic, authoritarian, and elitist in his views, Lienhard's rejection of political activism antagonized radical conservatives in the period of growing politization after World War I.

Lienhard was born in 1865 in the Alsatian village of Rothbach, near Zabern, the town that in 1913 was to lend its name to one of the recurring crises pitting progressives against nationalists in Wilhelmine Germany.[3] He was the eldest son of a Protestant elementary schoolteacher whose own parents had still been peasants. Lienhard's earliest memories went back as far as the Franco-Prussian War of 1870–1871. He remembered being impressed by the grandeur and discipline of the German conquerors, who had previously been portrayed to him—in French Alsace—as barbarians living on potatoes, sauerkraut, and pumpernickel.[4]

Like Heinrich von Stein, Lienhard was only eleven years old when his mother died. On her deathbed she extracted from her son a promise to become a parson. In later years Lienhard felt that at least in spirit he had fulfilled his promise, even if he had spread God's word through literary works rather than from the pulpit of an Alsatian village. Religion was an important part of young Lienhard's life. His father was swept up into the Old Lutheran pietist revival movement led by the Alsatian country preacher Michael Huser in the 1860s and 1870s. After the appointment of a liberal parson, a number of Old Lutheran adherents decided to build their own church in the village. Lienhard's father, who served as church organist, was caught in the middle of the dispute. Although his sympathies lay with the so-called "protest church," his position as teacher and civil servant put him under pressure to support official policies. To solve this dilemma, young Friedrich (or Fritz, as he was called until he adopted the more dignified Friedrich in 1903) played the organ in the protest church while his father continued to perform his duties in the official church. Noting that liberalism was no more tolerant than orthodoxy, Friedrich claimed to have acquired from this dispute a permanent distaste for the "plague of party politics."[5]

Aggrieved by the loss of his mother, Lienhard did not enjoy an easy

youth. He was teased and bullied at school, where he felt himself misunderstood by his teachers. Twice he was forced to repeat a class at the
local gymnasium. At home his father was severe and sometimes contemptuous toward him. When Lienhard wrote him a poem for his birthday one
year, his father asked where he had copied it. Parental coercion and lone-
liness pervaded the years of his upbringing. He found solace in books of
poetry, for which he sometimes sacrificed his lunch money, and in
daydreams of leaving Europe forever. The melancholy Austrian Romantic
Nikolaus Lenau (1802–1850) was the favorite poet of his youth.[6]

Shy and inhibited, young Lienhard worshipped from afar a "French"
Alsatian girl (the same girl, according to his account, whom he married in
1915, the year of his fiftieth birthday, after the circumstances of war had
coincidentally brought them together again). In the recollections he
published in 1918, Lienhard bitterly recalled the sexual conflicts that
plagued his adolescence: "Suffering, shame, and shattered nerves are today
lodged in this realm, which ought actually to be a temple and a holy grove.
Here divinities and demons fight each other: spiritual love and animal
drives. The important thing is that the divine remain victorious."[7] The
legacy of his upbringing and unresolved adolescent conflicts was a lifelong
prudishness, which grew into self-righteousness and intolerance.

In his imagination, young Lienhard delivered his beloved from the bonds
that tied her emotionally to France, like the prince in the legend who
releases his sleeping princess with a kiss. Unlike the majority of Alsatians
Lienhard identified himself with a Germany whose culture—and power—
he admired. He deplored the folly of those who protested German domination, thereby only depriving themselves of a voice in the future of their
country. His first publication, a poem in the *Strassburger Post* when he was
nineteen, made up in patriotic enthusiasm what it lacked in literary quality:

> . . . .
> A cheer to Germanic Alsace!
> A roaring cheer to Pan-Germany
> And the heroic German Kaiser![8]

Like Stein before him, Lienhard abjured theology after only one
semester of study at the University of Strassburg. Instead he received his
father's permission to study history and literature in Berlin. But the university, where he occasionally heard the lectures of Treitschke, served
Lienhard mainly as a camouflage for his literary interests and activities.
Inspired by a reading of *Moderne Dichter-Charaktere*, an anthology of
poems by young writers in revolt against the formalism and complacency
of an older generation, Lienhard wrote in his diary about the emptiness and
superficiality of most contemporary German literature and the need for

more greatness, dedication, and passion.[9] He felt keenly the disparity between a Goethe or a Schiller and the literary "dwarfs" of his own day. Despite doubts about his own talent, he decided in 1889 to leave the university to pursue a literary career. By that time his first publications had appeared.

In a two-part article entitled "Reformation der Literatur," appearing in the influential new literary journal *Die Gesellschaft* in 1888, Lienhard launched an attack on naturalism and formalism in art.[10] Through the good offices of the neo-Romantic novelist and publicist Karl Bleibtreu, a coeditor of *Die Gesellschaft*, Lienhard succeeded in 1888 in publishing his first play, *Naphtali*. Aside from a favorable review in *Die Gessellschaft* by Conrad Alberti (1862–1918), a firebrand leader of the generational revolt against the staid poetry of the Munich court, the play received little notice and was never performed on stage. In it Naphtali, a young Hebrew in the time of the Babylonian Captivity, fails to join the Exodus of his people to Israel because of his sensuous love for an Egyptian girl. Having betrayed his ideal by surrendering to sensuality, he commits suicide by throwing himself into the Red Sea. Although this theme of remorse for disloyalty to an ideal frequently recurred in Lienhard's later works, never again would he cast a Jewish character in so idealistic a role.[11]

In another early work, *Die Weisse Frau*, published in the form of a diary in 1889, Lienhard contrasts the peacefulness of the village to the hectic life of the big city. Lienhard's first reaction to Berlin was one of awe. The Imperial palace rose directly opposite the university, and one of the first questions that students asked each other was, "Have you seen the Kaiser yet?" Lienhard was impressed by the deep personal attachment that Berliners felt for their monarch. His landlord, who wore his beard in the style of William I, cried bitterly when the emperor died in 1888. From his balcony Lienhard could see Bismarck's dominant silhouette in the unforgettable funeral procession. Like so many disaffected conservatives of his generation, he came to view Bismarck's dismissal in 1890 as symbolic of a major cultural break. When Lienhard sought refuge in the countryside, he identified his lot with that of the aged Bismarck, rancorously following the politics of the capital from his retreat in the *Sachsenwald*. A spiritual Bismarck was needed, Lienhard wrote in 1891, to master Germany's cultural fragmentation as Bismarck had mastered its political disunity.[12]

In spite of his fondness for imperial grandeur, Lienhard felt lonely and out-of-place in Berlin. He could not get used to the tempo of city life and to the cold indifference with which people passed each other in the streets. Keenly aware of his provincial background, Lienhard imagined that people regarded him with derision. He felt a recurrence of his childhood fear of making a fool of himself. Lienhard could not bear the superciliousness and assumed superiority of his city-bred contemporaries. Lounging in cafés and foyers, they joked about women and talked about making money. Nothing was sacred to them, and even art seemed only a matter of business.[13]

From 1890 to 1892 Lienhard supported himself as a tutor to the blind, epileptic son of a professor (whose name he does not mention in his memoirs) at the University of Berlin. Social functions made him uncomfortably aware of his lack of savoir faire. His insecurity was reinforced by a sense of failure as a writer. He felt as if the naturalist literary revolution, now in full swing in Berlin, had passed him by. With a twinge of regret Lienhard recalled the opportunities that he had been temperamentally unwilling or unable to seize. Even the innovative theater director Otto Brahm (1856–1912), discoverer and patron of the naturalist dramatist Gerhart Hauptmann (1862–1946), expressed interest in his work. Although Lienhard's early work exuded too much pathos for Brahm's taste, he invited Lienhard to submit further efforts to his literary journal, *Freie Bühne für modernes Leben*, the journal that subsequently became the prestigious *Neue Deutsche Rundschau*. Ludwig Jacobowski (1868–1900), editor of *Die Gesellschaft* from 1898 to 1900, invited Lienhard to participate in his avant-garde literary circle, *Die Kommenden*. But Lienhard did not feel comfortable in this milieu. "These people," he wrote home to a friend in 1890, "are so cold, so sober, so modern and rational, so un-German, so scientific, so lacking in religion."[14] Throughout his life Lienhard would compensate for lack of talent by cultivating superior virtue and an aggressive nationalism.

Lienhard turned to journalism in 1893, becoming an editor of the Berlin monthly, *Das Zwanzigste Jahrhundert* (*The Twentieth Century*). From 1896 he served as a *feuilletonist* of Friedrich Lange's pan-German periodical, *Deutsche Zeitung*. Disgust with the competitive literary life in Berlin and his failure to achieve recognition frequently induced Lienhard to seek solace in such isolated regions as the Bavarian Alps, the Scottish highlands, and the Norwegian fjords. A hike through the Vosges mountains of his native Alsace in the summer of 1895 gave rise to his first major publication. *Wasgaufahrten* (*Travels through the Vosges*) is a slim volume of idyllic travel pictures interspersed with acerbic commentary on the literary culture of Berlin. The book was, if not inspired, at least strongly influenced by Julius Langbehn's anti-modernist tract, *Rembrandt als Erzieher*, which Lienhard, like so many of his contemporaries, had read with avid interest after its appearance in 1890.[15] *Wasgaufahrten* anticipated the later nativist *Heimatkunst* movement by seeking to mobilize such rural values as austerity, deference, duty, patriotism, and religious faith against the hedonism, intellectual culture, and social democracy of Berlin. The heart of the social problem, Lienhard contended, lay in the individual's oppressive feeling that in a mass society he was no longer free to determine his own growth toward God.[16]

Lienhard exhorted German poets not to subvert their vocation by descending into the realms of economics or politics. "The Gods of art have ever been the Gods of light," he wrote; "like the penetrating sun, they looked deeply into the cares and sufferings of the earth, but they stayed in the pure heights of their heaven."[17] From Langbehn Lienhard derived the term *Reichsbeseelung* ("ensoulment of the Reich"), a euphemism for national unity and social harmony, goals requiring the suspension of agitation for political reform. Lienhard ascribed to German artists the grand task of creating a "soul" for the empire by revivifying spiritual and moral ideals in an age that was able to build an Eiffel Tower but not a Strassburg Cathedral.[18]

Enthusiastically reviewed by Heinrich Sohnrey (1859–1948), founder of the journal *Das Land* in 1893 and vociferous opponent of urbanization, *Wasgaufahrten* endeared Lienhard to nationalists disgruntled by the more liberal course of German politics since Bismarck's dismissal in 1890. Lienhard's mixing of personal experiences, cultural criticism, and citations from favorite authors was to become characteristic of his method. He devoted several pages to quotations from Treitschke's attacks on democracy, party politics, and French opposition to German aspirations abroad. Describing his emotional crises to his readers, Lienhard viewed his own recovery as a therapeutic model for the maladies of the age. In the peace of the Vosges forest he rejoiced to be shielded from the political controversies of the day. He resented the Berlin literati: "To possess a finely developed feeling of honor, to feel oneself a hundred times more intelligent than this presumptuous, insolent people, and nevertheless to have to run the gauntlet as a lonely provincial between the superior smirks and glib verbosity of the big city market fixers—that is a hellish school!"[19] In nationalist ideology Lienhard found both a prop for his rumpled self-esteem and a weapon with which to beat his adversaries.

Lienhard's frustrations were reflected in his choice of dramatic themes. He turned to his native Alsace for the protagonists of his historical dramas *Gottfried von Strassburg* and *Odilia*, performed in Strassburg in 1897 and 1898 respectively. Disappointed in love, the *Minnesänger* Gottfried von Strassburg heroically renounces luxurious life at court. The saintly Odilia, committed to a religious vocation, rebuffs her tyrannical father's command to marry, and through the strength of her faith persuades him to permit a religious revival in his territories. Such examples of triumph through renunciation must have consoled Lienhard for his own disappointments.

Eulenspiegels Ausfahrt, the first play of a trilogy published in 1901, was performed in Strassburg in 1896. Through comic escapades Till Eulenspiegel wages a lonely struggle against a corrupt and degenerate society on the eve of the Reformation. The one-act middle play of this trilogy, *Der Fremde* (*The Stranger*), was the only play of Lienhard's to be performed in Berlin. It was given a single performance in 1903 at the royal theater, the *Königliche Schauspielhaus*, under the direction of Max Grube (1854–1934), and was performed again in 1922. According to Lienhard's account, Grube had rejected *Eulenspiegels Ausfahrt* some years before, not on aesthetic grounds, but because he feared the adverse reaction of the Berlin press to a play by an author reputed (with some justification, as we shall see) to be anti-Semitic. Fantasies of unfair discrimination occasionally helped Lienhard to explain away his lack of literary acclaim.[20]

Strident criticism of the Berlin theaters and those who controlled them constituted the major part of *Die Vorherrschaft Berlins*, the set of polemical essays with which Lienhard hoped to promote *Heimatkunst*. The term *Heimatkunst* (literally, "art of the homeland") was coined in 1897 by Lienhard's friend and later fellow-resident in Weimar, the anti-Semitic literary historian and polemicist Adolf Bartels (1862–1945).[21] Feeling that *Heimatkunst* was being too narrowly construed as regional or local art, Lienhard resigned in September, 1900, as editor of *Heimat*, a journal he had helped to found only eight months before at the instigation of his Leipzig-based publisher, Georg Heinrich Meyer (1872–1931). *Heimat* survived for only one more issue, and Meyer himself was forced by bankruptcy to sell his right to Lienhard's works to the Stuttgart firm of Greiner and Pfeiffer in 1903. The frequent commercial failure of such literary ventures only fueled the resentment of nationalists.

Lienhard's best-known single work, *Hochzeit in Schilda* (later reprinted as *Die Schildbürger*), a set of poems idealizing life in a small town, first appeared in *Heimat*, as did his *Burenlieder*, poems in celebration of the Boer struggle against England. Although he regretted the failure of the kaiser to protect the Boers, he claimed that his poems lacked all political intent. He extolled the Boers for their attachment to the soil and their "manly virtues."[22]

Lienhard had originally wanted to name his journal *Hochland* (*Highland*), a title later adopted by his friend, Karl Muth (1867–1944) for the influential Catholic journal he founded in 1903. By advocating *Heimatkunst*, Lienhard meant not merely to promote rural subject matter, which he feared would still leave literature prey to the technical virtuosity of urban literati, but rather to encourage a more "natural" literary form than the allegedly artificial, theoretical, and abstract forms of the avant-garde. What he wanted was a more affirmative point of view to balance what he termed the negative, hypercritical intellectualism of urban culture. The primary goal of *Heimatkunst*—more political than literary—was to discredit social analysis and reformist social criticism. Lienhard appropriated no less a figure than Shakespeare to serve as his model. When he praised Shakespeare for addressing himself to the people as a whole rather than a particular segment, his target was the working-class sympathies of naturalists. Shakespeare did not spotlight the "average plebeian," Lienhard wrote, nor did he rigidly insist, as the naturalists did, that his characters speak in everyday language. Literature must be freed from the "Americanism" (by which he meant both commercialism and social leveling) that increasingly dominated public life. Creating culture, Lienhard said, is more important than carrying on business or politics.[23]

Lienhard rejected the charge of the neoclassicist drama-critic Samuel Lublinski (1868–1910) that *Heimatkunst* represented a reactionary movement. Once again Lienhard invoked holism as a rationale for conservatism. *Heimatkunst* did not oppose modernity in literature, he asserted, but sought only to extend literary boundaries in order to create a culture for the nation as a whole.[24] He preferred the term *Höhenkunst* ("art of the heights") to characterize his endeavors. With his play *König Arthur*, first performed in Leipzig in 1900, Lienhard offered an example of what he had in mind. He attributes the defeat of the Celts at the hands of the Saxons in the fifth century to King Arthur's misguided efforts, against the advice of his exiled counselor Merlin, to supplant the time-honored customs of his people with a new and alien civilization.

Although progressives and modernists were the chief targets of Lienhard's polemics, he also caricatured patriotic extremists who regarded Germany's preoccupation with culture as a hindrance to political action:

> Germany must awaken, is the word in these temperamental groups; the Germany of philosophy, poetry, and music must become a master-Germany of the fist and power politics; the dream world called "German Idealism" was inflicted on us by the Thirty-Years' War; the so-called "German mind" only developed as a result of our political impotence; the dawning century with its Greater Germany will no longer know this weakly inwardness![25]

Yet Lienhard's commitment to idealism did not prevent him from supporting German overseas expansion. His ambivalence toward power politics anticipated the quandary in which he and other conservative idealists would find themselves when confronted with the rise of National Socialism after World War I.[26]

The turning point in Lienhard's career came as the result of a feud with Ferdinand Avenarius (1856–1923), editor and publisher of the influential journal *Kunstwart*. In 1903 Avenarius opened his columns to a polemic entitled "Wollen und Können" ("to want and to be able"), in which Lienhard's work, for all its good intentions, was dismissed as deficient in quality. This attack embittered Lienhard, coming as it did from a journal which also subscribed to the tenets of idealism and shared his distaste for naturalism.

Moreover, the journal had carried a piece by Lienhard in the previous issue. *Kunstwart*, however, was not as unreceptive to modernism as Lienhard was. It had earlier drawn Lienhard's censure for recommending the
satirical journal *Simplizissimus* to its readers. Now Lienhard took the of-
fensive with articles in *Der Türmer, Deutsche Welt*, and *Tägliche Rundschau*, in which he accused *Kunstwart* of overvaluing art at the expense of
the human personality. Aestheticism subordinated the soul to the senses.
What did it profit man, Lienhard asked, if he visited a thousand art exhibits
and still lost his soul? Mere beautification or the development of aesthetic
taste did not go to the heart of Germany's cultural predicament.[27] Once
again Lienhard sought refuge from criticism in political orthodoxy, however much he might disguise his motives in the language of idealism. Lack
of innovative talent could be made to seem a virtue if the purpose of art was
to promote serenity and social quiescence.

The *Kunstwart* dispute reinforced Lienhard's decision to leave Berlin for
good. In 1903 he took up residence in the state of Thuringia, whose charms
and attractions he set forth in his *Thüringer Tagebuch* that same year. It became one of his more widely circulated books as it passed through several
editions. In format it resembles *Wasgaufahrten*, but its tone is less shrill.
On the hilltops and in the forests of Thuringia, romanticized in the overwrought style of the day, Lienhard claims to have found the peace and harmony he missed in the city. In neo-Romantic terms he extolls the lack of so-
phistication of country people and the innocence of children. He retraces
the trips that Goethe had taken in the neighboring hills. In a mock conversation in the park of Weimar, he relates how the ghost of Goethe advised
him to abandon the newspaper trade for more edifying literary activity.[28]

At the repeated invitation of the aged Adelheid von Schorn, a devotee of
his works, Lienhard finally settled in Weimar. He relished the thought of
occupying in her heart the place that Heinrich von Stein would have filled if
he had lived. He also took pleasure in emulating the German classicists.
Goethe and Schiller, he explains, had eschewed politics and the literary
traffic of Berlin in order to nurture personal growth within a circle of like-
minded friends and colleagues. Their withdrawal from mundane affairs
was not to be construed as an escape from the world, for they had first internalized the world and then penetrated it in turn with their spirit. Classicism
represents not merely a literary school, but a way of life that would lead to
the highest goal on earth—a noble community. Lienhard describes the
coming utopia with the aid of ominously oversimple dichotomies: "Then
mankind will form a sound and healthy community, free of bad vapors, living with each other, not against each other. Mankind will be a cosmos, not
a chaos. The current of divinity will then run undarkened through the veins
of mankind. The planet earth will glow more brightly, for it will be healthy
and pure."[29] This was the vision and the language that inspired *völkisch*

idealists. All too easily such idealism could serve to inspire right-wing political extremism as well.

Lienhard preached holism as the constructive alternative to corrosive intellectual skepticism and divisive social conflict. The need to reconcile opposing forces and achieve balance became his stock formula for the suppression of dissenting voices in culture and politics. From a synthesis of Christianity, classicism, and Nordic Germanicism he sought to create a usable ideology for mass consumption. This he disseminated in his mammoth publicistic work, *Wege nach Weimar* (*Paths to Weimar*), first published in quarterly installments from 1905 to 1908. Lienhard denied that idealism—the discovery of secret powers within, the tap-line to the supernatural—necessarily entailed rejecting external reality. But inwardness needed to be promoted vigorously to make up for its neglect in a one-sidedly materialistic civilization. Weimar, the geographical and figurative heart of Germany, symbolized the idealist values that had gradually lost ground in art and society since the death of Goethe in 1832.[30] In Lienhard's view the ideas of Weimar had been nurtured more faithfully by Thomas Carlyle in London and Ralph Waldo Emerson in Concord, Massachusetts, than in Germany itself, where realism had swept aside all other literary currents. Only islands of idealism remained, one of which was Bayreuth.

Although Lienhard criticized the followers of Richard Wagner for exaggerating the preeminence of Wagnerian opera over the spoken drama and for downgrading most great literary figures of the past into mere forerunners of Wagner, he admired the nondecadent, uplifting art of Bayreuth, and he saluted Houston Stewart Chamberlain and other members of the Bayreuth Circle as fellow-idealists in a common cause. Heinrich von Stein, whose works Lienhard excerpted in *Wege nach Weimar*, personified for Lienhard the spiritual link between Bayreuth and Weimar. Lienhard, like Wagner, celebrated the quest for the holy grail as the central motif of idealist art. Only through selfless deed or commitment could the grail—that symbol of religious certitude and salvation—be won, and thereby release from the tyranny of earthbound forces be gained.[31]

This was the motif of Lienhard's historical novel *Oberlin* (1910), the most popular of his works, which by 1935 had sold 169,000 copies.[32] The novel relates a young Alsatian's successful quest for religion against the background of the destructive, divisive, materialistically motivated French Revolution. The same motif reappeared in *Der Spielmann* (*The Minstrel*), a novel published in 1913 and set in the present. The protagonist, Ingo von Stein, finds new meaning in a previously aimless existence by accepting idealist values. Despite his growing disaffection, Lienhard was addicted to happy endings. In his drama *Wieland der Schmied* (1905), he changed the ending of the Germanic legend that served as the source of his play. Lienhard has his hero undergo a conversion of will—so characteristic of the grail motif—and renounce the revenge that according to the legend he exacted. This play was repeatedly performed at the open-air Harzer Bergtheater, founded in 1903 by his friend and fellow *Heimatkünstler* Ernst Wachler (1871–1944/45?).[33] The Harzer Bergtheater would serve as a model for numerous similar theaters constructed in the countryside under Nazi auspices after 1933.

Like so many intellectuals of his persuasion, Lienhard welcomed the outbreak of World War I—"this nation-cleansing, heart-purifying war"—for uniting the country around the "ideas of 1914."[34] Now the quest for the grail would take the form of a national crusade. He hoped that the war, whose coming he had foreseen in *Der Spielmann*, would purge the country of materialism and restore its moral fiber. "For the first time since 1870," he wrote, "we have in our great German national community a common, heart-rending experience that rises above the commonplace."[35] Only in unity could Germany fulfill its mission of leading the world back to God and spiritual values.

During the war Lienhard did his best to promote pro-German sympathy in his native Alsace. In *Schicksal einer Verschleppten* (*The Fate of a Deportee*), a typical wartime pamphlet, he denounces the maltreatment an Alsatian woman allegedly received at the hands of the French. Accusing France of having systematically subverted German rule in Alsace and Lorraine in the years before World War I, he unwittingly testifies to the predominantly pro-French sympathies of the Alsatian population. The conflict between pro-French and pro-German elements in Alsace furnished the theme of the novel *Die Westmark* (*The Western Frontier*), which was banned by the French administration in Alsace after the war.

Lienhard continued his agitation for the return of Alsace to Germany after the Great War. His primary concern, however, remained what it had always been: the dissemination of moral values to supplant materialism, which appeared to have triumphed as a result of Germany's defeat. He revived the symbolism of the Rosicrucian Order, the secret Christian sect of the seventeenth century. His sense of exclusion from the mainstream of his country's intellectual life attracted him to a doctrine attributing a secret wisdom to the initiated. Fascinated by the idea of uniting the nation's unrecognized spiritual leaders into a benevolent conspiracy, he interpreted the Rosicrucian symbol of roses entwining a cross as a reconciliation not only of joy and suffering but also of the many other conflicts and polarizations of life. "In the Cross and the Roses," he wrote, "Akropolis and Golgotha are reconciled: the Third Reich is entered, an empire of light and love, where these antagonisms no longer obtain."[36] His inspirational platitudes appeared as installments in the monthly journal *Der Türmer*, the editorship of which he assumed upon the death of its founder, Freiherr von Grotthus, in 1920. Lienhard's contributions to *Der Türmer* were also collected in a volume entitled *Unter dem Rosenkreuz, ein Hausbuch aus dem Herzen Deutschlands* (*Under the Cross and the Roses: A Book for the Home from the Heart of Germany*).

The title of *Der Türmer* ("the watchman in a tower") suggests the desirability of attaining a vantage point above the fray of everyday life. Subtitled *Monatschrift für Gemüt und Geist* (*Monthly Journal for Mind and Spirit*), the journal surveyed and evaluated for its Protestant middle-class readership the cultural and political events of the day from a distinctly conservative point of view. Founded in 1899, *Der Türmer* served a purpose in the Protestant community similar to the function of *Hochland* among Catholics. After World War I, *Der Türmer*, like Lienhard himself, sought to reconcile traditional monarchism with *völkisch* ideology.

Lienhard's religious orientation brought him into conflict with the more activist and racist elements of the *völkisch* movement. His hopes for a revival of nationalism were expressed in his historical novel of the early nineteenth-century *Burschenschaft* movement, *Das Landhaus von Eisenach*. But in his last novel, *Meisters Vermächtnis* (*Meister's Legacy*), he rejects the tactics of violence advocated by right-wing extremists. This novel's eponymous hero was a fictional descendant of Goethe's *Wilhelm Meister*. Stressing the literal meaning of *Meister* ("master"), a term previously employed in his three-volume *Der Meister der Menschheit* (1919–1921), Lienhard proclaims that such masters exist in all ages. Following higher orders like the ultimate master, Jesus, they prevent the bestialization of mankind. Only from this spiritual elite can relief be expected from man's animal nature and Germany's present predicament.

Although he denigrated all the innovative literary figures and movements of his day—from Zola and Ibsen to Hauptmann, Thomas Mann, and the expressionists—Lienhard achieved considerable recognition and honors by the time of his death in 1929. The universities of Strassburg and Jena awarded him honorary degrees. Public acclaim reached its zenith in a *Festschrift* on the occasion of his fiftieth birthday in 1915.[37] The sixty-five contributors to this volume included such distinguished names as the 1908 Nobel Prize-winner in literature, Rudolf Eucken (1846–1926), the historian Karl Lamprecht (1856–1915), and the Jewish biographer of Goethe, Georg Witkowski (1863–1941). Witkowski's better-known brother, Maximilian Harden (1861–1927), editor of the political journal *Die Zukunft* and critic of William II, was not among the contributors. Hans von Wolzogen and the racial historian Ludwig Schemann represented Bayreuth on a list that included Lienhard's old friends Karl Muth and Ernst Wachler. Heinrich von Stein's editor, Friedrich Poske, contributed a selection in which he compared Stein's and Lienhard's efforts to prepare the *Volk* for higher tasks. Conspicuously absent was the name of Adolf Bartels, the erstwhile champion of *Heimatkunst*, who criticized Lienhard for neglecting the dimension of race.[38]

Reflecting at least to some degree the wartime atmosphere in which the *Festschrift* was published, Lienhard's well-wishers paid homage primarily to his patriotic *völkisch* convictions, not the literary merits, of his works. These were too programmatic in design and propagandistic in intent to survive as works of literature. Judged on their literary quality alone, his works have deservedly been forgotten. But as an acknowledged arbiter of taste and opinion for a loyal following, Lienhard remains of interest to the historian.

7

FOE OF MODERNIZATION: LIENHARD'S ASSAULT ON NATURALISM AND PROGRESSIVISM

Away with the material [*Stoffliche*]! The soul, the eternal, the inner life alone is abiding and is therefore the only worthy subject of serious poetry for men.

Lienhard, "Reformation der Literatur"

Although Lienhard broke into literature as a brash iconoclast, his radicalism was deceptive. His neo-Romantic attacks on philistinism and materialism masked a reactionary, not a revolutionary, temperament. Indeed, Lienhard condemned revolutionary sentiment as itself symptomatic of materialistic corruption. His earliest models were the so-called *Jüngstdeutschen* ("Youngest Germans"), writers of his own generation who proclaimed the need for a more creative literature to counteract the stultifying materialism of middle-class culture. Members of this self-consciously iconoclastic literary group collaborated to put out the poetry anthology, *Moderne Dichter-Charaktere*, a typical product of young writers obsessed with the apparent decline of heroism and genius in modern times.

Karl Bleibtreu's tract, *Revolution der Literatur*, published in 1886, became the manifesto of the *Jüngstdeutschen*.[1] Bleibtreu exhorted German writers to address themselves to the two most important problems of the century: the social question and the dissimilarities among nationalities. Lienhard would come to deplore the fact that writers of the naturalist school neglected the latter in favor of the former.

Although only six years older than Lienhard, Bleibtreu exercised a decisive influence on Lienhard's early works. His career resembled Lienhard's in its commitment to nationalistic values. Fascinated by heroism on the battlefield, Bleibtreu represented a generation for whom the Franco-Prussian War and the unification of Germany would remain the dominant experience of their lives. In a literary career spanning almost half a century Bleibtreu celebrated the exploits of Bismarck, Frederick the Great, Napoleon, Cromwell, and Lord Byron. More intensely even than Lienhard's, Bleibtreu's development reflected growing disenchantment with a culture that failed to perpetuate the grandeur of the German Empire. Like Lienhard, he sought to combat materialism by propagating a form of theosophy, but he failed to achieve peace of mind. Like Dühring, whose brash egotism and embittered isolation Bleibtreu shared, Bleibtreu's resentment took the form of increasingly virulent anti-Semitism. In the 1920s he went so far as to accuse Chamberlain of underestimating the importance of race. He disputed Chamberlain's contention that religion could ennoble race on the grounds that race produced religion and not vice versa.[2]

This was a far cry from his youth when he emerged into the limelight as a champion of the literary avant-garde. With the Munich-based writer Michael Georg Conrad (1846–1927), an admirer of Zola, he founded the journal *Die Gesellschaft* for the express purpose of promoting modern ideas in literature. Conrad and Bleibtreu admired Zola not for his concern for the impoverished masses or his egalitarian politics, but rather for his successful defiance of an overly refined and sentimental literary tradition, against which the *Jüngstdeutschen* were also girding to do battle. They acclaimed Zola's courage in writing about subjects previously taboo. Zola, the passionate and imaginative *Kraftmensch* ("strongman"), became a moral, not a literary, model. They admired his truthfulness and *Vokstümlichkeit* ("closeness to the people") as weapons in their fight against both the blandness of popular literature and the formalism of serious art. Zola sounded the call to leave the ivory tower. But Conrad and Bleibtreu called for a distinctively German literary form, a blending of Romanticism with realism, as an alternative to Zola's naturalistic method.[3] Germany's military victory over France in 1871 seemed to young Germans to require some demonstration of German cultural superiority as well. This helps to explain why Bleibtreu would open the columns of *Die Gesellschaft* to Lienhard's attack on Zola in 1888.

Young Lienhard had written to Bleibtreu to say how much he admired his *Revolution der Literatur*, which heralded a "Christian-Germanic-modern literature" to supplant the "pagan-Greek-antiquated aestheticism" of Germany's literary establishment. Bleibtreu published a segment of Lienhard's letter as an anonymous "voice from the public" in the preface to his novel *Grössenwahn*. This flattered Lienhard, and he was further encouraged when he discovered that the leading character of the novel, a poet of great promise, bore the name Friedrich Leonhart.[4]

Lienhard's article, "Die Reformation der Literatur," echoed not only Bleibtreu's title but also his point of view. In his attack on Zola's *roman expérimental* Lienhard went beyond Bleibtreu's more general indictment of muckraking naturalists. In a defiant, youthfully declamatory style, Lienhard propounded a critique of materialism that he would reiterate, in one form or another, throughout his life. According to Lienhard, contemporary literature needed to undergo a Lutheran Reformation to revive an earlier, more authentic perspective that had gotten lost in the race for worldly goods.

Rationalizing, perhaps, his own missed vocation as a pastor, Lienhard asserted that creative literature (*Dichtung*), like religion, is only concerned with the soul. Struggle against sin and sensuality is the eternal lot of man on earth—no less today than in the days of Noah's Ark. This eternal struggle is what makes a person truly human; not to give in is the mark of the idealist. The task of the poet, who must be priest and also prophet, is to awaken and strengthen man for this struggle. It cannot be the sole task of literature to draw attention to social abuses. "An unfortunate person," Lienhard wrote, "despairing of himself and God, who after violent inner struggles jumps into the Spree, moves me and every spiritual person more than some dead worker who doesn't have enough to eat."[5] A millionaire or a statesman can help the starving worker, but not a poet. Although the poet need not be indifferent to external needs, his primary function must be to show the effects of these externals on an individual's inner being.

Like Bleibtreu and other contributors to *Die Gesellschaft*, Lienhard rejected the "morphium-like" escapist literature of such representatives of the older generation as Paul Heyse, and he commended Zola for cultivating close observation of reality. But the poet cannot be content with recording the external experiences of others; he must record his own inner experiences with equal fidelity. These inner conflicts are of especial importance to the German mind. The trouble is that the materialist cannot adequately portray such idealistic traits as self-sacrificing love or yearning for a higher form of life because he has no experience, and hence no comprehension, of them.

Lienhard denounced naturalism as a materialistic form of literature because it depicts only external experiences. It debases the human being, eliminating guilt, free will, and conscience by explaining all human acts as the products of heredity and environment. Naturalism is more tyrannically deterministic than ancient tragedy, Lienhard wrote, for even the triumph of the individual soul in the face of tragic fate is attributed by naturalists to the natural laws governing human behavior. Lienhard rejected the adage "To understand all is to forgive all." The poet must not suspend judgment, but must put himself into his work. The modern poet must be to his people what the Old Testament prophets were to theirs. Literature must be united not with science, as in the naturalist approach, but with religion. An idealist *Weltanschauung*—a religious disposition—is a precondition of great art. Only he who finds no peace in purely temporal activity has the makings of a poet. Affirming the dictum of the *Sturm und Drang* poet Jacob Lenz, which also served as the motto for *Moderne Dichter-Charaktere*—"The spirit of the artist outweighs the work of his art"—Lienhard contended that a poet's personality is more important than his finished product.[6] Throughout his career this anti-formalist argument would serve as his defense against critics who pointed up the inadequacies of his own creative efforts.

In excoriating philistinism and public indifference to art Lienhard reiterated a favorite theme of Bleibtreu's, who, like Wagner before him, charged
the Prussian state with cultural barbarism. Undaunted by the contradiction in their argument, these artists accused the state of materialism for failing to reward them sufficiently with material benefits. Their opposition to
bourgeois culture was rooted in Romantic elitism, not in socialist sympathies. Lienhard contemptuously assailed the "stupid rabble" who permitted
a genius to lead an impoverished existence in the midst of plenty:

> Better to starve than to beg for a crumb of bread from the overloaded table of a
> spiritually dead, fat-bellied, beer-swilling philistine! We, too, have our pride!
> Stay with your treasures and cling to them—we will persist with ours! Between us
> there is no connection. Phew, you fat-bellies down there, how can you compare
> yourselves to us?! On your marble gravestones will be written: "He is no longer,
> and never was!"[7]

Such inflated pathos was typical of Lienhard's early style. His denunciation of industrialism was couched in similarly turgid language:

> Flatten, sensualize, externalize as much as you like; deride us, let your machines
> and hammers drone so that the mountains tremble and the animals of the forest
> flee; let your factories smoke until the cities threaten to suffocate in the fumes—I
> tell you, you will never suffocate or drown out idealism! Yes, the more feverishly
> you chase after external possessions and pleasures, the more fanatically we will
> cling with eagle's claws to the eternal, the ideal.[8]

Idealism merged with nationalism and reaction in what Lienhard described as a return to the authentic tradition of German culture. He claimed
that materialism was both recent and foreign in origin. It was symptomatic
of the modern age that its "poetic God" should be the "frivolous" Heinrich
Heine—"Harry Heine, the Paris Jew"—who represented the antithesis to
Lienhard's ideal "Christian-Germanic poet-thinker." In fulsome and self-
congratulatory language Lienhard acclaimed the good fortune that had
delivered his native Alsace from pernicious French domination:

> Oh, my treasured people! With tears in my eyes, I, the Alsatian, utter my heart-
> felt thanks that you did not leave us in this pestilential foreign atmosphere! I utter
> ardent thanks to you, divine guide up there, for having experienced this time of
> liberation! I utter thanks to you that I am German, German to the most inner
> core! . . . Hail us! The oaks in the Vosges forests are German! The long-
> repressed Germanic consciousness has awakened again on the western frontier,
> from the Vosges forest to the old German Rhine! A marvelous Spring is dawning,
> a Spring of the spirit. . . . Oh, German poets, never forget to be Germanic,
> Germanic to the core! Tenacious and serious, loyal and candid and full of sub-
> lime faith like our powerful ancestors! And we will journey into a flourishing

Germanic age, and be the guiding star of peoples, a green-bordered river bestowing life and bliss on all peoples![9]

Nationalism was to provide the solution to the vexatious "social problem." Lienhard's play *Weltrevolution*, the story of an abortive workers' revolt, was prompted by Bleibtreu's advice not to ignore modern social themes. Disillusioned and repelled by the destructive forces he had unleashed, the idealist young leader of the revolt rejects class hatred and seeks to rekindle love by returning to his home. When the police come to arrest him he commits suicide. Many years later, Lienhard's biographer asserts that in this play Lienhard had anticipated the defeat of international socialism by the healthier emotional forces of nationalism in 1919.[10] Materialism is indicted twice in this play, for it is the selfish greed of the top ten-thousand that causes the uprising, and the equally selfish greed of the lower classes that leads to its demise.

As with Bleibtreu and Conrad, Lienhard's concern with the "social question" in no way signified sympathy with the labor movement or the Social Democratic Party, which continued to gain adherents among the working class, despite the legal restraints placed on the party. These writers rejected Social Democracy for allegedly promoting uniformity. Lienhard traced the source of class antagonisms, not to economic exploitation, but to the loss of love and sympathy between people. The "social problem" was never posed in terms of how to correct economic imbalances, but rather in terms of how to reduce the bitterness and brutality displayed by the working class. The concern of conservative publicists was not to dismantle the class structure that had produced an impoverished urban proletariat, but to defuse the attitudes that led to animosity and warfare between the classes. Since materialism, in the sense both of economic avarice and lack of religion, spawned and promoted these attitudes, only a revival of idealism seemed to offer the promise of reconciliation. These conservatives did not view the labor movement as an instrument for the rectification of social abuses, but rather as a cause of such abuses. They desired social peace, not social reform.

For Lienhard, as for Bleibtreu, Conrad, and other early "naturalists," pungent descriptions of "social reality" offered a convenient means to shock philistines out of their complacent materialism. In *Die weisse Frau* Lienhard expresses his contempt for both the bestiality of urban workers and for the smugness of their bourgeois counterparts:

I frequently wander through the northern precincts, stroll between factories and tenements and wonder why the emaciated creatures who vegetate there are still accorded the honorary title "human." Be honest and call them slaves, beasts of burden, refuse, and rubbish—but not humans! Not your brothers! Single laws and measures don't improve things. They only aggravate social conditions. The thick-skinned philistine rubs his hands in relief and continues to lull in arrogant safety. Change your attitude [*Gesinnung*]! Only out of this will lasting help be born! The embitterment of the lower millions will not be mitigated through cold little laws of the upper ten-thousand. Not the situation itself—the mutual attitudes harbor the danger. Only the spirit of love can overcome the spirit of bitterness.[11]

Die weisse Frau (*The White Woman*) derives its title from a legendary figure of the Alsatian forests, the personification of rustic serenity. This book caused a break in Lienhard's friendship with Bleibtreu, who condemned the work as a plagiarism of a collection of short stories he had published in 1885. Lienhard in turn deplored Bleibtreu's increasing bitterness, though he sympathized with what he took to be its cause, namely, the failure of the *Deutsche Bühne* in Berlin, a theater founded by Bleibtreu in 1890, to compete with Otto Brahm's naturalistic *Freie Bühne*. It was on Brahm's stage that Hauptmann's important naturalistic dramas *Vor Sonnenaufgang* (1889) and *Die Weber* (1894) were first performed. Brahm, who also staged the works of Ibsen, Strindberg, and Tolstoy, was accused by Bleibtreu, Conrad, Alberti, and other disappointed playwrights of discriminating against German writers in his selection of plays.[12]

Lienhard, too, moved toward a more rigid conservatism in the years after 1890. His aversion to innovation and modernization became more pronounced. In an article entitled "Persönlichkeit und Volkstum als Grundlagen der Dichtung" ("Personality and Nationality as the Foundations of Literature"), written in 1894, he now criticized both the *Jüngstdeutschen* (Bleibtreu, Conrad, Alberti, Conradi, and Henckell, among others) as well as their naturalist successors (including Hauptmann, Arno Holz, Johannes Schlaf, Hermann Sudermann, Max Halbe, Richard Dehmel, Otto Julius Bierbaum, Otto Ernst Hartleben, and Detlev von Liliencron) for insisting that a writer take a position on the social issues of the day. Equating modernity with faddishness, Lienhard compared modernists to snakes that constantly changed their skins.

Not just in technique and subject matter, but in their realistic Weltanschauung [the naturalists] became "modern." Steam engines, electricity, Berlin tenements, urban misery, sexualism, piquant adultery in the stock exchange district, the boudoir, and the salon—social, sexual, and conventional values were to be poured into new molds. . . . Due to so much modernity and metropolis we have forgotten history and the Empire, the eternal and the ideal.[13]

Once again Lienhard used the vocabulary of holism to plead the nationalist cause. Masters of microscopic observation, the naturalists allegedly lacked telescopic vision of the whole. Taking social misery out of its larger context, the naturalists destroyed the harmony that is a people's greatest need. In an argument that recalled Heinrich von Stein's definition of idealism, Lienhard asserted that a fragment of nature presented in isolation is no better than a lie. By their embarrassing insistence on truthfulness (*peinlicher Wahrheitsfanatismus*), naturalists neglected the more important functions of art, which are to beautify, to edify, and to give joy and strength.[14]

Lienhard deplored what he termed the naturalist practice of simply transferring reality onto the stage. Naturalists distorted this reality by leaving out the many distractions that make life bearable. If naturalist principles were consistently applied, the audience would be forced to do something about the social misery it witnessed on the stage, for watching human misery without offering to help violates human nature. Hence by its own logic naturalism could lay no claim to art. Undue emphasis on social forces fails to take account of the importance of the human personality. Significant events are not produced by new systems, organizations, or technology, but by great personalities alone. According to Lienhard, it was Luther who gave the Reformation its force; and it was not the Prussian army that won the Seven-Years' War, but rather Frederick the Great, the leader who knew how to inspire that army.[15]

Lienhard also took aim at the psychological realism of Ibsen and Paul Bourget (1852–1935). Isben's seventy-fifth birthday drew from Lienhard an attack on the tradition of bourgeois realism.[16] He accused Ibsen of lacking warmth and feeling (*Gemütskraft*) on the grounds that he viewed his characters with the same "loveless" detachment with which a scientist might view bacteria. Whereas Dante had gone through a naturalist Hell and a realist Purgatory in order finally to reach a harmonious Paradise, Ibsen remained enmired in Hell. If Ibsen had written a *Romeo and Juliet*, it would have turned out to be a study of family relationships, not a tragedy of love and fate. Lienhard did not hide his opposition to the Enlightenment tradition. The bourgeois drama had originated in eighteenth-century England when Deism and rationalism held sway; it was also, significantly, when newspapers first exercised their corrosive effects. Bourgeois realism was then imported into France by Diderot, and into Germany by Lessing— Lessing, who showed so little appreciation for Goethe's *Sturm und Drang* works, *Götz von Berlichingen* and *The Sorrows of Young Werther*. Lienhard intended no compliment when he called Ibsen the Diderot of the nineteenth century and Nietzsche its Voltaire. In all of these writers, he concluded, there was too much brain and too little heart at work.

Lienhard's anti-intellectualism was closely tied to his failure to achieve critical recognition in Berlin. His frustrations increasingly took the form of attacks on the city as a seedbed of materialism, skepticism, and cosmopolitanism. Even established conservative institutions began to come under attack for their failure to stem the progressive tide. Thus he berated the *Königliche Schauspielhaus* for having failed to promote idealism, as Kaiser

William had demanded. Because its selection of plays was based primarily on commercial considerations, it remained largely without influence in theatrical life. Lienhard attributed these distressing conditions to the profit motive, which dominated the German theater, just as it threatened to dominate every aspect of German life. He pointed out that in one year, 1899, Oskar Blumental's shallow comedy, *Das weisse Röss'l*, was performed more times than all of the plays of Schiller were in a decade. This incongruous situation reminded Lienhard of the Napoleonic era, when Kotzebue and Iffland enjoyed greater success on the German stage than the patriotic Heinrich von Kleist.[17]

No theater, Lienhard complained, could afford to offend the momentary fashions of the day, which indulged the theatre-going public's lust for novelty and sensation. The size of the paying public, and hence the success of a play, depended in turn on the state of the stock market at any given time. His attack on commercialism in the name of artistic quality echoed Langbehn's charge that Berlin, like the United States, suffered from the flow of new immigrants, who brought with them over-rapid growth and the devaluation of traditional culture.[18] Lienhard expressed the hostility to large-scale capitalism so characteristic of Germany's declining *Mittelstand*:

> From the formation of pools and cartels, especially in American business, to the large-size department stores and emporiums, a dangerous trend toward a new tyranny can be observed. It is no longer the absolutism of princes that is dangerous and even Byzantinism [a reference to the pomp of the imperial court] seems harmless to me: dangerous is the terrorism of cliques and groups, of large-scale capitalists, of party fanatics with all their means and methods to either despoil or exclude the independent person and the individual. This, too, is a result of the social fever, the struggle of all against all.[19]

Rejection of self-interest in favor of the good of the whole was also to form the anti-capitalistic core of Nazi ideology.

Posing the rhetorical question, "Where are the national Berliners?" Lienhard called for the establishment of a state-supported national theater to combat the new "particularism." All regions of the empire would have to participate in a new artistic revival; this was the meaning of *Heimatkunst*. Lienhard had a ready answer to the question why regional art could not at present compete successfully with urban culture: theaters in the provinces were handicapped by the predominance of the Berlin press, which ignored everything that happened outside the capital. He thought that Theodor Fontane's novels of aristocratic foibles enjoyed greater success than Conrad Ferdinand Meyer's novels of aristocratic heroism only because Fontane lived in Berlin. Even a dismal flop on a Berlin stage received more publicity than a ringing success in the provinces. The provincial stages were further disadvantaged by the concentration of wealth which permitted Berlin theaters to engage the best actors and launch the most effective publicity campaigns.[20]

Lienhard envied Gerhart Hauptmann's success, which he attributed not merely to talent but also to the loyalty, tenacity, and tactical skill of his Jewish friends: his director, Otto Brahm, his publisher, Samuel Fischer (1859–1934), and his critical advocate, Alfred Kerr (1867–1948). Lienhard remained objective enough, however, not to blame his own disappointments on Jewish discrimination. His professional rebuffs had come at the hands of non-Jews. Nor did he deny Hauptmann's talent. What he criticized was the democratic bias most clearly exemplified in Hauptmann's sympathetic treatment of rebellious Silesian weavers, *Die Weber*, a play that also aroused the Prussian censors. Lienhard preferred the heroic individualism of Ernst von Wildenbruch (1845–1909), whose bombastic historical dramas of German imperial grandeur were particular favorites of William II. Lienhard's suggested synthesis of Wildenbruch's and Hauptmann's dramatic methods was intended to make nationalistic literature more popular. Just as Wildenbruch's salutary sense of the past provided a needed balance to Hauptmann's present-mindedness, his emphasis on aristocratic grandeur offered an appropriate corrective to Hauptmann's social bias. Lienhard praised Wildenbruch for emphasizing "healthy and typical" elements, whereas Hauptmann focused excessive attention on pathological aberrations. Wildenbruch portrayed his characters as valiant (*mannhaft*), while Hauptmann's protagonists too often went down in the struggle for survival.[21] Yet even Lienhard could not deny that the dramas of Wildenbruch or those of Joseph Lauff (1855–1933), another of the kaiser's favorites, were out of touch with popular concerns of the day. *Heimatkunst* was designed to add that missing populist dimension to the literature of patriotism and moral uplift.

Lienhard's rejection of modernity in art extended to the major literary figures of his time. He censured Tolstoy for excessive psychologizing, Strindberg for depicting relations between the sexes as a struggle, and Verlaine and the French Symbolists for their attachment to a doctrine of *l'art pour l'art*. He similarly disparaged the aestheticism of Hugo von Hofmannsthal, Rainer Maria Rilke, Stefan George, and Thomas Mann. With the exception of the Swedish Nobel Prize-winner Selma Lagerlöf (1858–1940), whose revival of ancient legend Lienhard admired, the only writers of stature to gain his approval belonged to an earlier generation. These included the novelist Wilhelm Raabe (1831–1910) and the Provençal poet Frédéric Mistral (1830–1914), whose works expressed a sense of rootedness in their native soil. Lienhard praised Walt Whitman's *Leaves of Grass* for its disdain of formalism—an irony in view of Lienhard's own rigid adherence to conventional meter and rhyme. But he chided Whitman for his unabashed treatment of human sexuality.[22]

Invoking moral standards to measure excellence in art, Lienhard dignified the important role that kitsch played in the lives of his readers. An insignificant picture that evokes pleasant memories possesses more beauty
than the most perfect drawing or design.[23] Lienhard deprecated the importance of *Literatur*, a term that bore a distinctly negative connotation when
juxtaposed with *Dichtung*. The genre he prized above all was the *Märchen*,
the fairy tale, in which a childlike purity of heart had not yet been supplanted by corrosive intellectualism. In attributing souls even to objects the *Märchen* marked a triumph of idealism over materialism. Its prayerlike mood
(*Gebetsstimmung*) provided a salutary antidote to the nervousness of modern literature. Arising organically out of the heart of the *Volk*, the *Märchen*
affirmed the positive values of reverence, simplicity, innocence, and awe.
Not coincidentally, these were also the values that would preserve an hierarchical social order.[24]

In Lienhard's works, attitudes rooted in the Romantic tradition became
transformed into self-righteous nationalism. The innovative thrust of Romanticism was lost in the evolution of *völkisch* ideology toward the end of
the nineteenth century. Industrialization and its attendant social conflicts
served as the crucial catalysts in this transformation of idealism into a reactionary doctrine. Young Lienhard advocated change, but it was change oriented toward the past. Many of the attitudes he championed would become normative under the sanction of force in the period of Nazi
domination after 1933. His disparagement of modern literature anticipated
the arguments the Nazis would use in their suppression of "decadent art."
His intolerance of opinions that failed to accord due respect to monarchy
or family echoed the intolerance of blasphemy in an earlier, more religious
age. His insistence that only a resolutely affirmative literature should be
permitted the right to public dissemination and popular support upheld the
tradition of censorship in the modern age. Lienhard rejected engagement as
a valid artistic objective. Literature must not mirror life, but rather eternal
ideals. It must point the way to concerns more important than the redistri-
bution of material wealth or the struggle for political rights. Lienhard's
aristocratic bias was the source of his attraction to German classicism. In it
he discovered the sublimity that would sustain and elevate mankind and
deflect popular aspirations for social and political reforms into more ac-
commodating channels.

8

ELITISM AND EVANGELISM: LIENHARD'S *WEGE NACH WEIMAR*

Redemption lies precisely in no longer asking questions.
Lienhard, *Wege nach Weimar*

With *Wege nach Weimar*, subtitled *Beiträge zur Erneuerung des Idealismus* (*Contributions to the Renewal of Idealism*), Lienhard launched a major propagandistic effort to revive and disseminate apolitical values. Issued from 1905 to 1908 as a quarterly journal and reissued later as a book, *Wege nach Weimar* was designed to serve an inspirational purpose. Its format was apparently patterned on the evangelical journal, *Grüne Blätter für persönliche Pflege* (*Green Pages for Personal Cultivation*), of Lienhard's friend, the *völkisch* evangelist Johannes Müller (1864–1949), who founded *Grüne Blätter* in 1897 as a means of disseminating his sermons. Combining excerpts from the works of exemplary historical figures with a commentary setting forth their message for the present, *Wege nach Weimar* made only slight intellectual demands on its readership. Lienhard's earnest but amiable tone resembles the conversational approach of a pastor addressing his flock. His uncomplicated language, far less abrasive than his earlier, more polemical style, matches his avowed purpose of fostering equanimity and quietism in the German populace.

Each volume presents one or two major historical figures as models to be emulated or preceptors to be followed. The first volume is built around selections from Heinrich von Stein and Ralph Waldo Emerson. Subsequent volumes feature Shakespeare and Homer, Frederick the Great, Herder and Jean-Paul Richter, Schiller, and Goethe, respectively. At the conclusion of each volume Lienhard appends a section headed *Tagebuch* ("Daily Journal"), in which he guides his readers through literary and political controversies and recommends certain recently published works. He offers his readers advice on how to acquire classical discipline and strengthen the German nation in the process. This section also contains correspondence from such well-wishers as Chamberlain, Schemann, Hans von Wolzogen, the pedagogue Christian Muff, the racialist Heinrich Driesmans (1863–1927), the Austrian Catholic author Richard von Kralik

(1852–1934), and the editor of the influential Protestant journal *Christliche Welt*, Martin Rade (1857–1940).

Wege nach Weimar was published in six volumes over a span of three years as a consequence of Lienhard's obsession with numerical symbols. Like Chamberlain, Möller van den Bruck (1876–1925), and other *völkisch* publicists, Lienhard was fascinated by the use of triads, which, in the words of Fritz Stern, "incorporated the hope that the great antitheses of German life—the antitheses of confessions, classes, regions—could be subsumed under some higher and harmonious synthesis."[1] The frequent references to a third Reich in the literature of the first decade of the twentieth century attest to this hope. Lienhard, too, used this figurative concept in advising his readers how to achieve peace amidst the polarized tensions of mass society: "Endeavor to ascend into a 'third Reich' and to become free of the irritations of pros and cons. Embody in yourself ingenuousness [*Unbefangenheit*] and serene fortitude."[2] For philosophical dualists, the use of triads was virtually unavoidable if a reconciliation between the realms of the ideal and the real was to be effected. But while most idealist philosophers employed triads as a dialectical device to achieve conceptual symmetry, Lienhard attributed to numbers themselves (specifically the numbers three and seven) a mysterious mediatory power. This obsession with the occult, which reached its culmination in the elaborate Rosicrucian symbolism after World War I, served Lienhard as a substitute for intellectual rigor. He sought to create harmony not by analyzing and synthesizing contending forces so much as by invoking the appropriate propitiatory symbol.

Another such symbol was Weimer, which Lienhard frequently linked with Wittenberg, the city in which the Reformation had originated, and the *Wartburg*, a medieval Thuringian castle, to form an alliterative triad. Lienhard also indulged his penchant for alliteration in coupling such symbols as *Sans-Souci* (the palace of Frederick the Great) with the *Sachsenwald* (Bismarck's forest retreat) and by pitting Bayreuth against Berlin. *Wartburg*, the symbol for the fortress that each person was enjoined to create in himself, provided the title for a trilogy of plays that Lienhard published in 1905. Each play was set in the *Wartburg* at a different historical period. *Heinrich von Ofterdingen* dramatizes a contest between the wandering troubadours (*Minnesänger*) of medieval Germany, a period that Lienhard admired for its chivalry and religious faith. *Die Heilige Elisabeth* celebrates the fabled charity of Saint Elizabeth, whose life Heinrich von Stein had also dramatized in *Dramatische Bilder und Erzählungen*. The theme of the final play, *Luther auf der Wartburg*, is Luther's refuge from emperor and pope. Lienhard describes the genesis of Luther's great hymn, "A Mighty Fortress is Our Lord." The marks of the inkwell which Luther had thrown at the devil to ward off temptation could still be seen on the wall of one of the castle chambers.

Lienhard popularized idealism as a victory in the struggle that every man must wage against the devil within. In this struggle the culture of Weimar could serve as a source of strength. Lienhard denied that his fixation on Weimar meant turning back the clock to an earlier epoch. Weimar, he explains, lies within us and before us: "Just as Schiller, Körner, Humboldt, [and] Goethe made a transition from conventional literary forms to the more rigorous and purer contours of the ideal of humanity and became harmonious personalities: so today it is up to us to overcome the crushing literary bustle and to find the higher humanity [*Menschentum*], in order then to create forms inspirited with new life."[3] Lienhard assures his readers that a person did not have to possess artistic talent in order to profit from the example of Weimar culture, for every man could emulate the creative artist by modeling his own personality as if it were a work of art. Both Weimar and Bayreuth envisaged a utopia in which every person would have the temperament of an artist, and not of a merchant or a politician.

Lienhard's work exemplifies the "culture of rejection" that pervades so much of German literature in the last half of the nineteenth century, a culture that found it hard to reconcile involvement in day-to-day reality with the demands of artistic and human integrity[4]: "Superior persons [*hohe Menschen*] . . . maintain a distance between themselves and the world. They renounce the scramble of proximate details [*nahe Einzelheiten*] and gain a perspective of the whole."[5] Yet Lienhard cautions against seeking happiness through thought or intellect: "Happiness is always there; only learn the most difficult art: to grasp the happiness that is close by! Here dewlike purity of soul helps more than all the murky and complicated powers of the intellect."[6] Nothing better illustrates the vulgarization of idealist culture than this typical effort to discredit intellectual activity.

Whereas German idealist philosophy may be read as a secularized version of the Christian world view in highly sophisticated form, Lienhard formulated this world view in forebodingly simplistic terms. Torn between the contending forces of spirit and matter, the human condition remains the same in all ages. A state of inner equilibrium marks the victory of spiritual forces. Classicism provides a model of how to achieve such a state of maturity:

> Classical means to us maturity, balance, poise, over which the ineradicable lower powers of this earth—and of the earthly components in ourselves—never again can gain perpetual or essential mastery. . . . This balance of powers yields the classical state of mind; this balance which must ever be maintained, assisted by grace from above, represents the victory of the spirit; and victory of the ever-active spirit is the goal. It is the problem of equilibrium, as mankind, poised between God and animal, strives to attain the level of divinity: using the means of the earth, not despising them.[7]

The struggle between Lucifer and Christ is repeated in the life of every individual. But only the "masters of mankind" emerge triumphant over the devil.

Although writing with the avowed purpose of simplifying the overly intellectualized culture of modern times, Lienhard's appeal to his readership was consciously elitist. In promoting traditional aristocratic values as the proper social norms, *Wege nach Weimar* exemplified on an ideological plane the marriage of convenience between the *Besitz- und Bildungsbürgertum*—the propertied and educated upper middle class—and the aristocracy in the latter part of the nineteenth century. For Lienhard—as for such other *völkisch* popularizers of Goethe as Chamberlain, Möller, and Bartels—the emphasis on character and personality made class distinctions seem irrelevant.[8] Citing Goethe's precept, "The greatest happiness of people on earth derives from personality alone,"[9] a quotation cherished by Stein and Chamberlain as well, Lienhard assured his readers that true nobility is attainable by all, regardless of family lineage. The aristocratic traits of pride, moderation, and inner stability need not be inbred, but can be acquired, with God's help, through training and self-education.

Lienhard proposed the formation of a new aristocracy of persons in whom the divine element had triumphed. By positing an idealist attitude as the only criterion of memberhsip, Lienhard's elitism was peculiarly suited to popular consumption. Propounding a diluted version of the Calvinistic doctrine of the elect, Lienhard in effect sought to restore to religious values a normative function in an increasingly secular society. In an essay entitled "Christentum und Moderne" (1912), Lienhard claims that Jesus had directed his sermon on the mount to an elite, not to the masses.[10] A spiritual elite, "an aristocratic community of magnanimous hearts," is needed to form the soul of a people, the soul that the German Empire sorely lacked.[11]

Lienhard revived Heinrich von Stein's appeal to like-minded persons of all classes to form a community that could exert greater influence on culture and society. He called for the creation of a national academy to give the values of idealism an institutional base. This was to become one of his favorite projects after the war, as he unsuccessfully tried to expand the *Goethe-Gessellschaft* in Weimar into a national institution for the formulation and propagation of ethical norms for society.[12]

Although he spoke of the creation of a new race of "truly ingenuous, truly noble and free elite persons [*Elitemenschen*]," Lienhard rejected the racial determinism of Gobineau or Chamberlain, whose aristocratic elitism he otherwise endorsed.[13] The elite of all nations and races, he contended, were related to each other through their shared love for spiritual values. Was not the Frenchman Gobineau closer in spirit to Wagner than the German aesthetic formalist Eduard Hanslick? "Leave me in peace with too much 'Aryanism'!" Lienhard wrote. "Prove your nobler race through nobler words and works."[14]

These apparently enlightened views did not, however, show his tolerance so much as his opposition to materialism. To Lienhard, more consistent than Chamberlain in an idealism that promoted spirit over matter, even the pseudo-scientific myth of racialism seemed too great a concession to materialism. Did everything have to have a scientific explanation? Whereas the mystery of Christ used to be approachable only through the profoundly inward avenue of prayer, now the novelty of his message was explained by his "Galilean" race. To insist that only the "Aryan race" (the existence of which Lienhard did not question) had made important contributions to culture was to revert to the ancient Israelite conceit of a chosen people, with which Christ was supposed to have made a definitive break. The goal of idealists must be to create a race based on nobility of souls, not a race based on blood. Race as a category applicable to mass populations offended Lienhard's elitism and his desire to perpetuate class distinctions. However, since such racists as Gobineau and Chamberlain shared his view of privilege, Lienhard endorsed their views. By interpreting their racial categories symbolically he helped to make them respectable. Gobineau's superior white race stood for the pure "white soul"; when Gobineau attacked the "darker" races, he meant only to attack the darker, baser, more sensual and sinful elements in man's nature.[15]

Lienhard's exaltation of German idealism led him to advocate a doctrine of national superiority as extreme as the doctrines sustained by racial superiority. The propensity of idealism to create hierarchy and rank led in Lienhard's case to the same kinds of discriminatory attitudes that racists justified on racial grounds. Although the explanation of his prejudices differed from that of biological determinists, he was equally contemptuous of the culture (or lack of culture, as he would have put it) of such "inferior" races as Negroes or Jews.

Lienhard's anti-Semitism stemmed from opposition to the progressive doctrines of liberalism and socialism.[16] Characteristically disdaining reality in favor of essential ideas, Lienhard saw in Jewishness a symbol of materialistic attitudes. Jewishness thus interpreted stood for stereotyped traits that were not restricted to Jews, nor applicable to each individual Jew. Healthy minded persons with the necessary *Verarbeitungskraft* ("the ability to assimilate and to alter ideas") need have no fear of what Lienhard nonetheless saw fit to term the "Semitic plague."[17] In advocating assimilation as a solution for the "Jewish problem" he differed from such *völkisch* extremists as Chamberlain or Bartels, whose racial determinism effectively eliminated assimilation as a feasible way of reconciling the alleged incompatibility of Jewish and German culture. Lienhard's attitude harked back to religious anti-Semitism, which aimed at the elimination of the Jewish community through conversion, not destruction.

Yet it was not Judaism that he and other right-wing anti-Semites feared, but rather the inordinate influence of secularized Jews in modern society. Lienhard approvingly cited Viktor Heyn, who had dated the onset of the "Jewish age" from the death of Goethe in 1832. It was in this period that scientific socialism, philosophical materialism, and literary realism emerged as the cultural determinants of modern Europe. Lienhard did not hesitate to label materialistic movements as "Jewish," even when a majority of their proponents were not of Jewish origin. He confidently expected the rise of the Youth Movement to usher in a new age in which so-called Jewish values would be repudiated. Presumably such plays as Shakespeare's *The Merchant of Venice* would then be presented differently on stage, for only an immoral age could make out of Shylock a tragic hero. For Lienhard, Shylock represented the Talmudic tradition of formalism and legalism which Christ had fought when he said that even a man with sinful thoughts is a sinner.[18]

A striking example of idealist anti-Semitism was furnished in the play *Ahasver am Rhein*, in which Lienhard attacks the materialism and monism of the biologist and popularizer of Darwin, Ernst Haeckel (1834–1919). Ahasver, the eternal wandering Jew, is personified both by the restless German scientist Adam Hasse (meaning "hate"), who had devoted the scientific efforts of a lifetime to the discovery of a remedy to that "childhood disease," religion, and by his nervous and cunning assistant, Laban. Feeding his master's hubris in order to be named as his heir, Laban hoped to use Hasse's findings to gain power and wealth. Then, to get rid of Hasse, he tries to drive him insane by stirring up the conflict between materialism and metaphysics, a hunger for which, as a German trait, lay latent in Hasse's mind. Laban's schemes are foiled by the return of Hasse's son from India, where he had been sent to gather the archaeological proofs of man's evolution from the apes. Instead, he had returned imbued with Indian religion. Through the restorative powers of his newfound faith, he rescues Hasse from the clutches of Laban, who falls to his death in the Rhine.[19]

Not only does Lienhard equate materialism with Jewishness without regard to the religion or background of the person holding materialistic attitudes, but the play is also subtly anti-Semitic in the use of an apparently Jewish name for the villainous assistant, even though Laban is never explicitly identified, much less vilified, as Jewish. This frequently used device enabled Lienhard to avoid attacking Jews for being Jewish, while at the same time enabling him to indict the values that Jewishness supposedly stood for.

Idealist anti-Semitism, an ostensibly benevolent bias against materialism shared by large segments of Germany's *Bildungsbürgertum*, prepared the soil in which, under different conditions, more extreme forms of anti-Semitism could flourish. Yet this kind of anti-Semitism did not appear negativistic to persons who subscribed to it. Epitomizing opposition to materialism, anti-Semitism could seem to idealists to be grounded in high principles. Chamberlain would attempt to prove that Goethe and Kant had adhered to similar convictions. The aim of idealists was moral improvement, which Jews, who had not enjoyed the benefits of Christianization, were felt to require most.

If anti-Semitism was implicit in Lienhard's campaign of moral uplift, his opposition to movements which sought to liberate mankind from the age-old restraints of tradition was quite explicit. Devoting his efforts to resurrecting and restoring the ethos of a time long past, Lienhard made no secret of his preference for the good old days. "It seems to me," he wrote in his recollections, "that people were more trustful [*traulich*] and affectionate [*gemütvoller*] before 1870."[20] A note of nostalgia for a more elegant and cheerful—as well as a more quiescent and deferential—epoch pervaded *Wege nach Weimar*. Lienhard's values harked back to a predemocratic age in which, as he put it, the individual had not yet lost his power to a collectivity. Yet he saw no contradiction in his defense of benevolent autocracy. "The ideal is the patriarch," Lienhard wrote after World War I, "the fatherly friend, master, and protector of persons and animals, plants and objects—possessions entrusted to him and formed and inspired by him. . . . His royal virtue is mastery of life."[21] Lienhard's prescriptions for social improvement envisaged a hierarchical society in which an elite would be freed to pursue self-fulfillment through the deference accorded to them by the masses.

Lienhard's views on the role of women in society reflected the values of an age that resisted women's suffrage and other forms of feminine emancipation. While idealizing the grace, charm, and purity of women, Lienhard portrayed women as finding fulfillment only as helpmates to men in their struggle for idealism. The Valkyries, bearing the slain warrior to Heaven, symbolized the power of women to heal and redeem men exhausted in their valiant struggle against materialism.[22] Insulated from the world of male aggression, woman embodies the spirituality toward which the male aspires. Mediating between God and depraved man, the selfless woman is a means to grace. In his play *Odysseus auf Ithaka* (1911), Lienhard idealized the feminine virtues of domesticity and steadfastness. Nausicaa and Penelope personified for Lienhard "what with tenderness and esteem we like to call 'German girl' and 'German woman.' "[23] In spite of a sentimentalization of womanhood that today appears condescending, Lienhard apparently attracted a high proportion of women readers. In 1921 a selection of his writings on women was collected by his protégé Paul Bülow into a paean to domestic piety entitled *Über Weibes Wonne und Wert* (*On the Delight and Value of Women*).

The veneer of romanticization concealed a contempt for woman and for the lack of autonomy to which she supposedly was consigned by her nature. Because of her essential ethereality, woman who falls into sin becomes more odious than corrupted man. A woman who gives in to sexual appetite—the materialistic desire to touch and possess—has denied her true nature of selfless love more completely than man, who is saddled with sexual drives by nature.[24] Like so many of his contemporaries, Lienhard subscribed to a doctrine of male supremacy in which man is the agent of history, while woman's proper role remains instrumental. For all the purity he ascribed to women, Lienhard revealed his contempt for them by the derogatory connotation he attached to allegedly feminine characteristics in culture and society. He held the "creative masculinity" of a Schiller to be far superior to the "feminine degeneration [*weibische Entartung*] of the present."[25] Despising the passivity and dependence to which he himself had relegated idealized woman, Lienhard called for an "idealism of the deed" (*Idealismus der Tat*). The one-sided ideality personified by woman must be forged into reality by active man.

In excoriating feminine passivity in literature, Lienhard may have been reacting to critics who accused him of constructing a dream world in his revival of idealism. Classical idealism was not opposed to realism, Lienhard contended, but rather to rationalism.[26] Nothing galled Lienhard (or Chamberlain) more than the charge that idealism impeded action. By mobilizing the powers of the soul, idealism makes resolute activity possible. Idealism is not a system of thought, Lienhard contended, but a way of life. The ideal is not a realm to be explored or analyzed; its precepts are revealed to us and spur us on to action. The consistency of Lienhard's dualism—a consistency exemplified by his rejection of Rudolf Steiner's *Anthroposophie* on the grounds that man could never gain knowledge of the ideal realm, no matter how great the refinement of his senses[27]—left man utterly free in his choice of means to implement ideals in the realm of temporal reality. The activist, antinomian thrust of idealism emerged in full force in the period after World War I. Trapped in the logic of their own dualism, conservative idealists would be unable to harness the forces they had helped to unleash.

9

THE CONSERVATIVE REVOLUTION: LIENHARD'S ROLE IN THE RISE OF NATIONAL SOCIALISM

Gather your strength, German people! And keep the dual goals in sight: the Greater German Empire and the divine empire of wisdom, beauty, and love.

Lienhard, *Unter dem Rosenkreuz*

In the years before World War I Lienhard's apolitical idealism served to defend an embattled social order against threats from the left, but such quietism proved to be anachronistic after the war. With the advent of the republic, conservatives intent on restoring (or maintaining) the social structure of the Empire and its concomitant ideology found themselves in the unaccustomed role of political revolutionaries. Many idealists of more liberal persuasion than Lienhard became *Vernunftsrepublikaner*, supporting the republic out of prudence, if not out of conviction. Only Social Democrats, pariahs under the Empire, rallied to the new state with any enthusiasm.

Lienhard's late works are of historical interest for the light they shed on the relationship between traditional conservatism and right-wing extremism in the declining years of the Wilhelmine Empire and in the Weimar Republic. His postwar novels expressed the bewilderment of conservatives who found that the apolitical idealism they had preached as a defense of the status quo before the war seemed to obstruct the counterrevolutionary task of rolling back democratic gains after the war. While they supported the Nazis' proclaimed goal of a national regeneration and a return to authoritarian government, Lienhard and conservatives of like mind displayed an ambivalent attitude toward right-wing extremism and violence.[1] The debate as to the degree to which force could legitimately be applied to achieve the desired objective originated in the period before the war and can be traced in Lienhard's novels and publicistic works.

The novel *Der Spielmann* (1913), rigidly plotted and didactic in intent like all of Lienhard's works, describes the clash between proponents of cultural and political imperialism. Both sides agree on Germany's mission to regenerate a materialistic world, but they disagree on the extent to which political and military means could be employed without endangering the goal of moral regeneration. The novel's protagonist, Ingo von Stein, spokesman for Lienhard's own views, seeks to reconcile both camps. Lienhard had previously written that German political expansion on land and sea was no hindrance to the development of a new German idealism, just as after the war he would emphasize that Germany's "ensoulment" need not be at the expense of political power.[2] Goethe's spirit alone would never have sufficed to create a unified German Empire. The political engagement of Fichte and Arndt and the practical energy of Freiherr vom Stein, General Blücher, and Bismarck provided the necessary complement to idealism.[3] Lienhard decried pacifism as a Social Democratic vice. When war broke out in 1914, he made cultural imperialism serviceable to the war cause in a pamphlet entitled *Deutschlands europäische Sendung* (*Germany's European Mission*).

In *Der Spielmann*, Ingo von Stein's close friend, Richard von Trotzendorff, described in the novel as "German to the core" and a "splendid representative of vigorous Bismarckian Germanity," acts as spokesman for those who urge preventive war: "Enemies around us! If only it would break out at last! I fear that with these diplomatic delays we will miss the right moment to let fly. For we can not avoid a European war in any case."[4] Although Lienhard caricatured Trotzendorff's militarism, he did not hide his sympathies for Trotzendorff's manliness and partiotic indignation. Trotzendorff, Stein, and Konsul Bruck, the novel's incarnation of otherworldly idealism and the renunciation of political activism, are of one mind in their opposition to the materialism personified in the Jewish brothers Otto and Samuel Marx, to whom Lienhard ascribed the traits of intellect, cunning, lasciviousness, energy, and nervousness. The careers of Otto Marx, a publisher who becomes a millionaire by skillfully advertising second-rate books, and Samuel, a successful scholar, provoke from the committed idealist Konsul Bruck the comment that modern Jewry could be divided into two categories: Mammonists and Spinozans. While avoiding such anti-Semitic remarks, Ingo von Stein resents the fact that Kommerzienrat Otto Marx had access to the Imperial Court merely because he was rich.[5]

Much as he admired Trotzendorff's sound Germanic instincts, Ingo von Stein did not share his advocacy of military action. Nor did he share Trotzendorff's faith in racial eugenics, a faith Trotzendorff combined with love of military parades in which thousands of strapping soldiers could be trained (and bred) to move as one. Yet Stein also welcomed the prospect of war—despite his premonitions of German defeat: "A war today would purify the European air, and then there would be space and receptivity for a new mood of life."[6] Asserting that people feared war only because it endangered their comfort and prosperity, Lienhard deplored the absence of the idealistic fervor of 1870. The sinking of the luxury liner *Titanic* in 1912 symbolized the approaching fate of a materialistic world. Perhaps an excessively clamorous Germany would have to pass through humiliation in order to remember its spiritual mission.[7]

Both Ingo von Stein and Trotzendorff reappear as secondary characters in Lienhard's novel *Westmark* (1919), the story of an Alsatian pastor who chooses to leave his homeland after the war rather than live under French domination. Wounded in the war, Trotzendorff now agrees with Stein that Germany's soul had been unduly neglected. Yet he maintains the stab-in-the-back legend which Lienhard helped to spread in *Der Türmer* after the war: "The hunger blockade, the blockade of lies, superior numbers from outside, and sedition from inside will perhaps achieve their goal—but this I know: we German soldiers will withdraw from the battlefield unconquered!"[8]

Through Trotzendorff Lienhard rails against industrial workers who had supposedly extorted excessive wages through strikes and threats of violence during and after the war. "Are we not all workers?" Trotzendorff fumes, expressing a favorite theme of future Nazis.

> What devil and demon has for decades sung to the German people this insane refrain of the oppressed worker? Hasn't labor been coddled and pampered since the Kaiser came to power? Didn't he drive away Bismarck because of them?! And this is now their thanks! . . . Satan has led these people for decades, not God. May our dutiful Hohenzollern have erred—this gang is truly not entitled to depose such a highly deserving royal house![9]

While concurring with his friend, Ingo von Stein expresses a point of view characteristic of Lienhard's stance above the realm of politics. He saw the working-class revolt as symptomatic of a moral decay afflicting society as a whole. Evidence of this decay also appeared among the upper classes, where women no longer shrank from smoking in public. Lienhard subscribed to an unabashedly patriarchal ethos. "The coarseness of the lower orders only reflects the spiritual nadir of the upper estates."[10] His antidemocratic bias led him to diagnose social discontent as a moral failing and to rely on moral improvement as a substitute for social reform.

Lienhard again rejected politics in favor of a spiritual regeneration in his strikingly propagandistic novel, *Meisters Vermächtnis* (1927), in which the eponymous hero is a fictional descendant of Goethe's *Wilhelm Meister*. Set in the present, this novel returns to Lienhard's favorite theme of a young man's quest for the symbolic grail of faith and serenity. Felix Meister, the son of the country's exiled emperor, is brought up incognito (to protect him from opponents of monarchism) in the household of the emperor's former councillor, Johann Wolfgang Meister. Having come of age, Felix must now decide how to fulfill the obligations of his royal descent. Colonel Lothar von Wulffen, the leader of a paramilitary troop called the *Spartaner-*

bund, advises Felix to lead a military revolt in order to regain his throne: "We need a leader, a dictator."[11] After much soul-searching and several traumatic experiences, including a visit to a castle converted by Wulffen's hedonistic ex-wife into a colony for the practice of free love, Felix decides instead to follow his stepfather's advice: to renounce political action in order to redeem the world by spiritual means. Reflecting the yearning for authoritarian leadership that pervaded conservative political thought in the years after the war, Lienhard's theme of a secret king who would rescue Germany in her hour of need perpetuated an age-old German legend.[12]

Felix's stepfather, himself a target of right-wing ire because he would not sanction their tactics of violence (*Knüppelpolitik*), formulates the secret king's predicament: "Hate will await him: from the left, because he is of royal blood, from the right radicals, because he does not immediately attack with rolling drums."[13] Yet Colonel Wulffen, who takes the place of Trotzendorff in Lienhard's unchanging cast of stereotypes, enjoys the Meisters' respect and friendship. His ideals are, after all, sound, and his impetuosity forgivable in view of his fatherland's plight. While Lienhard faulted right-wing extremists for being hotheads at worst, the true villains of the piece are such subversive characters as Wulffen's sensuous ex-wife and the intellectual Dr. Kaliber, a columnist for a paper called the *Tageblatt*.[14] It was this type of person who had introduced the tone of mockery and malice which poisoned the social and cultural discourse of the nation. Their insolence and lack of idealism had provoked the justified, if overwrought, response of patriots.

Lienhard's protestations of quietism notwithstanding, his attitude toward authoritarian violence was ambivalent. His protagonists are quick to dispense righteous whippings when occasion demanded it. Despite their rhetoric of love, when confronted with opposition or criticism, particularly of an intellectual kind, his idealists emerge as self-righteous bullies. A neglected "idealist" poet slaps Dr. Kaliber's face; this is portrayed by Lienhard as the appropriate response to intellectual subversion, as is Trotzendorff's punch in the nose for a striker in *Westmark*. When a patriotic forester blows up the sinful castle (*Sündenburg*) of Wulffen's ex-wife, killing everyone of its inhabitants, Wulffen understandably exults. But even Johann and Felix Meister, while deploring the violation of law, display a remarkable callousness, both in attributing to the victims responsibility for their own violent end and in dismissing the event from their minds almost immediately. While careful not to justify a criminal act, Lienhard could not conceal his relief at so final a solution to the problem of immorality in society. In his handling of this kind of subject matter, always with didactic intent, Lienhard unconsciously reveals the brutality that lurked behind his veneer of respectability and moral virtue.

Although Lienhard rarely discussed current political events in his own articles, *Der Türmer* carried an unsigned political column showing a similar ambivalence toward right-wing extremism. Editorially as well as in its selection of articles, *Der Türmer* had always opposed the Weimar Republic. Originally close to the traditionally conservative German National People's Party (DNVP), despite that party's failure to adopt *Der Türmer's* suggestion for the inclusion of "Christian" in its name, *Der Türmer* increasingly expressed the need of a party more capable of attracting the allegiance of the masses.[15] In January, 1922, *Der Türmer* called for a synthesis of monarchism and socialism in a new Greater Germany. While expressing sympathy with the aims of Hitler's Beer Hall Putsch in November, 1923, *Der Türmer* doubted the wisdom of an act that could well have resulted in civil war. Anxious to exonerate Ludendorff from the charge that he knew of the putsch in advance, the paper identified itself with traditional nationalists rather than the Nazis. Yet in its description of the fray in front of the *Feldherrnhalle* in Munich, based largely on Nazi party member Gottfried Feder's eyewitness account, *Der Türmer* revealed its sympathy for the Putschists. "Germany will only become free when it maintains its *völkisch* power!"[16] *Der Türmer* enthusiastically seconded Hindenburg's admonition to both sides in the confrontation, the Nazis and the Bavarian state, to make up their differences and unite in a common cause. Advising Hitler to adopt more legitimate methods, *Der Türmer* anticipated the policy of legality that the Nazis were in fact to pursue thereafter.

While Lienhard opposed parliamentary government and party politics, he expressed his personal opposition to the Republic in characteristically euphemistic terms: at least the choice of Weimar as the seat of government symbolized the need to return to the ideals of German classicism. His ambivalent position between reaction and counterrevolution, between traditional and radical conservatism, may be seen in his attitude toward the Wilhelmine monarchy after the war. A staunch defender of the crown before the war, Lienhard looked back nostalgically at the Empire, without, however, considering a restoration of the Hohenzollern dynasty either feasible or advisable. A genius-statesman, another Bismarck or Freiherr vom Stein, was needed to enable Germany to overcome the humiliation of the Versailles treaty.

Lienhard's reservations about a Hohenzollern restoration did not imply a rejection of the social values of prewar monarchism. Indeed, like other *völkisch* ideologists, Lienhard criticized the Wilhelmine state primarily for its failure to defend effectively the traditional social order against its domestic challengers. Whereas in his prewar novel, *Der Spielmann*, Lienhard had portrayed the kaiser as valiantly battling against the "Americanization" of German life, his postwar strictures on the monarchy stressed the kaiser's own responsibility for the decline of the old order. While agreeing that the dismissal of Bismarck had been the kaiser's greatest mistake, Lienhard objected to the extreme attacks of such *völkisch* propagandists as the rabidly anti-Semitic literary historian Adolf Bartels, who called William II "the most calamitous phenomenon of modern German history."[17] In Lienhard's view, the moral depravity of an era could not be blamed entirely on the state or its highest representative. The forced abdication of the Hohenzollern dynasty exemplified the persecution that nobility and aristocracy always suffer at the hands of a basely materialistic world.[18]

The monarchy might not be treated as a scapegoat, but the Jews were a different case. Radicalization of political opinion is clearly evident in Lienhard's increased anti-Semitism after the war. He did not, however, subscribe to the conspiracy theories with which right-wing extremists sought to justify their campaign of violence and assassination after the war. "The enemy is neither here nor there," Lienhard wrote in 1922, "not this nor that stratum of the European people: the enemy is of a spiritual nature, the enemy is plebeianization [*Verpöbelung*]. 'Be proud!' the forgotten Rembrandt-German called out in his now forgotten book."[19] Just as *Der Türmer* editorially deplored the assassinations of Rathenau and Erzberger by right-wing extremists, Lienhard condemned the assassination of August Kotzebue by Karl Ludwig Sand in his novel on the *Burschenschaft* movement, *Das Landhaus bei Eisenach* (1928).

While continuing to advocate assimilation of Jews after the war, Lienhard increasingly expressed despair at the scope of the problem. He now described the influx of Jews from the East (the same group of immigrants to which Hitler traced his revulsion against Jews in *Mein Kampf*)[20] in uncharacteristically abusive language:

> It is a new kind of dangerously inconspicuous invasion of Tartars or Huns. The bacteria nests from Galicia begin to move, break out of their encystment, and these racial aliens, after immigrating with only a bundle on their backs, occupy important positions within a short time, whereby they skip the peasant and artisan estates. They then make public opinion; they teach German culture and literature. It is a problem of the first rank. We cannot stop this development. It can destroy Germany in its essential character, or at least distort it, if we are not strong enough to assimilate the Eastern Jews and carry its better components upward, so that they assist in the solution of human problems, instead of undermining them.[21]

Lienhard dissociated himself, however, from the virulently anti-Semitic diatribes of Colonel Wulffen, his spokesman for militarism in *Meisters Vermächtnis*. In this novel Felix Meister challenges Wulffen with the question—so momentous in light of the Holocaust—of how he proposed to dispose of the Jews. To this question Wulffen can give no answer.[22] Yet Lienhard's attitude suggested a similar impasse, for he was clearly unwilling to tolerate the existence of a separate Jewish community within Germany. He viewed the "Jewish question" as a test of Germany's strength to assert its own character in the face of alien influences. He, too, like other German nationalists, desired the *Gleichschaltung*—the regimentation—of national life.

If Lienhard's attitude toward race differed from the biological determinism of the Nazis (despite their claims that they, too, considered ideology the most important dimension of race), he had no difficulty in accepting racist assumptions and findings once he had translated them into "idealist" terms. Thus he commended the notorious racial anthropologist Hans F. K. Günther (1891–1968), whom the Nazis awarded a professorial chair at the University of Jena, for his efforts to create a Nordic race through eugenics. "From our spiritual standpoint," Lienhard wrote, "we support the heroic disposition expressed in this effort."[23] His easy acceptance of the practical consequences of racial determinism provides clear evidence of the usefulness of *völkisch* idealism in legitimating Nazi social and political goals.

A Nazi commentator writing in 1935 acknowledged Lienhard's contributions to the triumph of National Socialism, despite his failure to join the party: "Lienhard was no National Socialist, and it would be completely wrong to want to make him one after the fact, even though I am firmly convinced that he would have . . . embraced National Socialism, had it been granted to him to experience the decisive years of the National Socialist struggle. However, Lienhard's enemies were also the enemies of National Socialism, and they remain so today."[24] The commentator went on to commend Lienhard for having led the fight against un-German influences, even if he had fought with means inadequate to the task. If Lienhard's conception of the Reich had contained too much Christian dogma, at least he had opposed the foolish isms (*Ismus-Blödsinn*) of artists and intellectuals in the 1920s who had protested the desecration of Jewish cemeteries, the suppression of pornography, and the execution of Sacco and Vanzetti.[25]

No doubt Lienhard would have welcomed the "Day of Potsdam" in March, 1933, when Hindenburg and Hitler joined hands at the opening of the first *Reichstag* to be convened after the fire, so symbolizing the union of old and new conservatism. Dying in 1929 at the age of sixty-three, Lienhard did not live to see the Nazi catastrophe unfold. His ambivalence toward political activism in the 1920s provided an early model for "inner emigration," the withdrawal into privacy by which disappointed conservatives would later express their opposition to Nazi policies. Yet it would be quite misleading to absolve Lienhard entirely of the stigma of Nazi savagery. His works clearly demonstrate how fascism could be tolerated and promoted by intellectuals who prided themselves in carrying on a tradition of idealism. Far from providing a basis of resistance to Nazism, *völkisch* idealism served instead as a means of disguising and justifying its excesses.

The contribution to National Socialism of conservative intellectuals like Lienhard lies in the mental habits that they fostered. Like so many other self-styled idealists, Lienhard surrendered intellectual and artistic integrity in favor of *Schönfärberei*, the purveyance of ideological window-dressing for a social order threatened by modernizing change. By proclaiming contempt for the material aspects of life, Lienhard sought to stem the tide of social and political reform movements. Encouraging his readers to avoid rather than face social realities, Lienhard advocated idealism as an alternative to critical analysis and independent judgment. Lienhard's self-righteous intolerance of intellectualism anticipated on an ideological plane the campaign of exclusion and repression that the Nazis would launch in practice. His rejection of rational analysis and debate foreshadowed this predilection for solving social problems by force. Committed to moral rectitude rather than intellectual probity, Lienhard fed the hypocrisies and resentments of a middle class which would put the Nazis into power with untroubled conscience.

Houston Stewart Chamberlain during World War One. (*Courtesy Richard-Wagner-Gedenkstätte, Bayreuth.*)

PART THREE

Houston Stewart Chamberlain and Idealized Racism

I do not like these latest speculators in idealism, the anti-Semites, who today roll their eyes in a Christian-Aryan-bourgeois manner and exhaust one's patience by trying to rouse up all the horned-beast elements in the people by a brazen abuse of the cheapest of all agitator's tricks, moral attitudinizing.

NIETZSCHE, *The Genealogy of Morals*

10

PROPHET OF REGENERATION AND IDEOLOGUE OF NATIONALISM: THE LIFE OF HOUSTON STEWART CHAMBERLAIN

Recently I have often had to think about the peculiar whims of fate, which causes so subtle a spirit as Stein to work so soon and so briefly, at a time when the soil was not yet prepared for the seed, while it does not have such forest-uprooters as myself take up their duty until later.

Chamberlain to Eva Wagner, 1897

Houston Stewart Chamberlain (1855–1927), son of a British admiral and descendant of an aristocratic Scottish family on his mother's side, became the foremost propagandist of *völkisch* idealism in Germany. If Lienhard's role was to convert the middle class to aristocratic ideals, Chamberlain provided a rationale for the German ruling elite itself (which is not to deny that both authors articulated attitudes already held by the groups they addressed as much as they created these attitudes). While both Lienhard and Chamberlain popularized philosophical idealism as a doctrine of social conservatism, Chamberlain's tomes were designed to meet a higher intellectual standard than Lienhard's publications. His influence was greater than Lienhard's, for he attracted the serious attention of political, cultural, religious, and educational leaders in the Wilhelmine Empire. An extract from the *Kölnische Zeitung* indicates how widespread his influence became in the first decade of the twentieth century: "Of all the men who took the pulse of their times around the turn of the century, no one has even come close to exercising so broad and lasting an influence on the thinking of the upper intellectual stratum as this Englishman, who speaks to us so powerfully in the German language."[1] Chamberlain's crucial influence was acknowledged by such leading opinion-makers as Heinrich Class (1868–1953), head of the Pan-German League; Möller van den Bruck (1876–1925), author of *The Third Reich* (1923); Nazi ideologist Alfred Rosenberg (1893–1946); and Hitler's mentor Dietrich Eckart (1868–1923).[2] A confidant of William II, with whom he corresponded for over twenty years, and an early supporter of Hitler, Chamberlain personified the ideological link between the Second Empire and the Third Reich.

The substantial secondary literature on Chamberlain may be subsumed under three time-frames. During Chamberlain's own lifetime a number of scholars challenged his views on religion and race, while others rallied to his defense.[3] After going into partial eclipse during the 1920s, Chamberlain's works enjoyed an officially inspired renascence during the Nazi period. Eulogy supplanted criticism in a vast literature that acclaimed Chamberlain as the "seer of the Third Reich."[4] Adulation turned to revulsion after the debacle of the *völkisch* world view following World War II. Today Chamberlain is remembered only as the anti-Semite whose racial interpretation of history promoted policies culminating in the Nazis' "final solution."[5]

Chamberlain's career offers a striking illustration of the prolonged identity crisis to which great men, of either the conservative or destructive variety, are often subject before emerging with great impact on the historical scene.[6] Although born two years before Stein and ten years before Lienhard, Chamberlain's productive life began after theirs. At the age of thirty, the same age at which Stein had completed his life's work, Chamberlain had not yet published a single article. Out of his long incubation Chamberlain emerged with a newfound identity as an apostle of Wagnerian idealism and nationalism. His search for a secure identity paralleled the continuing identity crisis of the country he chose to make his own. This "most Germanic of Germans" found his life's work in the effort to formulate a coherent self-definition for a nation only recently unified and increasingly torn by class conflict and the tensions of rapid industrialization.

By identifying with the most reactionary segment of German society, Chamberlain repudiated the progressive traditions of England, the country of his birth, and also France, the country in which he was raised. No doubt his passionate affirmation of the German aristocratic tradition (and of Nordic racial superiority) provided some psychological compensation for the decline of his family fortunes. In other ways, too, his career was marked by frustrations. Finding his literary vocation only after a nervous ailment had aborted a career as a scientist, Chamberlain channeled his frustrated ambitions into an attack on scientific materialism. Prevented by poor health from pursuing the military career for which his father had intended him, he would leave his desk after a hard day's work feeling like an officer who had been in the saddle for ten hours.[7] Hypersensitive, intolerant, and consumed with a sense of mission, he conquered his personal neuroses in writing books that nourished the neurotic arrogance of Germany's privileged classes. An autodidact of encyclopedic knowledge with a gift for language (acknowledged by no less a master than Karl Kraus), Chamberlain provided an eloquent rationale for those members of the German upper classes who were determined to retain their prerogatives amidst rapid social and economic changes. More so even than Lienhard, Chamberlain became a virtuoso of eclecticism and synthesis, blending Wagnerian idealism, racial anthropology, and social Darwinism into an imperialistic doctrine perfectly fitted to promote quietism in domestic politics and expansionism abroad.

Born in 1855 in Portsmouth, England, Chamberlain, like Stein and Lienhard, lost his mother at an early age. Her death when he was only two left him with a lifelong feeling of desolation. Relations with his father were never close and were frequently strained. The emotional wounds of childhood intensified the affection he acquired for Germany. In racial solidarity with a country his mother particularly admired he found the emotional security his parental home failed to provide. Growing up in the house of his aunt in Versailles, Chamberlain absorbed her contempt for the French, who were often referred to in his family as "frogs." He was made to feel a stranger in the land. Yet occasional visits to England were even more traumatic. Even traffic regulations seemed to reflect differences in national character. In England every pedestrian had to look out for himself, while in France, at least, the carriage drivers were responsible for exercising caution. Chamberlain was always glad to return to the Continent.[8]

In 1866 his father placed him in a private school in England. Chamberlain's autobiography, published in 1919, conveyed the desperate homesickness of the eleven-year-old boy: "It was the unconditional, irremediable, hopeless misery of a lost soul, suddenly torn from love, goodness, gentleness, friendliness, and hurled into the Hell where fists ruled."[9] From 1867 to 1870 he attended Cheltenham College, where he became better acclimated and went through a phase of intense enthusiasm for Shakespeare. But Chamberlain never felt comfortable in the country of his birth. The humiliations he suffered reinforced a lifelong aversion to the "anarchy" and "egoism" of liberal society. By joining a "superior" racial and cultural community—at Bayreuth and in Germany—he belatedly gained his revenge. After 1870 he paid only brief visits to England, for the last time in 1908.[10]

Chamberlain first visited Germany at the age of fifteen, just before the start of the Franco-Prussian War. If his later account is to be believed, he was an unauthorized witness, from the safety of nearby bushes, to the historic meeting between William I and Count Benedetti of France at Ems.[11] His first impression of Germany was formed by its heroic, not its philistine, aspect. The sight of the Prussian elite troops marching off to war remained an indelible memory. Chamberlain's Germanophilism was reinforced by his admiration for the theology student who served as his tutor from 1871 to 1874. As early as 1873 Chamberlain wrote home of Germany's unique gifts, of her dignity and self-awareness, and of the contributions she could make to a worldwide moral regeneration, if only she would remain true to herself.[12]

Years of ill health and the lack of any clear aim impeded Chamberlain's pursuit of a vocation. An inherited income gave him the independence to cultivate the self-education he would later recommend as the exemplary life. His lack of financial worries may explain his lifelong insensitivity to the plight of the lower classes. It was not until the death of his father in 1878 that his life took a more purposeful turn. In that year he married Anna Horst, a woman of partly Jewish descent and ten years older than he. A native of Breslau in Silesia, Anna Horst taught school in Geneva, where the couple made their first home. They had first met on vacation in southern France four years before. Anna recalled how attractive she found his shyness. In his letters and poems (some of which are in English), his love for her and for Germany were fused.[13]

In 1879 Chamberlain enrolled at the University of Geneva as a student of botany, an interest he had previously pursued in his own private herbarium. Yet Chamberlain lacked the disinterested curiosity of the scientific temperament. He became impatient and frustrated by the myriad of differences which exact observation revealed. His talent, he felt, lay not in making distinctions but in perceiving relationships—in what he called *zusammenschauen* ("seeing syncretically"). His perfectionism proved too great a strain on his nerves. He compulsively kept an alphabetic record of everything he had done, seen, heard, or read, down to the exact number of pages. A nervous breakdown in 1884 abruptly ended his formal academic career. Although in 1897 he finally completed his doctoral dissertation, which was on the rising of sap in plants, too much time had elapsed for him to earn a degree.[14]

In the years following his academic failure at Geneva, Chamberlain made a discovery about himself: abstract thinking proved less of a strain on his nerves than any concrete task. In these years of enforced idleness, he read avidly in philosophy and literature, finding inspiration particularly in the works of Plato, Kant ("the true master of my thought"),[15] and Goethe, with whose avocational interest in botany and nature studies Chamberlain could identify. But it was in the works of Wagner that he found his greatest inspiration. Here he discovered not only stirring music but also a fully developed consciousness of the Germanity he admired so much.[16]

Chamberlain claimed to have loved Wagner, whom he called the sun of his life, even before he knew anything about him. Touring the Lake of Luzern in Switzerland on an excursion steamer in 1870, the same year in which he had first felt the impact of German culture, Chamberlain admired the isolation and dreamlike quality of Wagner's lakeside estate, *Tribchen*. He felt an instinctive affinity with the man who lived there, an affinity reinforced by the derisive comments he overheard among some of the tourists. His sympathy and respect were aroused for a man who could be so well-hated by vulgar people.[17]

Thus predisposed to appreciate Wagner's music, Chamberlain was not disappointed. In 1878 he joined the Munich chapter of the Bayreuth Patrons, an association of Wagner-lovers formed to support the Wagnerian drama festivals at Bayreuth. When shortly thereafter an article in *Bayreuther Blätter* asserted that only a German could truly understand Wagnerian art, Chamberlain felt personally rebuffed. "I feel as if I had been expelled from a sphere that was holy to me."[18] His feelings hurt, he threw himself into his studies.

Chamberlain rejoined the fold on his visit to Bayreuth for the première of *Parsifal* in 1882. It was a closed performance reserved for dedicated Wagnerians, and Chamberlain was pleased by the absence of the merely curious or frivolous. "No alien or alienating element disrupted the harmony of love."[19] Wagner's regal bearing and eloquent speech left as strong an impression as his art. Chamberlain was too awed at the time to seek a personal introduction. Three years later an article of his attracted the notice of Wagner's widow and gave rise to an intensive correspondence and a lifelong friendship. Their first meeting took place in Dresden, where Chamberlain had settled after leaving Geneva in 1885. "Since Stein left me," Cosima Wagner wrote, "no one has spoken to me with such sympathy, and I did not think I would hear such accents again."[20] She described Chamberlain as "an aristocrat through and through, in the best sense of the word."[21] For his part, Chamberlain was fully won over to the Wagnerian cause. "If it were useful to Bayreuth," he wrote in 1896, "I would without hesitation allow myself to be fried on a slow fire."[22]

His career as a Wagnerian publicist was launched that same year when the French symbolist Edouard Dujardin (1861–1949), whom Chamberlain had met through the *Wagnerverein* in Geneva, invited him to participate in his newly founded journal, the *Revue wagnérienne*. This innovative journal, a predecessor of the celebrated *Revue indépendante* (founded in 1888), numbered among its contributors such outstanding representatives of French symbolism as Stéphane Mallarmé, Paul Verlaine, and J. K. Huysmans. It was Chamberlain's task to summarize the monthly contents of the *Bayreuther Blätter* for Wagner devotees in France. His first contributions included synopses of Stein's "Schopenhauer Scholien." In 1886 Chamberlain branched out with commentaries of his own on various Wagner operas. Two of his articles constituted virtually the entire last issue of *Revue wagnérienne* in 1888.[23] That same year an article in the *Allgemeine Musik-Zeitung* launched Chamberlain on a decade of publicistic activity for Wagner in Germany and Austria, where he settled in 1889.[24] His reputation as a Wagnerian became so well established that he was invited to write two articles on Wagner for the American *Ladies' Home Journal* in 1898.[25] He declined, however, to undertake the long journey to the United States, where he had been invited to lecture by the Assyriologist Paul Haupt (1858–1926) of Johns Hopkins University that same year.[26]

Chamberlain's early writing efforts were accompanied by gnawing self-doubts and inhibitions induced by a premonition of a fame that would turn into notoriety. It was not until 1892, at age thirty-seven, that he was seized, as he put it, by a demonic urge to write that remained with him for the rest of his life.[27] He was also a prolific letter writer: "*Schreibfaulheit* [letter-writing lazyness]—from that modern disease I do not suffer."[28] Completing his correspondence and practical affairs in the morning, Chamberlain would write all afternoon, leaving his evenings free to read aloud with his wife and a circle of friends that included the writers Hermann Keyserling (1880–1946) and Rudolf Kassner (1873–1959), as well as diplomats from the German legation in Vienna. At Anna's urging he published his first book, *Das Drama Richard Wagners*, at his own expense. Appearing in 1892, the book remained largely unknown until Chamberlain's increasing fame stimulated sales in later years.

The book fervently proselytized Wagnerian aesthetic doctrines. Contrasting visualizing (*Schauen*) to thinking (*Denken*), Chamberlain followed Schopenhauer, Wagner, and Stein in emphasizing the importance of *Anschauung* ("visualization and intuition"). The artist intuits relationships and connections which he could not have realized by rational abstraction or combination. Even the object of one's thoughts can only be effectively communicated if it is visualized. Because true art conveys a concentrated picture of the world, at its best it contains all wisdom and acts upon the viewer like a revelation.[29]

Wagner's music-drama made possible revelations of man's inner life which even Shakespeare could only suggest but not achieve. In traditional opera, however, music and poetry were not organically related, the former addressing itself exclusively to feelings, the latter to the understanding. In Wagner's operas, the poetry and the plot were born out of music, the language of "the other world within."[30] Opera did not pose for Wagner the formal problem of how to combine music and poetry most effectively. Wagner sought instead to determine what kind of artistic content it was that required such sublime expression. In portraying natural man freed of all convention (*das von aller Konvention losgelöste Reinmenschliche*), Wagner's *Gesamtkunstwerk* differed from all preceding forms of opera. In contrast to previous versions, for instance, in which Tristan and Isolde meet their death by tragic accident, in Wagner's rendition their death became a consequence of inner necessity.[31]

In 1895 Chamberlain was commissioned by the Munich publisher Hugo Bruckmann to write a biography of Wagner. Chamberlain turned the project into a lengthy exposition of Wagner's social and political ideas.[32] He explained his method at the outset: he would put himself in Wagner's shoes so as to represent the world as Wagner viewed it. So greatly did he empathize with Wagner that while writing the book he felt he himself no longer existed. In a letter to a fellow-Wagnerian, the psychologist and eugenicist Christian von Ehrenfels (1859–1932), he defended his uncritical approach as "scientific": "The basic principle of natural science is the old *panta kala lian* of the first book of Moses; whatever is, is good. To want nature to be different than it is . . . would bring the scientist into a lunatic asylum."[33] Transferred to the social realm, Chamberlain's "scientific" attitude, a vulgarized form of positivism, served to promote the unquestioning acceptance of an undemocratic status quo.

Chamberlain's work on Wagner was a typical product of the highly charged political atmosphere of the 1890s, as the vigorous growth of the Social Democratic parties in Germany and Austria provoked conservative reactions on various fronts. Chamberlain's objective was no longer simply to convert readers to an appreciation of Wagnerian art, but to mobilize public opinion for conservative social policies. This occasionally provoked conflict with those Wagnerians, always in a minority, who did not share Wagner's political views. Chamberlain defended Wagner's doctrine of support for an absolute monarchy combined with a "free" people as inspired (*genial*), even if it was paradoxical. "I love what is drastic," he wrote to Ehrenfels; "in every area, everywhere we go to the bottom of things, we hit upon contradictions."[34] Embracing the nationalist definition of freedom from foreign dependence rather than the liberal conception of freedom from the overweening state, Chamberlain praised the absolute ruler (*Einherrscher*) who made freedom possible by creating a nation.[35] He thanked Ehrenfels for not having interrupted a lecture he gave on Wagner and promised that he would show similar forbearance when Ehrenfels propounded his "world-redeeming, evolutionary-socialistic ideas."[36]

Chamberlain's political motives were clearly revealed in a polemic against the aged materialist philosopher Ludwig Büchner in 1895. In an article entitled "Büchners Sturz" ("Büchner's Downfall"), published, surprisingly, in Otto Brahm's *Neue Deutsche Rundschau* in response to Büchner's "Sturz der Metaphysik" in Maximilian Harden's *Zukunft*, Chamberlain first interpreted Kant in a way that would render the Kantian defense of rationalism useless for liberal or progressive causes. He cited Kant's distinction between appearances (phenomena) and things-in-themselves (noumena) in the *Critique of Pure Reason* as proof that in seeking to explain the world, human reason can do no better than grope in the dark. "Kant deposed reason from its throne once and for all."[37] Chamberlain exhibited a debater's craftiness in formulating arguments against the rationalist faith in science. Descriptive, not explanatory in its function, science can increase human knowledge but never human wisdom. Science can only gather facts without closing the gap between human knowledge and the infinity of what is knowable. Science cannot comprehend nature as a whole because a process of perception without beginning or end can never lead to final truth (*Erkenntnis*). In personifying conceptual abstractions such as atoms, molecules, or cells, scientific materialists reveal themselves to be as dogmatic as the Neo-Platonists who explained the world through the existence of angels. Materialists never inquire into the truly important question—the question of the meaning of life—for to them the world contains no secrets. A true idealist, on the other hand, goes through life wondering rather than knowing. Reverence, not skepticism, was the attitude Chamberlain sought to inspire.

The nineteenth-century debate between religion and science, idealism and materialism, masked a political conflict in which Chamberlain sided firmly with the traditionalist forces. He denounced the implicit claims to omniscience of scientists who exceeded the bounds of fact-gathering by constructing world views. Besides Büchner, his favorite targets included the evolutionist Ernst Haeckel, the physiologist and liberal politician Rudolf Virchow (1821–1902), the physician Max Nordau (1849–1923), and the Dutch geneticist Hugo De Vries (1848–1935). Chamberlain was not content, however, to rest his case against scientific materialism on philosophic grounds. He accused Büchner of a psychological and indeed physiological incapacity for metaphysics. Materialists ignore the basic question of metaphysics, posed definitively by Kant, of how experience is possible in the first place. Failure to heed the proper bounds of science, Chamberlain asserted, was a physical disability, a function of inadequate genetic endowment.

It was this assumption of hereditary determinism, shared to some degree by the very positivists he attacked, that would lend to racialism whatever scientific plausibility it could command. Chamberlain's device of marshaling racial determinism against the rationalist faith in science foreshadowed the mobilization, in the decades to follow, of "German biology" against "Jewish physics." Moreover, his article revealed how closely an apparently academic dispute was tied to social and political concerns. A hierarchical social structure was the natural corollary of the rehabilitation of metaphysics. The Aryan Indians, "the metaphysically most gifted peoples on earth," knew that the metaphysical gifts of superior individuals must be cultivated by society. This is why they gave their wise men the leisure to devote a lifetime to thought.[38]

In 1899 Chamberlain continued his largely politically motivated assault on scientific rationalism in his most famous work, *The Foundations of the Nineteenth Century*. In it Chamberlain expounds the racial doctrine that became such a vicious instrument of destruction under the Nazis. In stressing biological determinism Chamberlain parts company with more squeamish idealists such as Lienhard. Chamberlain's main purpose in propagating racialism was to harness the immense prestige of the scientific laboratory to the conservative alliance of altar and throne. His own education in science lent his pronouncements an air of authority. He dedicated his book to the Jewish biologist and anti-evolutionist Julius von Wiesner (1838–1916), whose lectures he attended when he first moved to Vienna—his home for twenty years—in 1889. Through Wiesner he claimed a direct line to the pioneer of genetics, Gregor Mendel.[39]

Although garnished with the trappings of science and philosophy, *The Foundations* is in fact an elaborate political polemic. Chamberlain conceded as much in his memoirs when he described the book as expressing "the impulse of self-preservation in the spiritual sphere."[40] Written in the ethnic cauldron of Habsburg Vienna, *The Foundations* is the product of the same milieu that exercised such a formative influence on Hitler's political and racial views. The book reflects Chamberlain's emotional identification with the German ruling elite and his resentment of the liberal Viennese establishment from which he felt excluded. He exhorts Germans to defend their tradition of Lutheranism and Kantian idealism—a tradition that had reached its pinnacle in Wagnerian art—against the presumed threats of "Jewish materialism" and Catholic ultramontanism. This involved a defense of Germany's authoritarian political tradition and hierarchical social structure as well. Indeed, Chamberlain's primary, if unacknowledged, motive may be said to have been to provide a scientific-sounding and at the same time inspirational rationale for the perpetuation of the quasi-feudal monarchical order in Germany against the reformist challenge from egalitarian and libertarian movements of the left. *The Foundations* was designed to serve as a stimulus to action. "I do not want to act upon the mind," he told Prince Philipp Eulenburg, the German ambassador in Vienna, "but rather on the will." His ideal reader would throw the book away in order to act on its precepts.[41]

The Foundations might never have been written if Chamberlain had not been prodded by his publisher. Bruckmann was anxious to exploit the potential market for a work that would commemorate the achievements of a century drawing to its close. Instead, Chamberlain produced a wide-ranging historical and pseudo-scientific justification of Germany's claims to superiority. His original plan called for two additional works of equal scope on the nineteenth century and the world of the future, respectively.

Put off by his distaste for the "century of progress" and perhaps also by the difficulty of continuing to attribute all major cultural achievements to the "Germanic" races, he turned instead to propagating social conservatism in philosophical guise in mammoth works on *Immanuel Kant* (1905) and *Goethe* (1912).

The Foundations of the Nineteenth Century, reissued in twenty-eight editions through 1942 and translated into English, French, and Czech, won instant acclaim when it was published. Reviewers compared it to Herder's *Ideen zur Philosophie der Geschichte der Menschheit* (1784–1791), which had sounded the call for a German national religion in the previous century.[42] Even critics who took issue with Chamberlain's judgments acknowledged its erudition and readability. Nationalists esteemed its exaltation of Germanic superiority, conservatives appreciated its strong defense of tradition, and religious believers welcomed its affirmation of spiritual values. The Berlin University library ordered five copies, and Chamberlain personally presented one hundred copies to the Vienna *Volksbibliothek*. With sales of 20,000 copies by 1904 and 100,000 by 1914, the book's circulation reached a quarter of a million by 1938, by which time it had become established as a classic of National Socialist literature.[43] The English version, introduced by the diplomat and author Lord Redesdale (1837–1916), whose granddaughter married the British fascist leader Oswald Mosley, was reissued in several editions before World War I—a commentary on the international acceptance of racial doctrines in the era of imperialism. "It is of great value," the prominent American historian Carl Becker wrote in a favorable review in 1911, "among historical works, likely to rank with the most significant of the nineteenth century."[44] The Progressive senator Albert Beveridge (1862–1927), a spokesman for American imperialism, assured Chamberlain that *The Foundations* had made a great impression in the United States, albeit within a fairly narrow circle.[45]

Among the book's most enthusiastic admirers was Kaiser William II, who read portions aloud to his family and had copies distributed to officers in the army. In 1901 a meeting arranged by Prince Eulenburg led to a correspondence with the kaiser that lasted beyond the end of the war. From Count Ulrich von Brockdorff-Rantzau of the German diplomatic corps in Vienna, a member of Chamberlain's reading circle, he learned the formalities of addressing the emperor, which he scrupulously and at times obsequiously observed. At Eulenburg's country seat at Liebenberg Chamberlain spent several evenings in animated discussions with the kaiser and the queen, the German chancellor Prince Bernhard von Bülow (1849–1929), and the well-known Protestant theologian Adolf von Harnack (1851–1930), who had read the 1,200-page *Foundations* in five days. Eulenburg reported that the kaiser stood fully under the spell of Chamberlain's personality.[46]

The success of his book made Chamberlain a celebrity whose contributions were sought by such talented journalists as Maximilian Harden, editor of *Zukunft*, and the Viennese satirist Karl Kraus (1874–1936), founder and editor of *Die Fackel*. Chamberlain's contributions involved Kraus in a dispute with his rival Ludwig Bauer (1876–1935), whose journal *Don Quixote* was modeled on *Die Fackel* and completed for the same readership. In an effort to raise the circulation of *Don Quixote*, Bauer announced a contribution by Chamberlain on the binding of his journal in early 1903. The announcement led unwary readers to assume that Chamberlain had written an original article for *Don Quixote*. In fact, the selection consisted merely of excerpts from *The Foundations*. Incensed by this apparent exploitation of a name that people associated with the *Fackel*, Kraus published a letter from Chamberlain in which Chamberlain assured him that his name had been used by Bauer without his permission. Bauer countered with a column implying that Chamberlain had approved the honorable use to which his name had been put. Again Kraus sought reassurances from Chamberlain, who wrote that only his lawyer, to whom he had entrusted the matter, had communicated with Bauer. Although his lawyer had told him that there were insufficient grounds for legal action against Bauer, Chamberlain assured Kraus of his continued loyalty to *Die Fackel*.[47]

It may seem odd that Kraus should have held Chamberlain in such esteem (Kraus dubbed him *der Gelehrte*, "the scholar"), because as a Jew who would later convert to Catholicism Kraus represented the very categories Chamberlain assailed in his *Foundations*. Yet both Kraus and Chamberlain opposed liberalism and democracy in the name of culture, sharing a common disdain for the liberal Viennese press, especially the *Neue Freie Presse*. Both authors were primarily political publicists and culture critics for whom anti-Semitism grew out of hostility to liberalism. Both men were animated by an aristocratic scorn for mass culture. The potentially destructive consequences of Chamberlain's racialism went largely unrecognized by contemporaries. Certainly no one foresaw its eventual culmination in genocidal policies. What seemed more important to conservatives was the rebirth of cultural creativity and traditional standards of excellence that Chamberlain preached. It was also possible, as the Wagnerian conductor Hermann Levy did, to endorse wholeheartedly the spiritual message of *The Foundations* while ignoring or rejecting its racial argumentation.

In his contributions to *Die Fackel*, one of which constituted the entire issue of January, 1902, Chamberlain made clear that his opposition to Catholicism, like his anti-Semitism, rested on political grounds. Echoing the ideas popularized by the influential Austrian Pan-Germanist Georg von Schönerer (1842–1921), founder of the *Los von Rom* movement, Chamberlain denounced the Catholic Church as an anti-national force.[48] Yet he criticized Bismarck's *Kulturkampf*, based as it was on liberal opposition to

Catholicism, for it only served to strengthen political Catholicism and the subservience of the Catholic Church in Germany to the pope. Liberalism was a more dangerous enemy than Catholicism, Chamberlain insisted. If "Rome" was the code word for Catholic ultramontanism, "Jerusalem" served the same function for liberalism, even if, as Chamberlain conceded, many non-Jews were liberals and many Jews were not. Perhaps in deference to Kraus and other Jewish friends, Chamberlain emphasized that individual Jews could make outstanding contributions to "Christian-Germanic culture."

Chamberlain was well aware of the potential usefulness of Catholicism as a bulwark against liberalism. Hence he sought to wean German Catholics, not from their religion, but from the anti-national posture to which they allegedly were driven by liberal opposition. Indeed, he admired the religiosity of Catholics and advised them not to convert to Protestantism unless they felt an overwhelming personal need to do so.[49] Protestants must make common cause with Catholics, not, as they so often did, with Jews. He scathingly attacked the classical historian and 1902 Nobel Prize-winner Theodor Mommsen (1817–1903), who had criticized the appointment of the Catholic and nationalist historian Martin Spahn (1875–1945) to a professorial chair in Strassburg in 1901. Made against the recommendation of the Strassburg faculty, Spahn's appointment seemed to Mommsen to endanger the principles of value-neutral scholarship and faculty self-determination. Chamberlain, on the other hand, contended that scholarship should serve the culture of which it formed a part, by which he meant that it should serve the interests of the German monarchy. He deplored Mommsen's failure to carry on Treitschke's "courageous" work of national education. Instead, Mommsen had "pulled forth his 1848 phrases, pushed downward even deeper that dark, directionless conscience of the nation, which for the time being calls itself 'anti-Semitism,' and flattered the worst instincts of those elements of Jewry who have retrogressed to functional parasitism and who represent an equally destructive plague to both Semites and non-Semites."[50]

The controversy enabled Chamberlain to assume the anomalous role of defending Catholic scholars against alleged religious discrimination. He could even pose as the spokesman of equal representation: of thirty professors at Strassburg, a city that was 50 percent Catholic, sixteen were Jewish, twelve Protestant, and only two were Catholic. But for Chamberlain politics, not religion, was at issue. He would hardly have rallied to the Catholic cause if Spahn had not been an avowed German nationalist. Chamberlain cited the aborted academic careers of Dühring and Stein as instances of similar discrimination in the name of detached scholarship. The state had not only the right but also the duty to intervene in cases such as these to forestall "subversive professorial cliques."[51] When Chamberlain denounced Judaism as "materialistic" and Catholicism as "imperialistic," his real targets were liberalism and internationalism. Insofar as Catholicism itself stood for opposition to liberalism, Chamberlain was prepared to defend Catholic rights. To have done otherwise in Catholic Austria and a religiously divided Germany would hardly have served the cause of German nationalism.

As Chamberlain's celebrity increased, he grew personally more inaccessible, refusing to grant interviews or photographs that would damage his valued anonymity in Vienna. In private life, however, he became more self-confident, referring to himself half-humorously as the "foundation-layer" (*Grundleger*) of a new Germany.

The self-esteem that success conferred adversely affected his marriage. Chamberlain grew increasingly restive in his relationship with a wife who, though affectionate and attentive to his needs, lacked in his eyes the stature befitting his newly acquired prominence. Perhaps the difference in their ages that had made her attractive to him in his youth now became a source of growing estrangement. For Chamberlain, Anna increasingly came to personify a past that he wished to escape. "For me life is movement," he wrote her while she was vacationing in Italy in 1905; "I do not want to live on memories."[52] His method of securing a divorce typified his habit of avoiding unpleasantness or conflict in his personal life. Count Hermann Keyserling, the author and erstwhile disciple to whom Chamberlain had dedicated the first edition of his book on Kant, described the Chamberlains' parting in 1906 after almost thirty years of marriage:

> [Chamberlain] used a chance absence on her part in order suddenly to be no longer contactable or even existent for her. From one day to the next he no longer had an address for her. None of her letters reached him any longer; he refused every meeting through his lawyer; from one day to the next, without any discernible reason for the changed situation, the only way of communicating with her beloved left open to Anna was through a lawyer.[53]

Chamberlain's independence did not last long. In 1908 he married Wagner's daughter, Eva, and was welcomed into the inner Bayreuth Circle, whose cause he had so faithfully promoted over the years. Long his spiritual home, Bayreuth became his actual home where he found the status and sense of belonging he had been searching for all his life. "I have the feeling," he wrote to the kaiser, "as if this marriage brings me closer to Your Majesty both geographically and spiritually."[54] Keyserling described Chamberlain as having been captured and tamed by *Wahnfried* like a member of a harem, but Keyserling also acknowledged that Chamberlain had never been so happy.[55]

Chamberlain's happiness was marred in 1912 by the onset of a debilitating nervous ailment, possibly syphilis, which eventually led to paralysis and death.[56] Yet his mind remained clear to the last, and his literary productivity abated only after Eva could no longer read the words from his lips. In his last major work, *Mensch und Gott (Man and God)*, published in 1921, Chamberlain again called for the fusing of the Christian and Germanic spirits in a unifying national religion. For the kaiser, now exiled in Doorn, *Mensch und Gott* expressed, as had *The Foundations*, thoughts he had long harbored himself.[57] The book also drew praise from Albert Schweitzer, who felt drawn to the "elementary and sincere aspect" of Chamberlain's thought.[58] The work inspired the founding of a Houston Stewart Chamberlain Association for Germanic Christianity in 1940, with Eva Chamberlain and Winifred Wagner, Siegfried's English-born wife, as honorary members.[59]

With the coming of the Great War, Chamberlain's progressive paralysis paralleled the declining fortunes of the country he had made his own. Becoming a German citizen in 1916, Chamberlain churned out numerous wartime pamphlets to bolster German morale. Issued in "editions for the trenches" for the soldiers at the front, these pamphlets earned for their author the award of the Iron Cross, Germany's highest battlefield decoration. The outrage directed by Chamberlain against his native England fed the curious sense of betrayal with which so many Germans greeted the British decision to join in the war against them. The historic clash of world views, proclaimed in *The Foundations*, was now being fought on the battlefields of Europe. The prize at stake was no less than the shaping of the future of mankind. Chamberlain foresaw a struggle that would last at least thirty years, perhaps even a century or more. The peace that followed the war would only see a continuation of the struggle in a different form. The war convinced Chamberlain that Germany and the "Germanic world view" could only survive if they could dominate. In the heat of the battle, Chamberlain wrote, Germany must not lose sight of its long-range goal or jeopardize it through default or compromise.[60]

The war completed Chamberlain's conversion to fascism as the best hope for national integration and resurgence. On October 6, 1923, Chamberlain received the aspiring *völkisch* politician Adolf Hitler for a visit and was favorably impressed. He did not find Hitler the fanatic he had been told to expect. He admired in Hitler the "non-politician" whose love for his country rose above party. Writing to Hitler after his visit, Chamberlain expressed his faith in Hitler's ability to impose a new order in Germany: "You know Goethe's distinction between force and force! There is a force which originates in chaos and which leads to chaos, and there is a force, whose characteristic it is to shape the cosmos."[61] According to his aide, Hitler rejoiced over this letter "like a child."[62] A month later he launched his abortive putsch, while Chamberlain defended him in print.[63]

Dying in 1927 at the age of seventy-two, Chamberlain did not live to see the disappointment of his hopes in the Third Reich. An ideological manifestation of Germany's twentieth-century quest for the status of a world power, his works reflected and in turn affected the course of German history. They are of interest not because they caused the rise of National Socialism—causation of this kind is impossible to establish—but because they epitomize the shift in conservative mentality that after 1918 led to wholehearted support for *völkisch* extremism. Linked to Germany's imperialistic fortunes, Chamberlain's works have shared the eclipse of the national power they were designed to serve. There is historical justice in this, for Chamberlain conceived of himself as a warrior in the realm of ideas. Yet he was quite unwilling to trust mere intellectual persuasion. Through the doctrine of Germanic racial superiority he sought to decide the battle outside the intellectual arena. If Nietzsche was misused and distorted by the Nazis, the same cannot be said of Chamberlain. Irresistibly drawn to authority and power, Chamberlain willingly put his pen in the service of the authoritarian and militaristic state.

11

RELIGION AND SCIENCE IN THE SERVICE OF CONSERVATIVE POLITICS: *THE FOUNDATIONS OF THE NINETEENTH CENTURY*

> I can't tell you how often your name was mentioned in Berlin. At any rate, your *Foundations* is the book read most on all levels of society, and at the meeting we had with His Majesty, the Kaiser repeatedly said, "that's what Chamberlain thinks, too."
>
> Cosima Wagner to Chamberlain, 1902

Although presented as a work of history, philosophy, and anthropology, *The Foundations of the Nineteenth Century* was in fact a political tract. Chamberlain's avowed purpose was to promote the kind of national religious regeneration that Wagner had envisaged. His unacknowledged aim was to justify the suppression of liberalism, socialism, and democracy by portraying such doctrines as un-German.

Chamberlain interpreted history since the death of Christ as an ongoing conflict between the Aryan-Christian world view—sustained primarily by the Germanic races (including Celts and Slavs)—and "Jewish" materialism, to which he attributed the "degeneration" of the modern world. *The Foundations*, written in nineteen feverish months and issued in two volumes in 1899, is divided into two parts: "The Origins," which as the longer part takes up the entire first volume and a portion of the second volume, and "The Rise of a New World." The first part, further divided into three sections, headed "The Legacy of the Ancient World," "The Heirs," and "The Struggle," offers Chamberlain's panoramic view of history up to 1200, a key date in Chamberlain's scheme. The second part traces the development of Germanic culture—synonymous, in Chamberlain's view, with culture itself—from 1200 to 1800. "The Legacy of the Ancient World" comprises chapters on "Greek Art and Philosophy," "Roman Law," and "The Appearance of Christ." The section entitled "The Heirs" includes chapters on "The Racial Chaos," "Entrance of the Jews into Western History," and "Entrance of the Teutons into World History," and the third section traces the ensuing struggle in chapters on "Religion" and "State."

When *The Foundations* first appeared, Chamberlain's future brother-in-law, Henry Thode (1857–1920), the art historian who married Wagner's stepdaughter Daniela von Bülow, gently accused Chamberlain of having borrowed his main ideas from Wagner without sufficiently acknowledging his indebtedness. Chamberlain reacted angrily to this charge of plagiarism, pointing out that Wagner himself had drawn on ideas that had long been in general circulation.[1] While it reflected the general outlines of Wagner's *Weltanschauung*, this massive treatise had its own claims to originality. With brash self-assurance Chamberlain rewrote the history of Western civilization in terms of an as yet unresolved struggle between the forces of light and darkness, spirit and matter. With the zeal of a revivalist he exhorts his readers to awaken the religio-idealistic powers within:

> Experience teaches you that you possess autonomy and freedom in the inner realm—use them! The connection between the two worlds—the seen and the unseen, the temporal and the eternal—otherwise undiscoverable, lies in the hearts of you men yourselves, and by the moral conception of the inner world the significance of the outer world is determined. Conscience teaches you that every day; it is the lesson taught by art, love, compassion, and the whole history of mankind. Here you are free, as soon as you but know and will it. You can transfigure the visible world, become regenerate yourselves, transform time to eternity, plough the kingdom of God in the field—be this then your task! Religion shall no longer signify for you faith in the past and hope for something in the future, nor (as with the Indians) mere metaphysical perception—but the deed of the present! If you but believe in yourselves, you have the power to make the new "possible kingdom" real. Wake up then, for the dawn is at hand![2]

To have awakened man to the power of the kingdom within was the undying achievement of Christ. His actual existence could not be doubted, for his individuality stood out too much to have been invented. Nor was it within human powers to forget him, once the example of Christ had been perceived. Christ's appearance heralded a new religion of pure and immediate experience, as distinct from a historical, earth-centered, and hence materialistic religion, such as Judaism, and a religion of rituals and dogmas, such as Roman Catholicism was to become. Christ pointed the way to the possibility of regeneration by conversion of the will. Buddha, too, had shown the heroic strength to reject externals, to leave father, mother, wife, and child, but his search for Nirvana had ended in a complete negation of the will—a living death.

As much as he admired the renunciation of worldliness, Chamberlain disapproved of such total abnegation. Hence he also rebuked Schopenhauer, in whose philosophy the keenness of perception (*Erkenntnis*) completely dominated the will. But Christ's redemption was affirmative, constructive, full of the love of life. In him will and perception were balanced, and his renunciation of the world only disencumbered the will for more active service in the world. Christianity marked a radical break with the Jewish religion, in which the will ruled arbitrarily and supreme, through external laws rather than inner necessity. Christ was persecuted, Chamberlain claims, because his gospel of an inner kingdom disappointed the Messianic hope of inheriting the external world.[3]

It was not the temporal powers that Christ combated, but the false inner spirit expressed in the motives and goals of mankind. Christ did not turn the other cheek for the enemy's sake. Chamberlain interprets the ethic of the Sermon on the Mount as the necessary expression of Christ's converted will, whereas the Old Testament adage of an eye for an eye was merely a reflex action. By the same token, he holds that Christ's exclamation, "Forgive them, for they know not what they do," did not represent weak humanitarianism, but expressed instead an inner state in which pain and death had lost their power. Just as Greek culture had liberated man's intellect, Christ freed man's moral sense. If moral culture before Christ had been based solely on the fear of punishment or the hope of reward, now man had at least the possibility, the motive power, for the development of a moral culture in which the intent of an act, not its consequence, determined its value. Christ's revelation of the voluntary conversion of the will permitted for the first time the creation of a true nobility—a nobility of birth, moreover, in which only he who was endowed with the inner potential could become a Christian. The coming of Christ signified for Chamberlain the coming of a new human species as different from foregoing species in the coloration of their will as races were different in the pigmentation of their skins. To follow Christ requires, above all, moral courage. "Only heroic souls—only 'masters'—can in the true sense of the word be Christians."[4] Chamberlain's aristocratic and militant Christianity would provide a suitable religion for a master race.

But according to Chamberlain the message of Christ got lost in the long dark age of Catholic Church dominance. The Church fathers demanded absolute surrender to the universal authority of the Church and its ruling caste, stifling both the enjoyment of life and the individual's inner freedom. The punishment of hell threatened those who would not submit. Catholicism absorbed from Judaism the utilitarian doctrine of salvation by external works. The dogma of transubstantiation reflected the materialism of a church that had retained pagan rites in a more absolute form. The quest for unlimited dominion over the external world necessarily meant the drastic limitation of that inner freedom which could not be obtained without renunciation. Only through the drawing of external limits, as in the principle of nationalism (which was but the expression of a people's individuality), could unlimited inner freedom be gained. With arguments such as these, well-rooted in the German Protestant tradition, Chamberlain sought to free German nationalism from the restraints imposed by an international church.

Chamberlain acclaims Luther's heroic reassertion of the freedom of conscience through the doctrine of justification by faith as the most important historical event since the death of Christ. Yet the struggle between nationalism and universalism, strengthened by the regrettable Jesuit revival, still raged at the end of the nineteenth century. The Achilles' heel of modern German culture was the lack of a religion commensurate with this people's unique gifts of inner freedom and loyalty, for even Lutheranism had degenerated into pietism, which represented a scrupulous adherence to ritual rather than genuine mystical experience. It was passages such as these that led Bernard Shaw to call *The Foundations* "the greatest Protestant Manifesto ever written."[5]

What Christ and Luther had done for religion, Chamberlain continues, Kant did for philosophy. By demonstrating the fallacy of attempting to venture beyond the boundaries of experience with speculative reason, Kant freed the inner realm of ideals. By defining strict outward limits, he threw open the inner world of the limitless. Descartes's Cartesian dualism had already anticipated something of the kind. But Descartes made the mistake of drawing the boundary between man and the world, whereas the crucial boundary is within man himself: between his reason (which is still, like the external world, in the realm of nature) and that realm of ideals forever barred to the rational comprehension of man. The error of such thinkers as Hegel, Fichte, and Schelling, as of Thomas Aquinas, was to have believed that they could explain the cosmos by human reason, whereas reason can not even satisfactorily explain the realm of nature (though it does, of course, enable man to organize phenomena for limited purposes). For how could nature ever explain nature? Excessive reliance on reason condemns man to anthropomorphism and perpetual delusion. The further development of culture and personality is in peril, Chamberlain warns, if man ignores that realm of intuitive ideals to which art and religion provide the connecting links.[6]

Chamberlain's major objective in affirming religious values was to counteract reformist and revolutionary ideologies. The target of his philosophical polemics was the secular, rationalistic social theory that underpinned the ideologies of the left. Yet despite his opposition to scientific materialism, Chamberlain was not prepared to concede to liberalism and socialism their exclusive claim to science—a claim that conferred an important advantage in late nineteenth-century intellectual discourse. Chamberlain's sometimes brilliantly provocative analysis of the limitations of rationalism might not have passed into such discredit if he had not sought to give his biases a scientific sanction through the doctrine of race. Racialism enabled conservatives to enlist science in their cause without forcing them to accept those assumptions of science that tended to legitimate social reform. A scientific-sounding rationalization could be used to perpetuate hierarchical social structures in an increasingly secular age.

Because of its secular and materialistic implications, racialism was rejected by more traditional conservatives such as Stoecker, Langbehn, or Lienhard.

Race is the explanatory key to Chamberlain's interpretation of historical change. Random racial mixing led to the decline of the two great cultures of classical antiquity, both the artistic culture of Greece and the state-building culture of Rome. The racial chaos of the declining Roman Empire provided the soil in which Catholicism could grow and maintain its stranglehold on political and cultural life. In an era in which character and individuality had been weakened by racial interbreeding, the Church arrogated unto itself the right to universal dominion. The modern heirs to ancient culture were the Jews, who owed their racial purity and hence their strength to stringently enforced marriage laws, and the Germanics, a uniquely superior race that included Germans, north-European ethnic groups, Celts, and Slavs. Dismayed by growing British opposition to German naval and political ambitions, Chamberlain would later accuse the English of lacking racial consciousness.[7] Chamberlain's inclusion of Slavs in the Germanic race, an assumption the Nazis emphatically rejected, also illustrates the degree to which his racial postulates express political biases—in this case, the traditionally pro-Russian orientation of Prussian Junkers, as well, perhaps, as sympathy for Czarist autocracy. One of the characteristics that endeared Slavs to Chamberlain was their resistance to the Catholic Church, at least in those areas in which they had not yet been weakened by racial mixing.[8] Yet as German-Russian relations deteriorated in the course of the next decade, he increasingly spoke of the "Tartarization" of the Russian people.[9]

His broad definition of Germanic made it easier for Chamberlain to attribute most of the cultural achievements since 1200 to Germanic "blood." Even Dante was Germanic by Chamberlain's reckoning, though Dante, too, had been led astray by the pernicious influence of the Catholic Church. Germanics ushered in the Renaissance, which Chamberlain preferred to call not a rebirth but the birth of an entirely new culture.[10] His conception of Germanic was broad enough to include Marco Polo, Saint Francis, Giotto, and Lavoisier. Ignatius of Loyola, whose ascetic precepts were designed not to subordinate the body to the mind but rather to conquer the mind through the body, was not Germanic, but as a purebred Basque he was a worthy enemy. In France, on the other hand, the expulsion of the Huguenots had so depleted the racial stock that instead of a Reformation the French only had a Revolution.[11]

The struggle for religion and state continued at present. Europe at the end of the nineteenth century still languished in a middle age. The outcome of this struggle, which went on silently when it was not being fought out with cannons, depended on the resources which each race could muster. It was a struggle of ideas and values, but because people created and transmitted these values, it was a struggle between peoples, too. Germany must remain true to herself and avoid the seduction of foreign influences. Chamberlain cites Goethe to justify a politics of avoidance and exclusion: "That which disturbs your soul / You must not suffer!"[12] While Chamberlain admonished anti-Semites not to make the Jews the scapegoats for all the vices of the age, he insisted that they be treated as aliens. With the trappings of science and scholarship, *The Foundations* transformed anti-Semitism into a doctrine that educated people could accept. The "Jewish peril" lay not in the Jewish people, but in the hearts and minds of Germans themselves, and it was here that the challenge would have to be overcome.[13]

To Chamberlain the success of Jews in maintaining cohesiveness even when widely dispersed seemed to prove the validity of his racial doctrine. "Would one small tribe from among all the Semites have become a world-embracing power," he asks, "had it not made 'purity of race' its inflexible fundamental law?"[14] Chamberlain admired Sephardic Jews because he thought that they had best preserved the purity and hence the nobility of their race—a view that did not prevent him from stressing the mixed racial background of Jews when it suited his purposes. Vacillating between admiration and loathing, between a desire to emulate and an impulse to destroy, Chamberlain claimed that he wished to exclude Jews from German cultural life not because they were inferior but because they were different. "The Jew is, like other men, shrewd or stupid, good or bad; whoever denies that is not worth talking to. But there is something which is not individual, namely, *les plis de la pensée*, as the Frenchman says, the inborn tendencies of thought and action, the definite bent, which the mind takes from the habits of generations."[15]

Chamberlain's description of Jews as mercenary, calculating, and self-seeking revived familiar nineteenth-century stereotypes. In contrast to the Aryans' inward search for a meaning in life, Jews allegedly idolized the will that enabled them to seize external possessions and power. Affected by a desert existence that may have made egoism mandatory for survival, Jews supposedly pursued only immediate advantage, not ideal goals. What particularly enraged Chamberlain, as it did Lienhard, was the insolence (*Frechheit*) of Jews who refused to accept their properly subordinate position in culture and society. Yet Chamberlain considered Jews far superior to Arabs, whose Mohammedanism he called "the greatest of all hindrances to every progress of civilization, hanging like a sword of Damocles over our slowly and laboriously rising culture in Europe, Asia, and Africa."[16]

Chamberlain's doctrine of race was a political ideology disguised as a scientific theory. In present-day anthropological usage race is a broad biological category defined by certain readily observable physical characteristics, such as skin color.[17] It is true that Chamberlain's use of the term "race" as a synonym for ethnic or national group conformed with nineteenth-century practice. There are, of course, no solid scientific grounds for regarding psychological or mental traits of the kind subsumed under the concept of "national character" as biologically inherited. Even if it were possible to draw precise distinctions between races, let alone ethnic groups, as Chamberlain and other racialists assumed, it is virtually impossible to ascertain to what degree such differences are the product of heredity or environment. Since Chamberlain's aim was not to contribute to scientific knowledge but rather to develop a plausible rationale for conservative politics, the paucity of scientific evidence for racialist assumptions did not prevent him from setting forth his racial doctrine as established fact. He adopted what he took to be a common-sense approach, one supposedly similar to that employed by Goethe in his studies of nature. "What is clear to every eye," Chamberlain wrote, "suffices, if not for science, at least for life. . . . One of the most fatal errors of our time is that which impels us to give too great weight in our judgments to the so-called results of science."[18] Whether or not scientists could agree on the exact nature of racial inheritance, the layman could see racial distinctions plainly. In an era fascinated both by aristocratic pedigree and by the science of eugenics Chamberlain's concern for racial purity seemed plausible enough. One did not have to be able to give a causal explanation of racial dynamics in order to recognize the superiority of a purebred horse, dog, or plant. Why should this not be true of humans as well?[19]

Aware of his fragile scientific base, Chamberlain equivocated on defining race, an omission for which he was criticized when the book first appeared.[20] Like the colors blue and green, he wrote, race is a fact beyond definition. All one can do is to investigate the conditions under which facts such as this appear.[21] "Race is an intensified form of life, achieved by pure breeding, through which certain corporeal dispositions or even certain traits of the character and intellect experience a previously unsuspected, individually distinctive development."[22] He compared race to a magnetic field that gives harmony to a random mass. The unverifiability of his theories conferred the advantage of making them equally hard to disprove.

In the absence of definitive objective criteria Chamberlain was ready to resort to total subjectivity as the ultimate measure of racial purity: "Nothing is so convincing as the consciousness of the possession of race. The man who belongs to a distinct, pure race never loses the sense of it. . . . It is a fact of direct experience that the quality of race is of vital importance."[23] This was a definition peculiarly fitted to the requirements of German nationalism. Although some nationalists worried that Chamberlain's emphasis on race might weaken the idea of the nation, Chamberlain denied that there was any contradiction between the two.[24] A nation as a political entity creates the conditions for the formation of race.

Even if it could be scientifically proved that an Aryan race had never existed in the past, the important thing was to create a superior race from the superior Germanic stock already on hand. Chamberlain rejected Gobineau's pessimistic postulate of an originally pure white race gradually doomed to decline: "A noble race does not fall from Heaven, it becomes noble gradually, just like fruit trees, and this gradual process can begin anew at any moment, as soon as accident of geography and history or a fixed plan (as in the case of the Jews) creates the conditions."[25] The future development of European culture required Germanic racial solidarity, for the coming century would determine for years to come the direction that mankind was to take. "Why should we not," Chamberlain wrote in 1903, "before it is forever too late, work for the preservation of all that is most dear and holy to us by maintaining the physical foundations on which it grew and without which it cannot exist?"[26] It was this activist thrust which made his works so useful to the Nazis.

Chamberlain's five "natural laws" for the creation of a superior race read like a stockbreeder's handbook. As the first condition he posited the presence of excellent racial material, the origins of which are unknown to man. Second, there must follow a period of inbreeding coupled with, as a third condition, the deliberate selection of desirable traits. The fourth law decreed a mixture of blood as indispensable, while the fifth law stipulated that this racial mixing be of a definite kind and limited in time. Thus Chamberlain claimed that Prussia owed her racial strength to a limited infusion of Slavic blood. Yet Chamberlain shared the conviction, popularized by Gobineau, that racial mixing leads to degeneration; the indiscriminate crossing of unrelated types, he wrote, is as destructive as continuous inbreeding.

Chamberlain insisted that he owed his major intellectual debt to Darwin, a claim intended at least in part to exonerate himself from the charge of plagiarizing Wagner's and Gobineau's ideas. His racial program could be presented as a conscious effort to apply Darwinian selection to human populations. It thus gained plausibility at a time when throughout Europe and the United States Darwinism provided the scientific guise for theories that justified imperialism and social conservatism. But because Darwin's conception of mankind as a single species tended to legitimate humanitarian rather than nationalist goals, Chamberlain preferred to emphasize the subtitle to *The Origin of Species: The Preservation of Favored Races in the Struggle for Life*. Race was a less arbitrary category than species, he claimed, since distinctions between races were frequently more obvious than distinctions between species. Predictably, he also rejected the doctrine of evolution, since the idea of progress implicit in evolution posed a threat to the static social order that he wished to preserve. Once again he fell back on Kant's metaphysical critique to dismiss the inquiry into human origins as beyond the proper boundaries of science. The same injunction did not apply to racial determinism, however, since he held racial laws to be purely descriptive, not explanatory.

As it was Chamberlain's aim to perpetuate an elitist personality cult in an age of mass politics, he was ready to concede that individuals (though never races as a whole) could transcend the determinism of their racial makeup. "Race is for the collectivity," he wrote, "what personality is for the individual."[27] Race does not guarantee the proper ideals, though it makes them possible. "It certainly may happen that too much importance is attached to the idea of race: we detract thereby from the autonomy of the personality and run the risk of undervaluing the power of ideas. Besides, this whole question of race is infinitely more complicated than the layman imagines. It belongs wholly to the sphere of anthropological anatomy and cannot be solved by any dicta of the authorities on language and history."[28] Yet it was typical of Chamberlain's method to follow pages of anthropological data on racial differences, replete with illustrations, with a statement that the reaction of a child who begins to cry at the approach of a Jew was worth more than the judgment of an entire anthropological congress.[29]

The primacy Chamberlain accorded to ideology led him to deduce a person's race solely from the ideas that he held—a practice in keeping with the Viennese mayor Karl Lueger's well-known dictum, "I will decide who is Jewish." Thus Chamberlain argued that Jesus (and possibly David before him) was not a Jew (a contention Dühring had advanced fifteen years earlier), but Chamberlain did not go so far as to make Jesus Germanic, as some careless readers falsely (but understandably) assumed. He also cited with approval the French racial anthropologist George Vacher de Lapouge's "purely scientific" definition of the *homo Europaeus* as inherently Protestant. The telltale Germanic racial characteristic for Chamberlain was loyalty: "This loyalty to a master chosen of their own free will is the most prominent feature in the Germanic character; from it we can tell whether pure Germanic blood flows in the veins or not."[30] He goes so far as to argue that ideas have the capacity to induce racial changes in and of themselves, a notion that Hitler would also hold. One could become a Jew in Chamberlain's sense simply by reading Jewish newspapers. In any case, he asserted, it was far easier to become a Jew than a Germanic, for idealism is more demanding than materialism.[31]

Fearing as a consequence of his own logic that reproductive power may stand in inverse relation to the nobility of a race, Chamberlain suffered from the sexual phobias that so often motivate or justify racism. In a letter to the kaiser in 1902, he asserted that the greater sexual potency of Negroes irreversibly doomed the United States to ruin, despite the violent means employed by whites in the Southern states to avert their fate.[32] Citing the Swiss anthropologist August Forel on the alleged inferiority of blacks, Chamberlain pointed to South America for examples of the pernicious effects of random racial mixing. Ironically, he exempted the island of Puerto Rico: "Here the native Caribbees were exterminated, and the result is a pure Indo-European population distinguished for industry, prudence, and love of order: a striking example of the significance of race!"[33] Unconscious of the circularity of his argument, Chamberlain viewed social and political conservatism as constituting proof of racial superiority.

It was primarily to its political message that *The Foundations* owed its huge success. While often recognizing that Chamberlain's conjectures about race were dubious at best, most critics did not regard this failing as particularly important. The writer Ernst von Wolzogen (1855–1934) doubted the validity of Chamberlain's racial doctrine but dismissed this as a minor reservation.[34] The artistry of his treatment made mere factual details irrelevant. In an era increasingly impatient with overspecialization and narrow scholarly monographs, Chamberlain's frankly avowed dilettantism was widely admired, all the more because his conclusions merely reinforced prevailing prejudices.

Chamberlain expressed delight when his book was judged as a work of art: "To be right or wrong: what phantasmagoria! . . . Besides, it is necessary even in the realm of ideas to shape the world of knowledge, of perceptions, yes, even the world of abstract thoughts and dark presentiments in a beautiful way—if at all possible in a way that generates further beauty."[35]

Such notions found ready acceptance in a society conditioned to regard history as an inherently subjective discipline in which the methods of the sciences had only limited application.[36] Most German historians agreed that only through intuition and aesthetic contemplation (*Anschauung*), the attributes of the artist, could historical reality be grasped. In other ways, too, Chamberlain's approach satisfied prevailing historicist principles, according to which the search for chains of historical causation seemed ultimately fruitless. History is neither progressive nor circular. Historical events and past cultures are absolutely unique and never again recur in exactly the same form. Contrary to the assertion of historical materialists, the chronicle of historical events yields no general laws and contains no lessons for the present, for there is no guarantee, even if an exact duplication of conditions were possible, that things would not turn out quite differently the next time. People and races make history and culture, and people and races are everywhere different. But history is not therefore without meaning. Every great historical achievement, such as Greek art, represents a timeless ideal and remains alive in human consciousness. It was this "ever-present" aspect of history, rather than any illusory linear or dialectical development, that Chamberlain sought to capture.[37]

In stressing the uniquely creative quality of German culture and its superiority over the rational civilization of the West, Chamberlain also remained within the mainstream of the idealist and historicist traditions of the nineteenth century. To most of his readers, Chamberlain's racial doctrine, far from appearing pernicious, seemed only to corroborate the primacy of idealism and Christian values. *The Foundations* appealed even to readers for whom "race" remained a cultural, not a biological, concept. Racialism could be viewed as a modern, "scientific" prop for the idealist faith in the individuality of peoples, states, and cultures. Racialism commended itself to conservatives as a more benign doctrine of collectivism than social democracy, which tended to divide rather than unite the nation.

Chamberlain dismissed socialism as simply the most modern example of the Jewish talent for planning impossible Messianic empires "without inquiring whether they do not destroy the whole of civilization and culture, which we have so slowly acquired, by their childish belief that with decrees and laws the soul of the people can be changed from today to tomorrow."[38] Although he acknowledged that the doctrine of human equality originated in Christianity (Jewish egalitarianism allegedly having pertained only to Jews for the purpose of strengthening the Jewish nation against other nations), he insisted that this doctrine had meant only equality before God, a doctrine which did not free the slave of his duty to obey and revere. The distortion of this doctrine into a dogma of political equality resembled a sin against nature. "I fear," Chamberlain wrote in 1919, "through this cancer the human race must and will necessarily go to ruin."[39]

Chamberlain sought to restore reverence to the preeminent rank from which it had been displaced by the leveling forces of modernization. He admired the *homo religiosus*, unswerving in the pursuit of an ideal and impervious to worldly temptations. Yet for all the concern he expressed for individual salvation, the primary attractiveness of the religious mentality for Chamberlain lay in its social and political uses. Germanic Christianity was to provide a creed that would unify a fragmented society and sanction the purgation of all so-called un-German elements from the body politic. The Catholic Church could not fulfill this function, for it competed with the state for the primary allegiance of the masses. But even so loyal an arm of the state as the Lutheran Church in Germany seemed too ready to accommodate itself to the intellectual, cultural, social, and political changes that Chamberlain opposed. By accepting the democratic "dogma" of racial equality, he wrote to William II, the Christian churches "have become a true curse for mankind."[40] The humanitarian ethos and the doctrinal complexities of denominational Christianity seemed quite inadequate as a force to mobilize the masses for nationalist goals. His attacks on

Jewish self-will and the perfectibility of man notwithstanding, Chamberlain heeded political considerations in his own version of Christianity by leaving the will less encumbered by the onus of sin than in traditional Protestant doctrine.[41]

Even his loyalty to Bayreuth was not as strong as his loyalty to the political cause for which Bayreuth stood. Thus he was quite ready to overlook attacks on Wagner by publicists like Dühring or Bartels, whose political biases he shared.[42] This tolerance did not extend to Nietzsche, however, whose fame he deplored. A number of reviewers appraised *The Foundations* as a response to Nietzsche's attacks on Christianity and Germanic culture. "How firmly rooted and grandly sublime," wrote the *Bayreuther Blätter*, "the full Germanic personality [*germanische Vollmensch*] seen by Chamberlain looks beside Nietzsche's deranged superman!"[43] Chamberlain accused Nietzsche of lacking the originality he so desperately sought; he had derived his superman from *Faust*, while his "blond beasts" were bowdlerizations of Greek satyrs and nature deities.[44] Yet, aware of the degree to which his own work echoed conventional values, Chamberlain did not claim originality for himself. Indeed, he denied that originality was a goal worth striving for; the fever of innovation, so endemic to the nineteenth century, threatened to undermine all true culture.

The thread that runs through *The Foundations*, as it runs through Chamberlain's life, is a search for a realm where necessity rules, for a haven from the merely accidental, the random, the temporal, the distressingly arbitrary. He sought certitude in political authority, in the exclusiveness of race, in the realm of ideals, and in the definition of freedom as a duty to an inner law. He could not abide frivolity, skepticism, or irreverence, whether displayed at the Bayreuth Festival, in the writings of Heine or Nietzsche, or in the "racial chaos" of the late Roman imperial period. "Everywhere chaos is the most dangerous enemy," he wrote.[45] Neurotically addicted to purity and order, he sought to create a nation from which reformist change, social conflict, and political dissent were forever barred, a nation united in collective narcissism. Mobilizing the discontents and psychological insecurity of a society in the throes of modernization, *The Foundations* prophetically anticipated the coming of the Third Reich.

12

KANT AND GOETHE ENLISTED IN THE STRUGGLE AGAINST RATIONALISM

The lack of reverence for our great ancestors and their achievements is perhaps the only unconditional and irremediable crime in the intellectual realm. This is the true lese majesty. It should be atoned for by death through hanging—and whoever is unable to feel reverence should keep still and ventilate his lungs as a broker on the stock exchange.

Chamberlain to Eva Wagner, 1898

In his now-forgotten books on Kant and Goethe, tomes that absorbed his energies for more than a decade following the publication of *The Foundations*, Chamberlain sought to enlist the authority of Germany's foremost cultural heroes in the cause of German conservatism, a cause euphemistically expressed as Germanic regeneration. These books were animated by the same ideological fervor as his earlier works. "It is not enough to make Kant accessible," he wrote; "it must be done in such a fashion as will make him a real motive power in culture."[1] He set himself the task of "rescuing" Kant and Goethe from academic scholarship. But his purpose was not so much to popularize as to agitate. He conceived of himself as neither a scholar, nor a philosopher, but rather as a seer, whose function it was to provide an all-embracing world view. He compared such a *Weltanschauung* to mythology or religion, which differed from conventional philosophy in that they harmonized thought and deed. His overriding ambition was to redirect German, European, and eventually all human culture from the materialistic and relativistic courses upon which it had been set by Enlightenment rationalism. Chamberlain might have been speaking of the impact he hoped his own work would have when he wrote of Kant that "his *Weltanschauung* is heading us toward a revolution, against which all previous political revolutions shrink into insignificant episodes: he wishes to realize ideals . . . by the dispassionate and conscious change in direction of human thought and will, a change wrought slowly but surely from the humble study of the quiet thinker" (*Kant*, p. 564).

Chamberlain's Kant was not the Enlightenment philosopher who set out to defend rationalism against the British skeptics, but the critic of Enlightenment rationalism who circumscribed theoretical reason and accorded primacy to practical reason, or will. Kant and Plato engaged in theoretical philosophy only to be free of theory, Chamberlain claimed; the goals they pursued were practical. The anti-rational activist thrust of his work set Chamberlain apart from the academic neo-Kantians who contributed so greatly to the revival of interest in Kant around the turn of the century. Nonetheless, he praised the neo-Kantian philosophers Hermann Cohen (1842–1918), whom he called the Nestor of Kant scholars, and Paul Natorp (1854–1924) for accentuating the dualisms of morality and science, spirit and nature, freedom and necessity, and faith and knowledge (*Kant*, p. 706). Kant had refuted materialism on the grounds that human reality, the "phenomenal" world, was mere appearance and thus incapable of providing the guide to the truth. Behind this reality, hidden from ordinary consciousness or scientific investigation, lay the "noumenal" world, a link to which was vouchsafed mankind only through moral commandment, the categorical imperative.

Chamberlain tried to exploit this dualism to restore the metaphysical basis for social and political conservatism in an age of declining religious faith. In doing so he ignored the democratic implications of Kantian ethics which had aroused the suspicions of the royal censors in Kant's own lifetime. Chamberlain's works, by contrast, continued to enjoy the highest official esteem. Stressing the authoritarian rather than the humanitarian dimension of Kantian ethics, Chamberlain portrayed Kant as the seminal thinker who marked out the limits of knowledge in order to make room for faith. Conveniently disregarding Kant's democratic sympathies, he praised Kant for rendering rational theory and natural law forever irrelevant in the realm of ethics and human conduct. In Goethe's naïvely descriptive and at the same time highly imaginative ruminations on plants and colors, Chamberlain found an alternative to the rational science he wished to discredit. As in Lienhard's biography, though on a higher intellectual plane, his Goethe became a model of how to achieve harmony by reconciling polar opposites, accepting the world as it is, and nurturing personal growth rather than social reform.

Kant and *Goethe* run to roughly eight-hundred pages each, a length attributable at least in part to Chamberlain's anxiety that his works be considered superficial. Despite the pleas of his publisher, he declined to cut the length of *Goethe*, but insisted that it appear in one volume instead of two.[2] The books sold remarkably well considering their difficulty and size, *Kant* reaching a distribution of close to 30,000 by 1923, with *Goethe* lagging slightly behind. Despite their tendentiousness, both books enjoyed considerable critical acclaim, some of which has lasted into the present. A recent Goethe scholar commended Chamberlain's biography as a book which, in contrast to *The Foundations*, contained "a great deal that is

right, and much that was unquestionably new."[3] An English translation of
Kant was issued by Lord Redesdale in 1914, but the outbreak of World
War I precluded wide circulation. Although *Goethe* was not translated into
English, a plagiarized portion of the book was awarded top prize in an
essay contest on Goethe sponsored by the Carl Schurz Memorial Founda-
tion in Philadelphia in 1933.[4]

These books were designed not so much to make new converts as to
fortify conservatives by providing them with sophisticated arguments for
nationalism and authoritarianism. As in *The Foundations*, Chamberlain
did not debunk his readers' prejudices but offered a rationale in their
defense. "Once again," he announced to the kaiser, "the hymn to great
German deeds shall sound forth."[5] His flattering tone and protracted prose
offer a sharp contrast to the aphoristic pungency of Nietzsche, against
whom he also polemicized. Like Lienhard (though in a more sophisticated
way), but quite unlike Nietzsche, Chamberlain told his readers what he
knew they would like to hear. In an age in which leveling forces threatened
traditional social relations, in which technology transformed time-honored
habits, and science seemed to undermine religion, Chamberlain soothed
and dispelled anxieties with an epistemology that sanctioned the ways of
the past. Claiming to defend human dignity, he offered a comforting
alternative to the doctrine of man's descent from the apes. His works fed
the hope that the unsettling progress of "civilization," with its seemingly
inexorable trend toward greater democracy and collectivization, could
once again be subordinated to an idealist culture rooted in the autonomy
of the human soul.

Subtitled *Die Persönlichkeit als Einführung in das Werk* (*The Personality as Introduction to His Works*), Chamberlain's *Kant* does not deal with
the philosopher's substantive works any more than his *Goethe* deals with
the literary works of the great German classicist. In six lengthy chapters, or
"lectures," as he called them, he compares Kant's way of seeing the world
with the viewpoints of Goethe, Leonardo, Descartes, Bruno, and Plato.
Attracted to Kant above all by the practical applications of his philosophy,
he chose as the motto of his book Kant's maxim, "The greatest concern of a
human being is to know what one must be in order to be human."[6] Kant's
dualism gave him a weapon against "monistic" explanations of the world,
whether religious, as in the case of Bruno's Hermetic philosophy, or
scientific, as in the case of Darwin's and Haeckel's evolutionary doctrines.

Doggedly Chamberlain belabors his main thesis, namely, that rational
theory offers an inadequate guide to the knowledge of reality and a totally
invalid guide to human conduct. If the superstitions of the past had been
largely supernatural, those of the present appear in the guise of all-
explanatory scientific theories. He derides the presumptuousness of scientists who purvey abstractions as real: "There is no need for me to believe in

God. It matters little whether I am a morally strong, energetic, and free man. But I have to believe in the hypothetical medium, the waves that are rays and rays that are waves, in the amplitudes and oscillations and polarizations and such hobgoblins, together with the descent of man from apes and of apes from jelly-fish, as if all these things were real, or otherwise I am sneered at" (*Kant*, pp. 132–33). By persuading humans to surrender their moral autonomy to the causal mechanisms of nature, scientific materialism, the most pernicious form of rationalism in Chamberlain's view, threatens to introduce a new era of barbarism.

In Goethe's approach to nature Chamberlain discovers an alternative to the rational method of modern science. Calling Goethe an explorer of nature (*Naturerforscher*) rather than a scientist (*Naturforscher*), he argues that Goethe confronted nature, as Kant had demanded, in the role of lawgiver and not as the slave of abstractions. He confidently expects Goethe's spurious method, more akin to art than to science, to determine the future course of human culture. Goethe would teach mankind

> to cast a free eye upon the wide field of nature, that is to say the eye of the conscious human creator, who no longer stands in dull obedience at the command of idle matter, but who is able to "hold his own with nature": and that means at the same time the eye of the man who is no longer blinded by his own compulsive hallucinations, but who, thanks to Kant's efforts, has won together with his own freedom the freedom of nature. [*Kant*, p. 107]

Chamberlain refuses to classify Goethe's own erroneous doctrines, such as that of plant metamorphosis, as hallucinations, for they result not from an excess, but rather from a total lack of theory. He concedes that Goethe had been wrong to conclude that all plants evolve from a basic leaf, but this idea was valuable nonetheless for it enabled him better to see and to experience nature. Only the inner eye of the imagination can "hold its own" with nature, Chamberlain writes, for the senses are taken in too much by nature to do so. Goethe's intuitive idea of plant metamorphosis must not be confused with a conceptual theory, such as the doctrine of evolution (the efforts of evolutionists to claim Goethe as one of their precursors notwithstanding), for it is characteristic of an idea to grasp things simultaneously and wholly, outside of space and time. An "idea" is not the product of sense perceptions, but rather a precondition for accurate and true perception. By recognizing the ideal element in reality, Goethe's intuitive approach preserved the holism that conceptualization destroyed.[7]

Chamberlain also tries to rehabilitate Goethe's doctrine of colors, which repudiated Newton's analysis of the spectrum. Again, Chamberlain does not try to prove the correctness of this doctrine, but defends Goethe's method on the grounds that it refined his ability to observe nature without the distortion that conceptualization supposedly entails. "The whole of

Goethe's natural science," he writes, "might be called an introduction to the art of seeing" (*Kant*, p. 123). Modern science explained color in terms of wave lengths and similar abstractions; in such terms a blind person can speak as knowingly of color as a Titian. Goethe, on the other hand, showed the way to a nonscientific comprehension of nature. His "childlike amazement" enabled him to see what duller minds could not. He approached nature as had the Christian mystics, in a spirit of love, aiming not to explain nature, but to understand it, not to master nature, but to possess it. Modern science not only deprived objects of their character by abstracting mathematically measurable properties; far worse, it robbed mankind of the direct sensual experience of nature. Rejecting scientific definition and rational theory as "systematic anthropomorphism," Chamberlain embraces a vulgarized empiricism as the sole reliable guide to nature and external reality. Scientific theories would all pass away, he predicts, but Goethe's empirical findings would last as long as the facts they reflected remained.[8]

Even Kant had relied more on perception (*Anschauung*) than on conception (*Begriff*), according to Chamberlain. Although Kant turned his glance inward rather than outward, he nonetheless adhered to experience even more faithfully than Goethe, whom Chamberlain rebukes for occasionally indulging an excess of creativity. Respecting the limits of both conception and perception more scrupulously than Goethe, Kant never confused mind and matter, as Goethe occasionally did (due, in Chamberlain's view, to his youthful preoccupation with Spinozan pantheism). By severely limiting its pretensions, Kant made a truly mechanistic and empirical science possible. Descartes had anticipated Kant's dualism, Chamberlain argues, even though he had remained too encumbered by religious preconceptions to achieve the insights of Kant. But Chamberlain does not sympathize with the rationalism of Descartes's Cartesian followers, whom he accuses of distorting the dualism of their mentor as thoroughly as Fichte and Hegel, by projecting consciousness upon reality, distorted the dualism of Kant (*Kant*, pp. 176ff.).

According to Chamberlain, Descartes was a skeptic in the original sense of one who examines, rather than in its modern sense of one who doubts. Unlike Spinoza, whom Chamberlain accuses of never leaving his desk or the realm of abstraction, Descartes went hunting and enjoyed close contact with nature. Perfecting mathematics as a means of communicating between the senses and the understanding, the visible and the invisible, Descartes exemplifies for Chamberlain the Germanic faculty for balancing both worlds. Despite his rejection of logic and abstraction, Chamberlain loved geometry as a deductive discipline based on a priori assumptions and as a tool for translating concepts into images and vice versa. He ridicules the arrogance of persons who laid claim to a special kind of genius because they could not understand mathematics. But his ire was mainly directed at those who failed to bear in mind that mathematics could never furnish an explanation of the underlying structure of reality.

This was the major failing, in Chamberlain's view, of those who uncritically accepted the Newtonian model of a mechanistic and mathematical universe. However useful this model might be in practical application, it could never explain reality in the ultimate sense that philosophical naturalists assumed. To avoid the naturalist fallacy, a metaphysical critique of human reason was required, yet this was what the purely inductive method of inquiry lacked. One-sided *ratiocinatio* tainted not only the monadism of Leibniz, but also the empiricism of Locke, Berkeley, and Hume, all of whom supposedly proceeded from one purely cogitative conclusion (*Vernunftsschluss*) to another. By confusing their thoughts with reality, Chamberlain charges, they followed in the footsteps of Giordano Bruno rather than Descartes (*Kant*, pp. 185ff.).

If Goethe was right even when his scientific doctrines were wrong, Bruno was wrong even when his doctrines were right. Undaunted by paradox or contradiction, Chamberlain argues that Bruno had accepted the heliocentric theory (as one of the first of his time) not on the valid basis of external observation, but on the specious basis of inner dreams. For Chamberlain Bruno embodies the fanaticism of reason that culminated in scientific materialism. Even though positivists like Ernst Mach (1838–1916) might claim that in modern science the study of reality had supplanted mythology, Chamberlain maintains that modern science only represents myth in its most modern dress. "Except for a positivist, this pseudo-vegetative stuffing of a stomach and a purse, we are all dependent upon myths, as much today as thousands of years ago. And this because two-sidedness, twofoldness, is a fundamental characteristic of the human being, and because we have no other means of bridging the gulf between perception and understanding, between nature and the self, than by myths more or less consciously invented or dreamed" (*Kant*, p. 283).

Chamberlain traces the primeval myth (*Urmythos*) to the fallacious identification of consciousness with being, of mind with matter, of the human with the cosmic—as if the macrocosm could ever be interpreted and understood solely through the microcosm. "Every monism is a lie" (*Kant*, p. 254). Of the two forms of monism branching out from the primeval myth, one seeks to explain the world from the self (as in Indian culture), while the other seeks to explain the self from the world (as in the culture of ancient Greece). While Heraclitus and Thales still saw the Godhead everywhere in nature, Anaxagoras exalted reason at the expense of nature, assigning to God a role as first cause apart from the world. But Anaxagoras's creation of the *nous*—divine reason, mind, intelligence—did not signify a true break with the hylozoism of his predecessors, for isolation of the divine merely led to the hubris that made humans consider their intellect related to the *nous*. Like the early Nietzsche, Chamberlain holds Socrates primarily responsible for foisting the "tyranny" of rationalism on the world. Attributing to logic the importance of a law of nature, Socrates falsely supposed he had eliminated myth by replacing it with syllogisms. "From that time forth reason is dominant, believes itself to be of divine origin, sees nature at its feet, and deludes itself into the belief that it knows: that is why its assertions are dogmas, and faith is demanded for its dreams" (*Kant*, p. 300).

But myths, which are indispensable to bridge the gap between nature and the cosmos, do not just disappear. Through Socrates, Chamberlain contends, men became to a greater degree slaves of their mythical preconceptions than their ancestors had been. Socrates mistakenly confused what is reasonable with what is true. As a result, mankind turned their backs on nature for more than 1,600 years, until in the thirteenth century the Germanic renaissance burst into life. Even those thinkers who did not accept the Socratic supremacy of reason, such as Lucretius or the neo-Platonists, loved nature but did not think it necessary to delve into her secrets (*Kant*, pp. 297ff.).

According to Chamberlain, Socrates found his true successor not in Plato, but in Aristotle: it was he who perpetuated the supremacy of thinking over seeing in an elaborate world view shaped solely by the demands of reason. Like the Aristotelian conception of the cosmos, western man's conception of divinity became dogmatically fixed. In the theology of the Catholic Church the Greek *Nous* assimilated the Jewish *Jahve*. It was Kant who finally toppled *Nous-Jahve* forever, even if the world did not yet know it. Since Kant made man conscious of his own myth-making, his critical philosophy marked a Copernican revolution in the history of thought. Demonstrating that human conceptions relate only to the reflection of objects, never to the objects themselves, Kant exposed the primeval confusion of thinking and seeing, of self and the world. "Kant has mown down the dogmas for all time: Idealism, Realism, Materialism, Skepticism, Monism, Dualism, Pantheism, Solipsism, Theism, Atheism—all the 'isms' that ever were or ever will be! The chatter of thousands of years is swept away! For we are encircled all around by mere phenomena; Goethe's 'All that is transitory is but a similitude' is the quintessence of what the poet learnt from Kant" (*Kant*, p. 390). Gone is the delusion that the history of thought (or history itself) represents a progression from error to truth. Aristotelianism, Catholic scholasticism, scientific materialism—all shared the fallacy that Kant refuted.

For Plato, on the other hand, the philosophical idealist and political elitist, Chamberlain has warm admiration. Long before Kant Plato had already realized that sense perceptions can have no meaning for man unless recognized by the understanding. A dog perceived by man remains nothing more than a yellow or black or spotted outline until it attains being through the idea "dog." The dog that results from this moment of recognition, this transcendental bridging of two worlds, is more than the mere outline perceived by the senses, yet less than the generalized idea: it is a phenomenon (*Erscheinung*). Plato's failure to define ideas with precision had a good reason, for to attempt to penetrate behind ideas, as interpreters of Plato who attributed to ideas a material existence did, is to surrender critical philosophy to dogmatism. Therefore Plato resorted to the allegorical device of speaking of ideas as actually existent. "All that exists is relation," Chamberlain writes; "this is Plato's critical discovery" (*Kant*, p. 443). The transcendental union of two parts of the mind makes experience possible.

Chamberlain thus used Kantian metaphysics and Platonic idealism to attack empirical and rational explanations of reality. Since an objective and a subjective component are indispensable to experience, the thing-in-itself—the object separated from the observing subject—is never accessible to humans. Theories based on empirical knowledge alone can never lay claim to truth, as rationalists would have it, for such knowledge could never lead to apodictic certainty. Rational truth he held to be equivalent to opinion (he called such truth *Fürwahrhalten*); only revealed truth can inspire conviction (*Seelenüberzeugung*). Slumbering within, true knowledge can only be awakened, not communicated. Thus Chamberlain validated the subjectivism that complemented vulgar empiricism in his doctrine of race. On the one hand he dignified as "scientific" such grossly empirical practices as measuring cranial sizes or describing nose shapes; on the other hand he employed metaphysical arguments to deny the possibility of objective knowledge and to discredit empirical findings when these contradicted his prejudices.

Innate ideas furnished the instruments by which Chamberlain consecrates his prejudices. It is the God-given power of forming ideas, rather than intelligence or intellect, that distinguishes humans from animals. Ideas are fed by nature and in turn ascribe laws to nature. Defined by Chamberlain as the means through which diversity is reduced to unity, ideas are essential to knowledge, for without ideas man would be confronted only by blind empirical data. The paucity of creative ideas to offset such "empirical theories" as natural selection kept modern biology roughly at the stage of Ptolemaic astronomy. Chamberlain commended Darwin for collecting an enormous body of facts, but he denied that reality could ever be explained on the basis of such facts, for the data could just as plausibly support a theory of decline. The function of exact science is to describe phenomena, not to explain causation. Chamberlain denied that the so-called progress of science extends the boundaries of empiricism; it involves at best a methodically more exact dissection of phenomena within these inviolable boundaries. He spurned Darwin's conception of species as an arbitrary construct of the rational mind. It angered him that Darwin should have borrowed this concept from Linnaeus without at the same time accepting Linnaeus's static taxonomy.

Chamberlain denounces Darwinian evolution as merely the latest form of "primitive totemism," which throughout history had assumed a blood relationship between men and animals. In interpreting advantage as a cause for mutation, evolutionists project the mentality of the merchant into the scientific realm.

> If one could not say that this craze is only the belated straggler of Romanticism and Hegelism in alliance with flat English utilitarianism, and that a hundred years will not have passed before it will be judged as men today judge alchemy—the doctrine defended as plausible during centuries by the most talented scholars, a doctrine which had no inkling of the individuality of things; if we could not hope for a race of creatively great German biologists; if we did not see around us in a few individual investigators—at any rate in Germany—an energetic shaking off of this "English sickness" . . . we might abandon all hope for science and culture. [*Kant*, p. 514]

To supplant the doctrine of evolution, Chamberlain advocates a doctrine of vitalism sufficiently vague to exempt it from empirical refutation. He suggests that life be viewed *sub specie aeternitas* as unchanging form (*Gestalt*). Unlike Darwin's conception of species, *Gestalt* qualifies as an idea, for it is the product of *Anschauung*. He defines *Gestalt* as the principle by which a multiplicity of mutually conditioning parts are unified into a whole. It is wrong to think of a crystal as having *Gestalt*, he writes, for here each part is identical with the whole. Only in life does *Gestalt* in the true sense of the word obtain, for only in life is form an integral principle and not merely an effect of external causes. *Gestalt* brings out what he considered the truly important aspect of life, namely, constancy (*Beharrlichkeit*), not the mutability (*Veränderlichkeit*) so stressed by evolutionists.[9]

Chamberlain hypostatizes life as a whole, inside which shiftings, but not progressive development, take place. It is absurd to think that nature had to experiment in order to produce a certain species, as if it were suddenly able to do today what it could not do in the past. Life does not continually effect as many changes as possible, asserts Chamberlain, nor does it incline toward motion and becoming. On the contrary, it persists "as the only conservative principle in all nature, as the greatest imaginable repose, as the incarnation of the concept of Being" (*Kant*, p. 524). Chamberlain avers his readiness to dispense with the progress promised by Darwin in the last paragraphs of his *Origin of Species*, if Darwin would only "leave us a little leisure, a little air, a little composure, in order to get acquainted with the present, to make ourselves at home in it, to assimilate, contemplate, tend, nurture, the pregnant eternity slumbering within us and accumulated all around us!" (*Kant*, p. 515).

Chamberlain accuses evolutionists of fearing to look eternity in the eye. "True science touches upon being, upon the eternal, upon the universal," he writes; "every inquiry into origins is unscientific and barbarous [*neger-mässig*]" (*Kant*, p. 645). He saw no contradiction in his racial doctrine, for racialism sought not to explain origins but only to describe phenomena visible to all. He insists that science be restricted to asking "what" of nature, not "how." Since he considers purposiveness inherent in life, biologists should inquire why a fish has fins, not how the fish acquired them. Chamberlain affirms purposiveness, because he preferred to think of changes as the result of inner potentialities and laws rather than environmental causes. Even if materialists could provide convincing physiochemical explanations for organic processes, they could never explain why these processes occurred, for life can never be explained in terms of inanimate forces. Efforts to arrive at such explanations seemed to him not merely futile, but "insolent" (*Kant*, p. 249).

On one level Chamberlain's long-winded strictures may be read as a defense of human purpose and artistic creativity against the psychologically depressing and seemingly stultifying causal determinism of modern scientific method. What Chamberlain seems to have been describing in his elaborate dualisms of thinking and seeing is the creative process itself. Yet the scientists he attacked were straw men, for he failed to appreciate the degree to which creative processes not dissimilar to those in other fields underlie scientific discovery and advance.[10] In fact, the narrowly descriptive approach which he considered the only tenable scientific method eschewed creative insight far more than the empiro-rational method he attacked. This is not surprising, however, since his defense of human creativity and a purposive world had an ulterior motive. His major concern was to discredit the analytical methods of social reformers. Hence his insistence that facts be accepted as given and not be subjected to an analysis of the circumstances that gave rise to them. He was quite aware that doctrines based on given or intuitive truths cannot be questioned and therefore escape the obligation of being justified by reason.

Chamberlain's attack on rationalism and the "hubris" of scientific materialism was intended to forestall the acceptance of social doctrines based on natural law, universal human rights, and the principle of human equality. His attack on evolution constituted an attack as well on environmentalism and the belief in human perfectibility, the underpinnings of progressive social and political doctrines in the nineteenth century. Against the secular and naturalistic doctrines of socialism and liberalism, Kant's delimiting of theoretical reason seemed to offer a foolproof weapon. In establishing an unbridgeable gulf between science and religion, between theoretical knowledge and practical commandment, Kant overcame what Chamberlain called man's original "sin of thought" (*Gedankensünde*) and freed humans from the determinism of nature. The categorical imperative, enjoining man to act according to self-prescribed moral law, represented a liberation of human potential far more profound than the mundane emancipation of the French Revolution. Now the "advancement of culture" required that mankind proceed in the only direction in which there are no limits to human capacities: self-ennoblement through the cultivation of inner freedom and the realization in practice of intuitive (*eingegebene*) ideals.

> All this means a complete change in all those conceptions and habits in science, religion, morals, law, society, which show us to be intimately related to the Babylonians of six-thousand years ago: it means a "transvaluation of all values," such as the devotees of the fashionable jargon of our day never have dreamt of [a reference to Nietzscheans], a growing and strengthening of mankind, not by the mad unchaining of man's blind "will to power," but, on the contrary, by the finer molding of his consciousness, by the clear apprehension of his mental organization, and so (which is the same thing) of the organization of the world of his experience—in other words, by the still tighter fettering of the dumb, beastly instincts of his will in the service of a reason perfectly self-controlled and consciously creative. [*Kant*, p. 565]

The political uses of this seemingly benign defense of practical reason became evident when in 1915 Chamberlain inserted this very passage into his most important wartime publication, *Politische Ideale*, to underscore the need for a more tightly organized and disciplined polity.[11]

The inculcation and justification of deferential attitudes as the cement to bind a hierarchically ordered society were in the last analysis the major purposes of Chamberlain's voluminous treatises. Hence he slighted the content of Kant's moral law, to treat persons as ends rather than means, but emphasized instead the need to submit to authority rather than to surrender to natural inclinations or rational self-interest. Precisely because Kant's ethical precepts (especially his exhortation to act only according to principles that one could will to become universal laws) could readily be invoked for liberal and democratic causes, Chamberlain felt obliged to interpret his philosophy in a conservative, authoritarian vein. Adopting Goethe's maxim, "The deed is everywhere decisive," he likened Kant's ethical imperative to Parsifal's quest for the Holy Grail. Chamberlain regarded religion as but the means to overcome the human inclination to seek worldly happiness rather than moral virtue. Casting off the shackles of nature, the free man displays the virtues of the soldier, ever ready to sacrifice his life for the good of his nation: "He bridles his selfishness, he sacrifices himself for an idea, he goes to his death radiant with joy: in a word, he obeys the self-imposed law—duty. He proves himself autonomous" (*Kant*, p. 758). In defining service in subordination as the highest form of freedom, Chamberlain anticipated the equivocating slogan, "Work makes free" (*Arbeit macht frei*), a slogan the Nazis would post at the entrances to concentration camps.

Chamberlain's hostility to democracy was fed by a grandiose paranoia into which he projected all his accumulated resentments. The Germanic "empire of the spirit" (*Weltreich des Geistes*) would need all the moral strength it could muster to withstand the assault of the foes that Chamberlain saw all around:

> On the one hand a Church of Rome gaining in strength, which already stretches out its hand to our schools to inoculate the pure minds of the children forever with her poison destructive of all freedom; supported, moreover, by Catholics of the second degree, that is to say Protestants, who no longer protest, but bend and bow, and imitate Rome as well as a miserably crippled inconsistency will allow; and on the other side a so-called "empirical scientific world view" which has fallen further back than Thales in the conception and apprehension of the problem of existence; a world view which is nominally "empirical" but solves everything in abstractions and hollow balderdash . . . and robs us of form and personality, and of the redeeming thought of freedom. [*Kant*, pp. 694–95]

Compounding this menace in Chamberlain's troubled mind was the threat posed by inferior races all over the world. He saw Germanic culture endangered by "a swarming population of tartarized Russians," while farther away the "soulless yellow race" and the "weakly mongrels" (*kraftlose Mischlinge*) of Australasia and South America were girding for the showdown. Posing the greatest threat of all were the "millions of blacks, poor in intellect, bestially inclined, who are even now arming for pitiless racial war" (*Kant*, pp. 694–95).

At home the greatest menace loomed from the labor movement, which could prove as fatal to Germanic spiritual freedom as the rising of the slaves had proved fatal to Roman political freedom. "If that class should win," he wrote, "mankind in Kant's sense, as pure personalities, would stand at a lower level, rather than higher" (*Kant*, p. 736). Unlike the peasant, who lived close to nature and learned from it daily, the worker, torn from nature and corrupted by the doctrines of progress disseminated by the press, had lost all powers of independent judgment. "At present millions of such workers obey a handful of immigrant Jews, who find their amusement and their advantage in undermining the state which has been built up by the work and pain of centuries" (*Kant*, p. 697). Unconscious of the irony in his prophecy, Chamberlain warned that in the future these same workers could obey a different tyrant.

Like Stein and Lienhard, Chamberlain invoked Goethe in support of social conservatism. The tenuous equilibrium that the German classicists cultivated as a mode of adjustment to stultifying social and political conditions in the eighteenth century became for Chamberlain the model of exemplary conduct, precisely because such accommodation left social stratification and political autocracy unchallenged. If the classical ideal of self-cultivation at least implicitly indicted an absolutist system that permitted the majority of people no fulfillment beyond the personal sphere, Chamberlain promulgated this ideal in order to achieve (or maintain) such a system. The classical gesture of resignation became for Chamberlain an ideological weapon. He enthusiastically affirmed Goethe's conception of equality as the opportunity for individual development in whatever direction an individual's social and economic situation best permitted. On the authority of Goethe, he asserted that the function of politics lay simply in the maintenance of order. The means by which this was accomplished were matters of indifference. Goethe had wisely preferred a degree of despotism as most conducive to building character. The democratic revolutionary and the slave are identical, Chamberlain wrote, for both destroy personality, the basis of morality and culture. In the battle of redemption (*Erlösungskampf*) that Chamberlain proclaimed, Kant and Goethe were to serve as models and guides.[12]

Waxing more dogmatic than the theological doctrines he disparaged and more sophistic than the rational doctrines he despised, Chamberlain's books serve as reminders of the uses of the Romantic personality cult in defense of a social order which was battling an emerging democracy. His works satisfied a psychological need felt by many members of the educated middle class, persons alienated and confused by the growing abstruseness and specialization of science and by the seeming irrelevance of traditional religion in an era of rapid modernization.[13] Stripping science of its claim to objective truth, while affirming its usefulness as long as it did not transcend vulgar empiricism, Chamberlain sought to invalidate rationalism as a mode of dealing with social and political problems. The convolutions of his arguments notwithstanding, he offered grand simplification through the marriage of narrow positivism and virtually total subjectivism, of technology and myth. Invoking Goethe's paradox, "All thinking is useless for thought," he assured his readers that they need not seek rational solutions to social problems (*Kant*, p. 253). At the same time he offered a substitute religion of striking simplicity and practicality, designed to unleash sacrificial ardor in the cause of Germanic grandeur. World War I would reveal the naked ambitions that lay behind his plea for cultural reform.

13

FROM MONARCHISM TO NATIONAL SOCIALISM:
CHAMBERLAIN'S WAR PAMPHLETS

> You have mighty things to do. . . . My faith in Germanism had not
> wavered an instant, though my hope—I confess—was at a low ebb. With
> one stroke you have transformed the state of my soul. That in the hour of
> her deepest need Germany gives birth to a Hitler proves her vitality, as do
> the influences that emanate from him; for these two things—personality
> and influence—belong together. . . . May God protect you!
>   Chamberlain to Hitler, 1923

Chamberlain's conversion to *völkisch* extremism took place in World War
I. His shift of allegiance from monarchism to National Socialism paralleled
the transition of many erstwhile conservatives, whose major concern after
the war no longer lay in the defense of the Imperial status quo, but rather in
the overthrow of the newly founded republic. His fame well established
when the Great War broke out, Chamberlain was asked by German friends
to address a pro-German appeal to his English compatriots in the manner
of Thomas Carlyle in 1870. By this time, however, he was already too
estranged from his native land to play such a role. Instead, he addressed
himself to the German public in numerous articles and pamphlets justifying
the war as a selfless cultural crusade. These were distributed to hundreds of
thousands of soldiers at the front. Several pamphlets were translated into
English to bolster Germany's psychological war effort. The British government countered by issuing in 1915 an official version under the title, *The
Ravings of a Renegade*. As a result the German Foreign Office advised
against the use of his pamphlets for propaganda purposes in the United
States.[1]
  Though inspired by the transitory passions of war, these pamphlets are
worthy of scrutiny, for they reveal very clearly the frame of mind that gave
rise to *völkisch* extremism. They did more than incite to hatred or bolster
morale: they provided a platform for Nazi politics and German world
domination. The war had the effect of laying bare the political goals that
Chamberlain had previously veiled in the language of spiritual rebirth and
cultural creativity. His apolitical stance of the prewar years, an effective
vehicle of conservative politics in an autocratically governed state, was now

discarded.[2] When Chamberlain now reitereated his oft-proclaimed maxim, "Germany's rebirth can only take place from within,"[3] he meant not only a moral regeneration but also a political restructuring in which all democratic forces would be effectively neutralized. If the function of his prewar works had been to provide an ideology for Germany's educated elite, the function of these pamphlets was to mobilize mass support for nationalist and imperialist goals. They also provided a practical program to meet the political crisis.

Echoing the "ideas of 1914," Chamberlain greeted the outbreak of war as the long-delayed opportunity to purge the social fabric of materialistic self-seeking and unite the country in an idealistic crusade. Germany's quarrel was not with any particular peoples, but rather with the evil influence of "Mammon," which threatened to enslave mankind. In this fight Germany had become an "indispensable, irreplaceable instrument of God."[4] The cultural preeminence that Chamberlain postulated now served as the basis for Germany's claim to power. Germany's mission required that she become the "first power in the world."[5] Since Chamberlain made survival contingent upon expansion and expansion dependent on domestic unity, social conservatism and imperialism abetted each other in a vicious circle consummated by war.

Chamberlain echoed the fears of Germany's leaders that time was on the side of her enemies, both external and internal. Had the war come ten years later, God might no longer have found a warrior for his cause on earth: "Germany was already walking at the edge of the abyss. The excessive esteem of money, the derision of all ideal stirrings, the growing power of the un-German segment of the press, the systematic undermining of respect for the monarchy, for the army, for Christian convictions. . . . Perhaps this war will once be celebrated as Germany's rescue from mortal danger."[6] Significantly, Chamberlain viewed a lack of popular zeal as a greater obstacle to German imperial ambitions than the military strength of her opponents. To strengthen public resolve in the face of a long war, he asserted that a quick victory might have been fatal to Germany, for it would not have ensured "the purifying and steeling of her soul." "It may take a series of wars," he predicted, "in order to overcome France, England, and Russia and to promote the reconstituting of Europe, the opening of Asia, the population of Africa, the mastery over the yellow and black races to such a degree that we can speak of a 'German peace' in the sense that I mean."[7] Thus Chamberlain anticipated not only the Nazi goals of conquest, but also the Nazi dynamic of virtually constant war. For war held out more than territorial gain; it provided the ethos best suited to the defense of privilege and the suppression of equalitarian reform.

Chamberlain's visions of a world dominated by Germanic culture and power had emerged long before wartime passions gave them free play. In

his prewar books imperialistic ambitions were concealed behind a philosophical façade. In his letters, however, he advocated German world domination. Thus in *Politische Ideale* he was able to quote verbatim from a letter
he had written to William II: "Germany is destined to become the heart of
mankind; every other nation is now finally eliminated. . . . Of this I am
firmly convinced: Germany can succeed in dominating the entire globe
within two centuries (in part politically, in part indirectly through language, culture, methods) if she can be made to adopt the 'new course' early
enough, and that means to bring the nation to a final break with Anglo-
American ideals of government."[8] Like other *völkisch* critics of the Wilhelmine regime, Chamberlain would later deplore the failure of the monarchy
to achieve such a break.[9]

In his wartime attacks on England Chamberlain revived allegations
made more than a decade earlier in letters to the kaiser. Toward England
and the United States Chamberlain adopted the moralistic tone of one who
had renounced personal advantage for higher things. "It is a painful
privilege to love Germany the way I love it. How pleasant it would be to
dance around the star-spangled banner of the dollar dynasties! How
comfortable for the born Englishman to surrender himself to the ecstasy of
'Greater England!' "[10] Rationalizing Anglo-German naval and commercial
rivalry in cultural terms, Chamberlain plied the kaiser with assurances of
German superiority. The differences between Schiller and Byron, two
poets of equal talent, exemplified for Chamberlain the gap in cultural
potential between the two nations. He praised Schiller's constructiveness,
soaring spirit, firm footing, edifying morality, and fervent love of his
country, while disparaging Byron's destructiveness, frivolity, dissolution,
egotism, and cynical derision of his own country. "The highest thoughts,"
Chamberlain wrote to the kaiser, "of which the human intellect is presently
capable, can only find adequate expression in the German language."[11] He
assured him that no other culture was entitled to equal status. William II,
who occasionally worked Chamberlain's ideological suggestions into his
speeches and decrees, lauded Chamberlain for "that admirable trait, with
which providence has endowed you for the good of your fellow men: The
gift of finding the right external form for the thoughts which preoccupy and
permeate us."[12]

While in 1914 Chamberlain claimed (not without a degree of retrospec-
tive idealization) to have loved Victorian England, he blamed Edward VII,
in whose reign the Triple Entente was forged, for having "demoralized" his
country.[13] Although he commended the English for their reserve, helpful-
ness, and sensitivity in personal relations, Chamberlain charged that
money and power had become Britain's dominant ideals. The Norman
invasion in 1066 and the transition from an agricultural to a commercial
and seafaring nation in the sixteenth century marked the historical stages in

his account of Britain's moral and cultural decline. He accused the British of downgrading intellectual pursuits in favor of sports. Students in their early teens already chose their courses of study solely on the basis of the earning power such training would afford. He cited the popular contraction of the British Association for the Advancement of Science into "British Ass" to sustain his contention that educated persons were suspect in England unless they happened to be rich.[14] Yet in an apologia written to his brother in England several months after the outbreak of the war, he acknowledged that his ardor about Germanic culture could not fail but appear ludicrous to the English sense of humor.[15]

Although he considered democracy far inferior to autocratic government, Chamberlain at the same time refused to concede that Britain enjoyed a truly democratic system. The British system had degraded the king to a mere puppet (unless, like Edward VII, he could compensate for his loss of power through skillful intrigue), while political power rested with an aristocracy increasingly based on wealth. Chamberlain defended monarchy as the ideal form of government because it encouraged the popular mind to endow the nation's ruler with the highest qualities of character. "Whoever speaks of a republic in Germany," he wrote, "belongs on the gallows. The monarchic ideal is here the holy law of life." For Chamberlain, monarchy best expresses the subordination of the individual to the community, an ideal that National Socialism would seek to revive in modernized form. The British system, however, represented a "government by committee" from which king and people were excluded.[16]

Chamberlain dismissed the vaunted English ideal of freedom as a mere battle cry in the historical struggle between aristocracy and royalty—as if freedom consisted of the privilege of toppling the prime minister according to whim. The British aristocracy did not constitute a racial elite, but merely an interchangeable social caste to which money could always provide entry. American democracy represented an even more blatant form of plutocracy in which votes could be openly bought by political candidates. Here, too, democracy served as a façade to conceal anarchy and wanton individualism (*frevelhafte Einzelwillkür*), the most destructive effects of which could only be prevented by the despotic power of whatever president happened to be in office.[17] Chamberlain claimed to be quoting an American acquaintance when he wrote, a year before American entry into the war: "[The U.S.] is a satanic whirlpool [*Hexenkessel*] in which all the contradictions of the world, all the greed, all the envy, all the lust brew and bubble; a wild struggle of millions of egotistic, ignorant persons without ideas, ideals, or tradition, without unifying customs, without any capacity for sacrifice; an atomistic chaos, without any true national power."[18] Having assured William II as early as 1903 that the United States was a country without a future whose cultural sterility would become plain as soon as the influx of population from Europe ceased, Chamberlain encouraged that grievous underestimation of American strength to which German leaders also succumbed in both world wars.[19]

While Anglo-Americans allegedly sacrificed culture to practical considerations, Germans simplified practical life in order to promote culture. In 1903 Chamberlain had already written to the kaiser of the need for a more rigid organization of the state: "Germany can only outdo Anglo-Americanism by pursuing an entirely different method; by proceeding as a closed unit—disciplined and methodological."[20] In a letter to the future German chancellor, Prince Max von Baden, a month after the outbreak of the war, Chamberlain expressed hope that the war would lead to the elimination of the Reichstag, an institution allegedly imported from England and France.[21] Chamberlain was forced by the government's policy of maintaining the *Burgfrieden*—the suspension of partisan conflicts—to refrain from public discussion of annexationist aims. No objection, however, was raised to his attacks on the Reichstag, presumably because these could be construed as an effort to overcome partisan divisiveness. Nor were these attacks provoked solely by impending defeat; launched a month after the outbreak of war, Chamberlain's anti-parliamentary campaign formed an integral part of his war effort.

Analyzing its etymological origins, Chamberlain equated parliament with a talking-shop (*Schwatzbude*), to which not the most capable persons were elected, but rather those who happened to possess a gift for public speaking. The "mass psychosis" that made individual representatives vote against their better judgement constituted in his view an insuperable obstacle to effective government. "Compared to the tyranny of a parliamentary majority," he wrote, "Genghis Khan is an angel of God to me."[22] The Reichstag could take no credit for any of the political achievements since 1870; it was only thanks to the persistence of the various chancellors and the *Bundesrat* that anything had been accomplished at all. "The most pernicious alien influence [*Ausländerei*] is the belief in the indisputable dignity and decisive significance of popular assemblies elected by universal suffrage: on this Germany will yet go to ruin, if a complete change in public opinion does not take place in time."[23] Yet Chamberlain predictably defended that bulwark of agrarian conservatism, the Prussian *Landtag* (elected by a system in which the weight of a man's vote depended on his wealth); mass passions could not exercise their hypnotic effect in this chamber, because concrete interests, not merely opinions, were here represented.

Chamberlain's defense of property rights also accorded with Junker interests and anticipated the Nazi emphasis on "blood and soil." In passages that foreboded the Nazi attacks on international finance capitalism, he argued that land ownership, not the possession of money, formed the true foundation of the state. Since it recognizes no fatherland, moneyed wealth represents a threat to the state. "The enduring cultivation of the soil, in which every generation inherits from the previous generations and accumulates for coming generations: this is the prototype of every constructive cultural activity."[24] Landed property represents an advanced stage in the development of human dignity, guaranteeing stability and permanence, the main conditions of an effective state.

Contrary to the claims of theorists of social contract, from Locke to Rousseau, it was not mankind who invented the state, but the state that made mankind. Arguing that mankind without a state would be animals, Chamberlain judged policies according to their usefulness in promoting the stability and permanence of the state. Like so many other German intellectuals, he portrayed the war as a struggle against the seditious ideals of the French Revolution. According to Chamberlain, *liberté, egalité,* and *fraternité* pointed the way to chaos, for they contradicted truths of nature. He disparaged these values as "simply Gallic insolence, nothing more; insolence born of shallow thought paired with unbridled desire."[25] Man is not born free, but helpless and dependent. He can exist only in a community in which his inborn egotism is curbed. Freedom should not form the starting point of social and political organization, as in revolutionary doctrine, but rather the result of such organization. Only a strong state can guarantee the moral freedom of the individual. The Western ideal of political liberty stood indicted as "selfish" in contrast to the German ideal of freedom from egotism, material gratification, and sinfulness. True freedom does not consist of the right to walk on the grass, but in a lack of desire to do so. Citing Luther's "Flesh shall have no freedom," Chamberlain insisted that true freedom exists only where persons respect social and ethical norms without coercion.[26] By Chamberlain's definition a totally conformist society would be the most free.

In claiming that egalitarians must believe that all are born with equal abilities, Chamberlain set up a straw man that he could easily demolish. Egalitarians wrongly invoked Rousseau, he argued, for Rousseau had maintained, not that persons were equal by nature, but only that they suffered least from inequality in a primitive state. Since social institutions necessarily reveal the inequality of their individual members, revolutionaries would have to demand the dissolution of all institutions if they wished to remain consistent. Egalitarian politics were rendered invalid by the absurdity of such a demand.

Nor can fraternity form the basis of the state, for a state can only be based on duty if it is to function effectively. To counteract the appeal of a positive reform program, Chamberlain took pains to represent liberty, equality, and fraternity as negative values: the right not to obey authority, not to show respect toward superiors, and the right not to love or tolerate those who think differently. The consequence of such attitudes, as borne out by the French Revolution, must inevitably be tyranny, mediocrity, and heartlessness. If Germany was to avoid such a fate, it would have to develop new ideals: "The old ideals no longer suffice for Germany. Even the splendid loyalty to the king of the Prussian aristocracy of the sword is no longer relevant in Bismarck's Germany. Even less adequate are the other particularist residues from a beautiful past age."[27] Defense of the status quo no longer sufficed to save the "historical Germany" from the inroads of democracy and socialism. Existing institutions would have to be changed to make them more resistant to the revolutionary forces from the left.

Mapping out the coming transition to fascism, Chamberlain advocated a reorganization of the state on the model of the army, which had proven its worth in the war. As Germany had not yet become democratic, Chamberlain felt confident that a reorganization could be achieved by maintaining a wartime regimen after the war as well.

> This is the road that Germany must continue to take, in peacetime as well, in ever more complete organization: the individual free within, totally affiliated without; society as a whole delivered from the thousand inhibitions of inherited antediluvian democratic hallucinations, ready to construct a conscious, planned, scientific future out of the present. If Germany does this, then it will overcome all obstacles and—to the salvation of mankind—become the predominant world power, which means: she will fulfill her God-given destiny.[28]

Applying vulgarized positivism to political doctrine, Chamberlain argued that nature, not theory, must serve as the guide to mankind's future. Nature teaches mankind that unequal parts are essential to the creation of an organic *Gestalt*. His use of socialist vocabulary notwithstanding, Chamberlain dismissed planning as futile. Napoleon had failed to realize his great opportunities because he had pursued only plans, not ideals.[29]

Chamberlain envisaged a totally administered corporative state in which estates, not parties, would form the units of political organization.[30] He rejected a party system on the grounds that a person could compromise his interests, but never his convictions, if he wished to remain true to himself. Parties perpetuated disunity by espousing irreconcilable doctrines. Echoing the technocratic (though not the egalitarian) ideal of Saint-Simon, Chamberlain contended that policy must be determined by competent specialists who would guide the state with efficiency and impartiality. "There shall be no politics in its current sense in the new Germany," he wrote; "statecraft will take its place." Warning that a military victory alone would not ensure the victory of Germanic ideology, Chamberlain called for an "impetuous and ruthless Germanic man" to lead the fight against the forces of sedition and permissiveness, which were undermining the state from within. "An iron broom must sweep in Germany: whoever has the courage to wield it will find all popular forces behind him."[31] The kaiser now seemed too weak for such a task.

As before the war, the "social question" seemed to pose the major problem in the eyes of conservative publicists. Chamberlain confidently expected the war to "liberate" the working class from its attachment to socialism, the strength of which lay in the size and quality of its following, not in its program. He accused communists of being ultra-reactionaries who wished to return to prehistoric times.[32] At the same time he reiterated his belief, already stated in *The Foundations*, that economic privations remain largely constant throughout history. "That many must become poor for one person to become rich is obvious," he had written twenty years before; "nor do I find this a special misfortune, for wealth does not confer happiness."[33] Chamberlain showed how idealism could be bent to the defense of wealth and property; possessions do not preclude entrance into the kingdom of heaven, he wrote in *Mensch und Gott*, for what is important is only one's attitude toward possessions. Wealth is reprehensible only if used for pleasure.[34] Thus the poor who seek to escape their condition stand condemned as more materialistic than the frugal rich. Chamberlain diagnosed the plight of modern workers not as poverty, but as alienation from nature. Only a superior mind could compensate for the loss of bearing resulting from the separation from nature which industrialization and urbanization entailed. His proposals for the workers' movement of the future presaged Nazi labor policy. The reintegration of workers into a social order patterned on "natural models" would obviate the need for labor rebellion or agitation for reform.

To lend weight to his denunciation of war-profiteering, Chamberlain refused to accept remuneration for the sale of his pamphlets. Instead he transferred his royalties to a local army commander for use in boosting troop morale.[35] In 1917 Chamberlain agreed to become an editor of *Deutschlands Erneuerung*, a journal founded by the nationalist publisher Julius Friedrich Lehmann (1864–1938). He had declined to join a similar venture before the war, apparently fearing participation would tarnish his public image as philosophical sage. Now his wish to aid the war cause overcame his reluctance to enter the popular fray. "I am very interested in this project," he wrote to Lehmann, "as long as I may believe that it will proceed in a German, practical, ideal, and ruthless way."[36] The editorial board included the nationalist historians Georg von Below (1858–1927) and Dietrich Schäfer (1845–1929), as well as Heinrich Class, head of the Pan-German League, which Chamberlain joined in 1916. *Deutschlands Erneuerung*, which continued publication until the end of World War II as one of the leading periodicals of the *völkisch* movement, served as a vehicle for publicists who sought to channel wartime patriotism into support for ultra-conservative political objectives. Handicapped by declining health,

Chamberlain's role consisted primarily in lending the prestige of his name to the new journal. His occasional contributions included a eulogy of Hitler in January, 1924.

Although disappointed by the ignominious end of the war and by the revolution that followed, Chamberlain retained the unflagging optimism that made his works so useful to the Nazis. A month after the end of the war, Chamberlain reaffirmed his belief in Germany's mission: "Faith in German character, in what we will call the German idea, is for me a part of my faith in God. I am unswervingly convinced, now as ever, that God has permitted the German to grow and develop for the salvation of all mankind."[37]

Proclaiming hope as a duty, he denounced the defeatism of Spengler's *Decline of the West* (1918). Spengler saw Germany's defeat in the war as the final blow in the victory of the civilizing, rationalizing pragmatism of liberal Europe. "With the word 'West' the racial idea is to be undermined," Chamberlain lamented, "and with the word 'decline' all hope is to be cut off."[38] He also berated idealists who pursued the illusion that defeat had restored the Germany of Kant and Goethe. The fate of the German classicists depended on German political fortunes, for unless the German language became widely disseminated throughout the world, their works would in the future only be studied by a handful of scholars.[39] Chamberlain himself acceded to the demands of cultural nativists by substituting German expressions for foreign terms in the second edition of his *Goethe* in 1918.

Convinced that Germany had been defeated only from within, Chamberlain perpetuated fantasies of a German military victory. If Admiral Tirpitz had been chancellor and Hindenburg and Ludendorff had headed the Reichswehr from the start of the war, peace would have been signed in Paris in 1914.[40] Chamberlain's anti-Semitism, restrained for the sake of unity during the war, reemerged with a vengeance in the period of political unrest that followed. While in England and France the Jews had been among the best of patriots, in Germany they had been permitted to "capture power" despite their "unpatriotic" attitude. Chamberlain now called for the abrogation of Jewish political rights, thereby anticipating a key point in the National Socialist program.[41] In his efforts to justify discriminatory policies against Jews, he gave at least partial credence to conspiracy theories that he would earlier have dismissed as unfounded:

Whether there really is a Jewish secret covenant, which has set as its consciously pursued goal the physical, mental, and moral destruction of the Indo-European and his culture, I do not know; I believe the mere instinct of this plastic demon of the degeneration of mankind (as Richard Wagner called it), bred through thousands of years, suffices; the more so since here, as everywhere else, their direct business interests accord with this goal.[42]

Scoffing at sentimental doctrines of humanity (*Humanitätsduselei*), he preached xenophobia as a necessary condition of self-preservation.

Spanning the transition from the Second Empire to the Third Reich, Chamberlain's works provide a valuable insight into the ideological and political origins of National Socialism. The confident self-glorification of *The Foundations* reached its denouement in the desperate and pathological chauvinism of National Socialism as unreconstructed conservatives battled to retain control of a society in the throes of modernizing reform. Chamberlain's wartime pamphlets underscore the importance in this transition of a war originally welcomed by conservatives as a means to maintain and extend the sway of their social and political values. Defeat and the advent of the Weimar Republic turned many erstwhile conservatives into counterrevolutionaries bent upon restoring an elitist system in the modernized and populist forms necessary for success in an age of mass politics.

With the foresight of a participant rather than an observer, Chamberlain predicted the coming of the Third Reich and World War II, though vanity clouded his vision of its disastrous end. Chamberlain did not misjudge Hitler's politics but only his chances of ultimate success. Nor did Chamberlain's rejection of politics signify a renunciation of imperialistic aims. "This non-politics should be frankly professed," he wrote to Hitler, "and forced upon the world with might."[43] For Chamberlain nothing better confirmed the legitimacy of the National Socialist movement than General Ludendorff's decision to join it. Having searched all his life for a way to contain threatening change, Chamberlain found in Nazism the hope and comfort that monarchism could no longer provide.

14

CONCLUSION: THE DEBASEMENT OF IDEALISM

> It is a fatal error to assume that National Socialism came about in spite
> of Germany's intellectual greatness. It was the natural result of the par-
> ticular social—or rather asocial—orientation of its great men.
>
> Erik H. Erikson, *Childhood and Society*

It is likely that Stein, Lienhard, and Chamberlain would have welcomed
the national revival that the Nazi accession to power in 1933 appeared to
usher in. To millions of Germans steeped in the values of idealism, National
Socialism promised a way of achieving these values in practice. National
Socialism satisfied the yearning for national unity and order. It marked the
radical culmination of a long and bitter campaign—a campaign that
enjoyed the support of Germany's most influential intellectuals—to reverse
the modern trend toward greater democracy. At the same time the triumph
of National Socialism seemed to guarantee an end to sectarian fragmentation and squabbling within the *völkisch* camp.[1]

Völkisch intellectuals contributed their part to the "German Revolution" by articulating the insecurities and resentments of those strata of
German society that stood to lose status and privilege through egalitarian
and liberalizing change. A study of their works helps us to understand the
favorable reception that important segments of German society accorded
to Nazism. They succeeded in discrediting democracy as the "triumph of
inferiors."[2] The strength of *völkisch* ideology lay in marshaling the forces
of tradition against revolutionary changes. Even before World War I, but
especially after it, such changes had become so widespread that a wholesale
transformation of German (and European) society seemed required to
destroy the ground for revolutionary progress. Fascism in its various forms
attracted the support of those who desired a "conservative revolution" to
restore unity and stability. In a time of severe depression, the Nazis, the
völkish party with the best organization and leadership, gained the votes of
those groups, especially the *Mittelstand* of independent artisans, peasants,
and shop owners, for whom liberalism and socialism held out only the
prospect of further decline.[3] The Nazis also received at least the tacit
support of traditional elites, including Junkers and industrialists, who

feared that liberalism and socialism would lead to a further erosion of their wealth and power.

To such individuals and groups *völkisch* idealism provided a valid and coherent ideology because it accorded with their material interests. For those vulnerable to the fluctuations and the competitive squeeze of a laissez-faire economy (especially in a period of depression), the *völkisch* view of liberalism as a selfish and divisive system was reinforced by personal experience. Fear of proletarianization or of exorbitant union demands gave added credence to the *völkisch* denunciation of socialism as an even more divisive system based on the greed of a particular class. Static and archaic social models had special appeal for people threatened by social mobility and continuing industrialization. No wonder such people were particularly susceptible to the blandishments of "idealists" who invoked moral sanctions against groups and individuals that profited from social emancipation and technological progress.

National Socialism thus appeared to many as a benignly motivated, if radical, movement to rid society of its disruptive elements and of the attitudes that permitted disruptive elements to thrive. For generations, Germans and other Europeans had been conditioned to blame the disruptions of modernization on Jewish influence. Jewishness stood for selfishness, the corrosive force that in its various guises seemed to tear asunder the social fabric. The Nazis seemed radical not in their objectives, but only in the methods they proposed to use. Racialism seemed to complement rather than contradict idealism, for it provided the basis for the extreme policies that seemed to be required to purify a society in an advanced state of degeneration.

If the German idealist tradition lent itself readily to antidemocratic uses, this is not surprising since it was itself the product of an age hostile to democracy. German idealism may be interpreted as an effort to compensate for and overcome the constraints of social and political life in Germany at a time when religious beliefs no longer offered such universal consolation, at least not to educated people, as in the past. Idealism imitated religion by providing both an optimistic doctrine of ultimate harmony and a heroic creed for individual fulfillment. But if idealism originated as a response to the lack of democracy, it gradually became converted to a system of argument against democracy.

We have traced the last stages of this transition through the works of three representative authors, each of whom valued idealism in large measure for its conservative social and political implications. No doubt the idealist disdain for material values, however noble as a quasi-religious creed, is particularly susceptible to corruption as a political doctrine. Idealism could be used to discredit rational analysis and theory as merely products of intellect rather than intuition. It could be used to thwart social criticism, dissent, and reform, and to sanctify inequitable social arrangements. A degree of idealism in the conventional sense is, of course, indispensable for any constructive social or political critique, for it is impossible effectively to criticize what *is* without having some vision of what ought to be. The absolute idealist distinction between everyday reality and spiritual essence could, however, easily become a weapon for the suppression of social reform in the name of idealized entities such as the state or the *Volk*.

Idealism offered a "higher" alternative to the rational ethics of self-interest that underpinned social and political emancipation movements. The invocation of eternity and the absolute buttressed the authority of the state and of elitist values. By proclaiming contempt for the material aspects of life while preaching the virtues of cultivating the personality and the soul, *völkisch* publicists sought to harness the labor movement in a social order in which each person was to accept the station divinely allotted to him. The cult of inwardness fostered by *völkisch* authors was designed to contain social mobility and popular aspirations in a hierarchical community free of conflict and social reform. A system of values which, however sincere its propagators, reflected the interests of groups whose property and privileges were endangered by social change, made possible the easy acceptance of National Socialism by the German public. Fascism reaffirmed in radical and populist guise the values of aristocratic conservatism that *völkisch* authors transmitted from an earlier age.

Völkisch idealists like Stein, Lienhard, and Chamberlain thus helped to shape the further development of the tradition that had molded their outlook. Social and psychological factors interacted dialectically to shape their outlook. Members of a generation that came of age in the period following German unification, each in his way sought to fulfill the heroic aspirations of the *Gründerzeit*. Childhood memories of the brilliant military and political successes of 1870–1871 impeded their adjustment to mundane reality ever after. We can speculate that the loss of their mothers early in life may have abetted a lifelong preoccupation with an eternal realm where death and bereavement had lost their sting. Germans by choice and circumstance, Lienhard and Chamberlain reflected in their works the conflict of nationalities in disputed or mixed areas such as Alsace and Austria. For Stein, too, unity and wholeness were overriding concerns.

Whether Stein's intellectual and political development would have paralleled Lienhard's or Chamberlain's is impossible to determine. Perhaps he would yet have undergone the transformation that Nietzsche hoped for. Stein personified a transitional phase in which idealism had not yet become an instrument of demagoguery. His best works express an intensely personal commitment devoid of conscious political motive. But his attitudes were fraught with the political dangers inherent in the idealist mentality: the worship of intuition and the distrust of intellect and rationality, the denial of man's temporal nature and the rejection of the pursuit of happiness (and by extension of social reform) as a base inclination, and the flight from reality into fantasy and wish-fulfillment. Nietzsche unmasked a cast of mind that inclined toward righteousness rather than truthfulness, toward self-deception and self-congratulation rather than self-knowledge and self-criticism. With the perspicacity that perhaps only someone who was himself steeped in Germany's apolitical intellectual tradition could command, Nietzsche exposed idealist hypocrisy. For Nietzsche, to be sure, it was intellectual integrity, not democracy, that was at stake. Self-styled idealists failed to live up to their own avowed principles. Projecting their own egocentrism onto Jews, they either failed to realize or refused to admit that their hierarchical notions of triumphant spiritual forces were in fact self-serving.

If Stein's works still reflected a generalized malaise in the face of secularization and modernization, *völkisch* idealism became increasingly identified with political reaction in the turbulent decades following his death. In the works of conservative publicists like Langbehn and Lienhard idealism degenerated into the idealization of authoritarianism and nationalism. Lienhard entirely eschewed the intellectual rigors of philosophical idealism in favor of moral evangelism and elitism. Feigning disinterest in political affairs, he preached a pseudo-religious doctrine designed primarily to prevent social and political change.

Chamberlain represented a further stage in the developing counterrevolution. More brazenly than his predecessors he exploited the dualisms of spirit and matter, mind and body, and light and darkness for political ends. He carried to an extreme the idealist equation of freedom with submission to a higher authority. Racialism offered a "scientific" way to invalidate the environmentalism of reformers while making aristocratic conceptions of pedigree and hierarchy attractive to the lower classes. Most important, racialism provided a radical method for countering liberalism and socialism by attacking what conservatives perceived as their source: the Jewish community. Chamberlain repudiated the forcible assimilation advocated by more traditional conservatives like Treitschke, Lagarde, or Lienhard in favor of the exclusionary policies adopted by the Nazis.

There is no way of knowing, of course, whether Chamberlain, let alone Stein or Lienhard, would have supported Nazi policies after 1933. Even Chamberlain might well have shared the disenchantment of numerous "idealists" who originally greeted Hitler's appointment as chancellor with high hopes.[4] If for idealists power represented a means of achieving ideals, the Nazi leadership exploited ideals as a means of achieving power. Even before 1933 "genuine National Socialists" who wished to give conservative social reform priority over tactical measures designed solely to secure power were read out of the party.[5] The "blood purge" of 1934 further alienated principled Nazis and their sympathizers. In the interests of power the Nazis refused to introduce the corporatist institutions that many of their supporters had been led to expect. Moreover, even idealists who believed in a German mission feared Hitler's reckless determination to wage war. The conspiracy of July 20, 1944, was fueled largely by disillusionment with a Führer who had destroyed the very cause he purported to lead.[6]

Nonetheless, the disaffection of some idealists from Nazism should not lead us to underestimate the idealist content of National Socialism nor the capacity for ruthlessness of those who prided themselves on their idealism. The fanatical implementation of ideals usually leads to the violation of these ideals in practice, for he who regards himself as the instrument of higher forces feels himself freed of worldly scruples. Although Stein, Lienhard, and probably Chamberlain as well would have been revolted by Nazi genocide, their works justified anti-Semitism as well as the quest for "final" rather than pragmatic solutions to social problems. Apologists for the use of power rather than critics of its misuse, Lienhard and Chamberlain, and to some extent Stein as well, represent a paradoxical but frequent type: the intellectual as anti-intellectual. Throughout history an important social function of intellectuals has been to unmask hypocrisy, especially when officially propagated, and to reveal unpleasant truths, even against the opposition of those elites that profit from their concealment. Völkisch writers, however, not only abandoned the critical function inherent in intellectual activity, but sought to stifle criticism by branding it immoral. They thereby contributed to the illusion of respectability that the Nazis successfully cultivated.

The motive force behind the völkisch movement was not one of criminal impulses but of perverted moral energy. If philosophical idealism reflects a revulsion against disorder, against the pessimistic conception of the world as a product of chance, völkisch idealists rejected democracy as the institutionalization of such disorder. Their code word for democracy was "chaos." Their animus against democracy led them to deny the possibility of cultural or intellectual achievement in an egalitarian social order—a prejudice that history does not warrant.

The ideological antecedents of National Socialism are not to be found in doctrines of social or political revolution or in preachments of spontaneity, amorality, self-indulgence, decadence, or anarchism, but rather in the intellectual reaction to such "permissive" and excessively democratic precepts. The works of Lienhard and Chamberlain represent the triumph of squeamishness, of resentment, of purism and moral intolerance, of the need for rigid control and total order. It is precisely in such an atmosphere of moral absolutes that the ends could be viewed as justifying any means. To impose such a vision of order requires doing violence to life itself. Too convinced of their own virtue, *völkisch* ideologues lacked the moral under-standing that could come only from insight into their own nature and into the nature of their society. The ideological road to National Socialism was paved not by Nietzschean self-awareness and self-overcoming, but by *völkisch* self-congratulation.

NOTES

CHAPTER ONE

1. Jean F. Neurohr, *Der Mythos vom dritten Reich*, pp. 13–26.
2. Edmond Vermeil, *Doctrinaires de la Révolution Allemande;* William M. McGovern, *From Luther to Hitler;* Rohan d'O. Butler, *The Roots of National Socialism, 1783–1933.*
3. Robert Anchor, *Germany Confronts Modernization*, pp. 3–58.
4. Hajo Holborn, "German Idealism in the Light of Social History," *Germany and Europe: Historical Essays*, pp. 1–32.
5. Fritz Stern has coined the term *Vulgäridealismus* for the idealization of material interests, *The Failure of Illiberalism*, pp. xxxvii, 17.
6. Paul de Lagarde, *Deutsche Schriften*, 5th ed., p. 408.
7. Hans v. Wolzogen to Heinrich v. Stein, 10 January 1884, *Heinrich von Steins Briefwechsel mit Hans von Wolzogen* (Berlin, 1914), p. 81.
8. Gerhard Kratzsch, *Kunstwart und Dürerbund* (Göttingen, 1969), pp. 310ff., uses the term *Gesinnungsantisemitismus* (best translated as "principled anti-Semitism") to describe the kind of anti-Semitism that seemed benign because it stood for opposition to immorality. See Chapter 8 for a more detailed discussion. For a suggestive analysis of anti-Semitism as the stifled longing for a more natural and expressive life, see H. Stuart Hughes, *The Sea Change*, pp. 160ff. For anti-Semitism in Germany, see also Uriel Tal, *Christians and Jews in Germany*, esp. pp. 235–59; Léon Poliakov, *The History of Anti-Semitism*, vol. 3, pp. 380–457; and George L. Mosse, *Toward the Final Solution*, esp. pp. 128–49.
9. Hermann Rauschning, *The Conservative Revolution*, p. 53
10. For *völkisch* ideology see Fritz Stern, *The Politics of Cultural Despair* and George L. Mosse, *The Crisis of German Ideology.* Armin Mohler, *Die konservative Revolution in Deutschland 1918–1932*, 2nd rev. ed., provides the most extensive biographical and bibliographic information on *völkisch* authors. For a representative statement of the *völkisch* world view, see Hermann Ullmann, *Das neunzehnte Jahrhundert.*
11. R. R. Ergang, *Herder and the Foundations of German Nationalism*, esp. pp. 82–112.
12. An effort to link Romanticism to National Socialism was undertaken by Peter Viereck, *Meta-Politics: From the Romantics to Hitler.*
13. J. G. Fichte, *Addresses to the German Nation*, p. 208.
14. Rolland Lutz, " 'Father' Jahn and His Teacher-Revolutionaries from the German Student Movement," Supplement to *The Journal of Modern History*, 48 (June, 1976).
15. Otto Pflanze, *Bismarck and the Development of Germany*, esp. pp. 8–14. For a good brief review of the history of the German Empire, see Peter G. J. Pulzer, "From Bismarck to the Present," in *Germany*, ed. Malcolm Pasley, esp. pp. 249–300.
16. Heinrich von Treitschke, *Politics*, vol. 1, esp. pp. 19ff.
17. Anchor, *Germany Confronts Modernization*, pp. 117–23.
18. For the consequences of the depression of 1873, see Hans Rosenberg, *Grosse Depression und Bismarckzeit* and his "Political and Social Consequences of the Great Depression of 1873–1896 in Central Europe," reprinted in *Imperial Germany*, ed. J. J. Sheehan, pp. 39–60.
19. Peter G. J. Pulzer, *The Rise of Political Anti-Semitism in Germany and Austria*, pp. 88–101.

20.   For a suggestive analysis of 1879 as a turning point in German history, see Geoffrey Barraclough, "A New View of German History," *New York Review of Books* (16 Nov. 1972), pp. 25–31.

21.   For "bourgeois feudalization," see Michael Stürmer, ed., *Das kaiserliche Deutschland*, esp. pp. 265ff., and Gerhard A. Ritter and Jürgen Kocka, eds., *Deutsche Sozialgeschichte*, vol. 2, esp. pp. 67ff. For the alliance of "rye and steel" as reflected in nineteenth-century German literature, see Ernest K. Bramstead, *Aristocracy and the Middle Classes in Germany*, pp. 228ff.

22.   Klaus Bergmann, *Agrarromantik und Grossstadtfeindschaft* (Meisenheim am Glan, 1970), pp. 33ff.

23.   Daniel Frymann [Heinrich Class], *Wenn ich der Kaiser wär'*, p. 208.

24.   For post-Bismarckian politics and Wilhelmine imperialism, see Dirk Stegmann, *Die Erben Bismarcks*; Klaus Wernecke, *Der Wille zur Weltgeltung*; and J. C. G. Röhl, *Germany Without Bismarck*.

25.   Pulzer, *The Rise of Political Anti-Semitism*, esp. pp. 118–26. See also Richard S. Levy, *The Downfall of the Anti-Semitic Political Parties in Imperial Germany*, pp. 225–53.

26.   For Austrian Pan-Germanism, see Andrew G. Whiteside, *The Socialism of Fools*, and Carl E. Schorske, "Politics in a New Key: An Austrian Triptych," *Journal of Modern History* 34 (December 1967): 343–86.

27.   A good description of the ideology of antimodernism may be found in Shulamit Volkov, *The Rise of Popular Antimodernism in Germany*, pp. 297–325. For an overview of the literature on modernization, see Henry A. Turner, Jr., "Fascism and Modernization," *World Politics* 24 (1972): 547–64.

28.   Stern, *The Failure of Illiberalism*, p. 45.

29.   For Wagner's social views, see especially Winfried Schüler, *Der Bayreuther Kreis von seiner Entstehung bis zum Ausgang der wilhelminischen Ära* (Münster, 1971), pp. 1–27, and Jacques Barzun, *Darwin, Marx, Wagner*, rev. 2nd ed., pp. 231–317. For Wagner's contributions to *völkisch* ideology, see Hans Kohn, *The Mind of Germany*, pp. 189–221, and Peter Viereck, *Meta-Politics*, pp. 90–143. For a refutation of interpretations linking Wagner to National Socialism, see George G. Windell, "Hitler, National Socialism, and Richard Wagner," *Journal of Central European Affairs*, 22 (Jan. 1963), 479–97. For a suggestive description of the Wagner cult, see Peter Gay, *Freud, Jews, and Other Germans*, pp. 189–230. See also William J. McGrath, *Dionysian Art and Populist Politics in Austria*, pp. 58–61, 87–99.

30.   Quoted in Houston Stewart Chamberlain, *Richard Wagner*, 5th ed. (Munich, 1910), p. 166.

31.   Ibid., p. 157.

32.   Carl E. Schorske, "The Quest for the Grail: Wagner and Morris," in *The Critical Spirit*, pp. 216–32.

33.   For Gobineau, see E. J. Young, *Gobineau und der Rassismus*, and Michael D. Biddiss, *Father of Racist Ideology*.

34.   Houston Stewart Chamberlain, *Die Grundlagen des neunzehnten Jahrhunderts*, 2 vols., 10th ed. (Munich, 1912).

35.   H. Stuart Hughes, "The German Idealist Tradition," in *Consciousness and Society*, pp. 33–66; George L. Mosse, *The Culture of Western Europe*, 2nd ed., pp. 203–33; Wilson H. Coates and Hayden V. White, *The Ordeal of Liberal Humanism*, pp. 253–91; Jan Romein, *The Watershed of Two Eras*, esp. pp. 461–77; and John Weiss, ed., *The Origins of Modern Consciousness*, pp. 11–24.

36.   Friedrich Lienhard, *Neue Ideale nebst Vorherrschaft Berlins*, 4th ed. (Stuttgart, 1920), p. 105.

37.   H. S. Chamberlain, *Mensch und Gott* (Munich, 1921), pp. 15–16.

38.   Walter Z. Laqueur, *Young Germany*. For a more sympathetic account of the Youth

Movement, see Jakob Müller, *Die Jugendbewegung als deutsche Hauptrichtung neukonservativer Reform*.

39. Ernst Troeltsch, "Die Ideen von 1914," in *Deutscher Geist und Westeuropa*, pp. 31–58; see also Klemens von Klemperer, *Germany's New Conservatism*, pp. 47–55.

40. Fritz Fischer, *Germany's Aims in the First World War*, esp. pp. 3–92.

CHAPTER TWO

1. Günter Ralfs, ed., *Heinrich von Stein, Idee und Welt* provides a biography and excerpts from Stein's works. Houston Stewart Chamberlain eulogized Stein in "Un Philosophe wagnérien: Heinrich von Stein," *Revue des deux Mondes*, 831–58. The German version of this article was published with an essay by Freidrich Poske, the editor of Stein's posthumously published works, in *Heinrich von Stein und seine Weltanschauung* (Leipzig, 1903). An article on Stein by Ferdinand Jakob Schmidt was included in *Allgemeine Deutsche Biographie*, pp. 456–59. Stein personified the link between the traditions of Bayreuth and classical Weimar for Friedrich Lienhard, *Wege nach Weimar* (Stuttgart, 1905–1908), vol. 1, pp. 55–150. G. H. Wahnes, *Heinrich von Stein und sein Verhältnis zu Richard Wagner und Friedrich Nietzsche*, used Stein's works to promote the *völkisch* view in uncritical fashion. The Hegelian scholar Hermann Glockner's brief essay, *Heinrich von Stein, Schicksal einer deutschen Jugend*, offers a more convincing treatment within the *völkisch* frame of reference. The postwar literature on Heinrich von Stein is limited to a brief appraisal of Stein's career in Schüler, *Der Bayreuther Kreis*, pp. 94–98.

2. Glockner, *Heinrich von Stein*, p. 6.

3. Ibid., p. 474; Ralfs, *Idee und Welt*, p. 10; Nietzsche to Peter Gast, 27 June 1887, in *Werke in drei Bänden*, ed. Karl Schlechta, vol. 3 (Munich, 1956), p. 1258; Malvida von Meysenbug, *Memoiren einer Idealistin*, vol. 2 (Stuttgart, 1922), p. 305.

4. Quoted in Adelheid von Schorn, *Zwei Menschenalter, Erinnerungen und Briefe* (Berlin, 1901), p. 476.

5. Ralfs, *Idee und Welt*, p. 10.

6. Ibid., pp. 14–16.

7. Ibid., p. 26.

8. See Chapter 3.

9. Elisabeth Förster-Nietzsche, *Das Leben Friedrich Nietzsche's*, vol. 2, p. 495.

10. Meysenbug, *Memoiren*, pp. 304–5; Schorn, *Zwei Menschenalter*, p. 345.

11. Ralfs, *Idee und Welt*, pp. 102ff.; Chamberlain and Poske, *Heinrich von Stein*, pp. 11ff.

12. Ralfs, *Idee und Welt*, pp. 104 ff.

13. Stein to Wolzogen, 28 May 1883, in Hans von Wolzogen, ed., *Heinrich von Steins Briefwechsel*, p. 68.

14. Various versions of Stein's writings on Bruno were published in *Bayreuther Blätter* (1881); *Schmeitzners Internationale Mouatsschrift*, 1 (1882), nos. 1–3; and in book form under the title *Giordano Bruno*, ed. Friedrich Poske (Leipzig, 1900).

15. Ralfs, *Idee und Welt*, p. 115.

16. Ibid., pp. 197–98, 203, 212; Wahnes, *Heinrich von Stein*, pp. 54, 70.

17. Ralfs, *Idee und Welt*, pp. 205ff.

18. A collection of Stein's articles in *Bayreuther Blätter* was published in *Zur Kultur der Seele*, ed. Friedrich Poske (Stuttgart, 1906).

19. Quoted in Wahnes, *Heinrich von Stein*, p. 154.

20. Stein to Daniela v. Bülow, 1 October 1884, in Wahnes, *Heinrich von Stein*, p. 98.

21. Chamberlain to Cosima Wagner, 11 December 1896, in Ralfs, *Idee und Welt*, p. 391.
22. Nietzsche to Overbeck, 30 June 1887, ibid., p. 388.
23. Hermann Bahr, *Selbstbildnis*, p. 181.

CHAPTER THREE

1. Dühring's most important early works are *Der Werth des Lebens* (Leipzig, 1865); *Kritische Geschichte der Nationalökonomie und des Sozialismus* (Leipzig, 1871); *Kritische Geschichte der allgemeinen Prinzipien der Mechanik* (Leipzig, 1873); and *Cursus der Philosophie als streng wissenschaftliche Weltanschauung und Lebensgestaltung* (Leipzig, 1875). The last was revised and reissued as *Wirklichkeitsphilosophie* (Leipzig, 1895). For an overview of Dühring's career, see Gerd-Klaus Kaltenbrunner, "Vom Konkurrenten des Karl Marx zum Vorläufer Hitlers: Eugen Dühring," in *Propheten des Nationalismus* (Munich, 1969), pp. 36–55.
2. Friedrich Engels, *Herrn Eugen Dührings Umwälzung der Wissenschaft (Anti-Dühring)*. For a discussion of Dühring's social views, see Peter Gay, *The Dilemma of Democratic Socialism*, pp. 83–92, and Eugene Lunn, *Prophet of Community*, pp. 57–63, 68–69.
3. Dühring's main anti-Semitic tract, issued in numerous revised editions, is *Die Judenfrage als Frage der Rassenschädlichkeit für Existenz, Sitte und Kultur der Völker* (Karlsruhe, 1880). See Uriel Tal, *Christians and Jews in Germany*, pp. 264–66.
4. Dühring, *Wirklichkeitsphilosophie, passim.; Der Ersatz der Religion durch Vollkommeneres und die Ausscheidung alles Judenthums durch den modernen Völkergeist* (Karlsruhe, 1883), *passim.*
5. Chamberlain and Poske, *Heinrich von Stein*, p. 23.
6. Dühring, *Der Wert des Lebens*, 3rd ed. (Leipzig, 1881), p. 129.
7. Stein to Wolzogen, 5 November 1881, *Briefwechsel*, p. 30. Stein reviewed Dühring's autobiography, *Leben, Sache und Feinde* (Karlsruhe, 1882), in Schmeitzner's anti-Semitic *Internationale Monatsschrift*, 1 (1882), No. 4.
8. Chamberlain and Poske, *Heinrich von Stein*, p. 30.
9. Stein, *Über Wahrnehmung* (Berlin, 1877), quoted in Ralfs, *Idee und Welt*, p. 39.
10. W. M. Simon, *European Positivism in the Nineteenth Century* (Ithaca, N.Y., 1963), p. 4.
11. Stein, *Die Ideale des Materialismus* (1878), repr. in vol. 1 of *Gesammelte Dichtungen*, ed. Friedrich Poske (Leipzig, 1917), p. 3.
12. Stein, "Über Werke und Wirkungen Rousseaus," in *Zur Kultur der Seele*, pp. 41–56.
13. Stein, *Giordano Bruno*, p. 81.
14. Ibid., pp. 89–90.
15. Ibid., pp. 90–91.
16. Houston Stewart Chamberlain, *Immanuel Kant* (Munich, 1905), pp. 279–394.
17. Stein, *Helden und Welt*, vol. 2 of *Gesammelte Dichtungen*, p. 217.
18. Ibid.
19. Ibid., p. 32.
20. Ibid., p. 28.
21. Chamberlain, *Die Grundlagen des neunzehnten Jahrhunderts*, 21st ed. (Munich, 1936), vol. 1, p. 368.
22. Carl Friedrich Glasenapp and Heinrich von Stein, *Wagner-Lexikon* (Stuttgart, 1883), p. viii.
23. Stein, *Helden und Welt*, pp. 168–69.

24. Dühring, *Der Ersatz der Religion*, p. 55.

25. Stein, *Helden und Welt*, pp. 168–69.

26. Stein, "Luther und die Bauern," in *Zur Kultur der Seele*, pp. 57–80.

27. Ralfs, *Idee und Welt*, p. 309. For a discussion of conservative opposition to urbanization, see Bergmann, *Agrarromantik und Grossstadtfeindschaft, passim*.

28. Wahnes, *Heinrich von Stein*, p. 82.

29. Stein, *Helden und Welt*, pp. 226–27.

30. Stein, *Dramatische Bilder und Erzählungen*, vol. 3 of *Gesammelte Dichtungen*, p. 197.

31. Stein, *Karl Ludwig Sand*, ed. R. Buchwald (Willsbach, 1947).

32. See Richard Hamann and Jost Hermand, *Gründerzeit*, vol. 1 of *Deutsche Kunst und Kultur von der Gründerzeit bis zum Expressionismus* (East Berlin, 1965; repr. Munich, 1971).

CHAPTER FOUR

1. Chamberlain and Poske, *Heinrich von Stein*, p. 50; Lienhard, *Wege nach Weimar*, vol. 1, p. 89.

2. Stein, *Die Entstehung der neueren Ästhetik* (1886; repr. Hildesheim, 1964), pp. 6ff. Hereafter *Ästhetik*, with page references in text. For Chamberlain's commentary on Descartes, see his *Immanuel Kant*, pp. 176–275.

3. Julius Langbehn, *Rembrandt als Erzieher* (Leipzig, 1890).

4. See Schüler, *Der Bayreuther Kreis*, pp. 193–98.

5. Ibid., p. 405; Chamberlain, *Die Grundlagen*, vol. 2, p. 153.

6. Stein, *Goethe und Schiller* (Leipzig, 1893).

7. See Lienhard, *Wege nach Weimar*, vol. 6, and Chamberlain, *Goethe* (Munich, 1912).

8. Stein, *Goethe und Schiller*, p. 81.

9. Ibid., p. 50.

10. Ibid., p. 51.

11. Schüler, *Der Bayreuther Kreis*, p. 97.

12. For a discussion of the "conservative revolution," see Chapter 9.

13. Stein, *Vorlesungen über Aesthetik* (Stuttgart, 1897), p. 48.

14. Ibid., p. 60.

15. Ibid., p. 142.

16. Stein, "Schopenhauer-Scholien," in *Zur Kultur der Seele*, pp. 304–42.

17. Stein, "Schopenhauer-Scholien," cited in Ralfs, *Idee und Welt*, p. 290.

18. Ibid., pp. 251ff.

19. For the "culture of rejection," see Robert Anchor, *Germany Confronts Modernization*, pp. 117ff.

CHAPTER FIVE

1. Walter A. Kaufmann, *Nietzsche*, 3rd ed. (New York, 1968), p. 47.

2. Chamberlain and Poske, *Heinrich von Stein*, p. 1; Lienhard, *Wege nach Weimar*, vol. 1, pp. 71ff.

3. Elisabeth Förster-Nietzsche, *Das Leben Friedrich Nietzsche's*, vol. 2 (Leipzig, 1904), p. 499.

4. Wahnes, *Heinrich von Stein*, pp. 95ff.

5. Paul Rée to Nietzsche, June-July 1876, in Ernst Pfeiffer, ed., *Friedrich Nietzsche, Paul Rée, Lou von Salomé* (Frankfurt/Main, 1970), p. 15.

6. The correspondence between Nietzsche and Stein was first published by Elisabeth Förster-Nietzsche, "Friedrich Nietzsche und Heinrich von Stein," in *Neue Deutsche Rundschau* (*Freie Bühne*), 11 (1900), 747-62.

7. Nietzsche to Stein, undated [1882], ibid., p. 748. The last sentence of this passage reads: "Dies ist etwas *Unschätzbares*, vorausgesetzt, dass es seine Zeit hat." The deliberate ambiguity of the phrase, "dass es seine Zeit hat," suggests both, "provided the time for it is right," and "provided it is of limited duration."

8. Nietzsche to Stein, early December 1882, ibid., p. 748.

9. Ibid.

10. Ibid., pp. 748-49.

11. Ibid., p. 749.

12. Nietzsche to Ida Overbeck, 29 July 1883, Pfeiffer, *Friedrich Nietzsche, Paul Rée, Lou von Salomé*, p. 329.

13. Stein to Wolzogen, 14 October 1883, Ralfs, *Idee und Welt*, p. 152.

14. Nietzsche to Franz Overbeck, 14 September 1884, ibid., p. 160; Nietzsche to Peter Gast, 2 September 1884, in Karl Schlechta, ed., *Friedrich Nietzsche: Werke in drei Bänden* (Munich, 1956), vol. 3, p. 1222.

15. Nietzsche to Stein, 22 May 1884, ibid., p. 1220.

16. Ibid., p. 1221.

17. Nietzsche to Overbeck, 14 September 1884, Ralfs, *Idee und Welt*, p. 160.

18. Ibid.

19. Nietzsche to Stein, 18 September 1884, Schlechta, *Nietzsche: Werke*, vol. 3, p. 1223.

20. Nietzsche, *Ecce Homo*, trans. Walter Kaufmann (New York: Vintage, 1967), p. 227.

21. Nietzsche to Overbeck, 14 September 1884, Ralfs, *Idee und Welt*, p. 161.

22. Stein to Daniela v. Bülow, 31 August 1884, ibid., p. 158.

23. Stein to Wolzogen, 27 November 1884, ibid., p. 162.

24. Stein to Nietzsche, 24 September 1884, Förster-Nietzsche, "Nietzsche und Stein," p. 755.

25. Nietzsche to Stein, November 1884, Ralfs, *Idee und Welt*, p. 166. Translation of poem by Walter Kaufmann in Nietzsche, *Beyond Good and Evil* (New York, 1966), p. 241.

26. Stein to Nietzsche, 1 December 1884, Ralfs, *Idee und Welt*, p. 168.

27. Ibid., p. 169. Nietzsche's reference to Philoctetes occurs in his letter to Stein, 18 September 1884. Lou Salomé and Paul Rée may have been the other members of Stein's discussion group, although Stein makes no mention of this in his letter. If Nietzsche suspected this, as is suggested by Rudolph Binion, *Frau Lou*, p. 127, he had additional reason to be annoyed.

28. Nietzsche to Elisabeth Nietzsche, December 1884, Ralfs, *Idee und Welt*, p. 170. Although this and the following letter to his sister (see fn. 31) are among those cited by Karl Schlechta as containing changes made by his sister (*Nietzsche: Werke*, vol. 3, p. 1375), the passages referring to Stein appear to be authentic. Förster-Nietzsche had no motive to exaggerate her brother's disappointment with Stein, since she was anxious to portray them as like-minded battlers in a common cause.

29. Ralfs, *Idee und Welt*, p. 170.

30. Nietzsche to M. v. Meysenbug, 13 March 1885, Schlechta, *Nietzsche: Werke*, vol. 3, p. 1230.

31. Nietzsche to Elisabeth Nietzsche, March 1885, Glockner, *Heinrich von Stein*, p. 42. Stein had visited Nietzsche's sister in Naumburg earlier that year and had expressed his hope of seeing Nietzsche that summer (Förster-Nietzsche, "Nietzsche und Stein," p. 758).

32. Stein to M. v. Meysenbug, 11 January 1885, Ralfs, *Idee und Welt*, p. 171.

33. Diary entry, 30 September 1885, ibid., p. 172.

34. Stein to Nietzsche, 7 October 1885, ibid., pp. 172–73.

35. Nietzsche to Stein, 15 October 1885, Schlechta, *Nietzsche: Werke*, vol. 3, p. 1237.

36. Ibid. The last phrase in this passage, "denn eines schickt sich durchaus nicht für zweie," is a variation on the proverb, "denn eines schickt sich nicht für alle" ("the same thing will not do for all").

37. Nietzsche to M. v. Meysenbug, 30 July 1887, Ralfs, *Idee und Welt*, p. 388.

38. Nietzsche, *Der Fall Wagner*, in G. Colli and M. Montinari, ed., *Nietzsche, Werke*, vol. 6 (Berlin, 1969), p. 38.

39. Ibid., pp. 28, 30.

40. Nietzsche, *Ecce Homo*, pp. 317–18.

41. See the discussion of idealist anti-Semitism in Chapter 8.

42. Stein, *"Weltpolitik* von C. Frantz," *Schmeitzners Internationale Monatsschrift*, 1 (1882), 517.

43. Nietzsche, *Ecce Homo*, p. 321.

44. Ibid., p. 322.

45. Significantly, only the works of the younger Nietzsche could be readily constrained into *völkisch* ideology. See, for instance, Wilhelm Laubenthal, *Der Gedanke einer Geistigen Erneuerung Deutschlands im deutschen Schrifttum von 1871 bis zum Weltkrieg* (Frankfurt/Main, 1938), pp. 19 ff.

CHAPTER SIX

1. The best source of information on Lienhard's career is an adulatory biography by his protégé Paul Bülow, *Friedrich Lienhard, der Mensch und das Werk*. Lienhard's memoirs, *Jugendjahre, Erinnerungen*, 10th ed. (Stuttgart, 1918), provide detailed information only up to 1900. See also Karl Gruber, "Dichter-Erzieher, anlässlich eines Thüringer Tagebuchs von Fritz Lienhard," *Hochland* 1 (5 February 1905), 572–86, and Albert Soergel, *Dichtung und Dichter der Zeit*, vol. 1, 21st ed., pp. 879–91. Heavily biased sources are Hellmuth Langenbucher, *Friedrich Lienhard und sein Anteil am Kampf um die deutsche Erneuerung*, and Wilhelm Laubenthal, *Der Gedanke einer geistigen Erneuerung Deutschlands*, both published in the Nazi period. For a discussion of *Heimatkunst*, see Karlheinz Rossbacher, *Heimatkunstbewegung und Heimatroman*; Klaus Bergmann, *Agrarromantik und Grossstadtfeindschaft*, pp. 102–21; and Richard Hamann and Jost Hermand, *Epochen deutscher Kultur von 1870 bis zur Gegenwart*, vol. 4, *Stilkunst um 1900*, pp. 364–94.

2. For a discussion of the kind of readership to which writers like Lienhard appealed, see Gerhard Kratzsch, *Kunstwart und Dürerbund*, esp. pp. 336ff., and Karlheinz Rossbacher, *Heimatkunstbewegung*, pp. 93–98.

3. In this affair, the military commander of the Zabern district was accused of highhanded action in the detention of civilians.

4. Lienhard, *Jugendjahre*, p. 18.

5. Ibid., pp. 36, 68ff.

6. Ibid., pp. 26ff.

7. Ibid., p. 50.

8. Ibid., p. 67.

9. Wilhelm Arent, Hermann Conradi, and Karl Henckell, eds., *Moderne Dichter-Charaktere* (Leipzig, 1884). For a discussion of this influential work see Albert Soergel, *Dichtung und Dichter der Zeit*, pp. 91ff.

10. See Chapter 7.

11. For a discussion of *Naphtali*, see Adalbert von Hanstein, *Das jüngste Deutschland. Zwei Jahrzehnte miterlebter Litteraturgeschichte*, pp. 135–37.

12. Lienhard, *Jugendjahre*, pp. 160, 185; Bülow, *Friedrich Lienhard*, p. 116.

13. Lienhard, *Jugendjahre*, p. 165.

14. Ibid., p. 184.

15. Julius Langbehn, *Rembrandt als Erzieher, von einem Deutschen* (Leipzig, 1890). For a discussion of Langbehn's influence, see Fritz Stern, *The Politics of Cultural Despair*, pp. 131–227.

16. Lienhard, *Wasgaufahrten*, 23rd ed. (Stuttgart, n.d.), p. 13.

17. Ibid., pp. 13–14.

18. Ibid., pp. 57, 146–47. See Fritz Stern, "The Political Consequences of the Unpolitical German," *History* 3 (September 1960), 104–34.

19. Ibid., p. 3.

20. Bülow, *Friedrich Lienhard*, pp. 247, 252ff.

21. Bergmann, *Agrarromantik und Grossstadtfeindschaft*, p. 110.

22. Bülow, *Friedrich Lienhard*, pp. 155, 236.

23. Lienhard, *Neue Ideale nebst Vorherrschaft Berlins*, pp. 54, 66, 87–88, 92–93, 183.

24. For the dispute between Lienhard and Lublinski, see Erich Ruprecht and Dieter Bänsch, eds., *Literarische Manifeste der Jahrhundertwende, 1890–1910*, pp. 344–49.

25. Lienhard, *Neue Ideale nebst Vorherrschaft Berlins*, p. 107.

26. See Armin Mohler, *Die konservative Revolution in Deutschland, 1918–1932*, 2nd rev. ed. (Darmstadt, 1972), pp. 40–57, 364 (on Lienhard). See also Chapter 9.

27. For an account of this controversy, see Bülow, *Friedrich Lienhard*, pp. 240ff, and Karl Muth, "Oberflächen-Kultur," *Hochland* 1 (November 1903), 233–37. For a biography of Avenarius, see Kratzsch, *Kunstwart und Dürerbund*.

28. Lienhard, *Thüringer Tagebuch* (Stuttgart, 1910), pp. 52ff.

29. Ibid., p. 195.

30. See Chapter 7.

31. For a discussion of the grail motif at the turn of the century, see Jost Hermand, "Gralmotive um die Jahrhundertwende," in *Von Mainz nach Weimar (1793–1919), Studien zur deutschen Literatur*, pp. 269–97.

32. *Deutsches Bücherverzeichnis* (Graz, 1961), vol. 18, p. 105; Donald Ray Richards, *The German Bestseller in the 20th Century*, p. 62.

33. According to Mohler, *Die konservative Revolution*, p. 384, Wachler, one of whose parents was Jewish, was killed in the concentration camp Theresienstadt in 1944. Wilhelm Kosch, *Deutsches Literatur-Lexikon*, 2nd ed., vol. 4 (Bern, 1958), indicates that Wachler died in a refugee camp in October 1945. This is also the date given in Ruprecht and Bänsch, *Literarische Manifeste*, p. 328.

34. Lienhard, *Der deutsche Elsass* (Stuttgart, 1914), p. 31. For a discussion of the "ideas of 1914," see Klemens von Klemperer, *Germany's New Conservatism* (Princeton, N.J., 1968), pp. 47–55.

35. Lienhard, *Der deutsche Elsass*, p. 21.

36. Lienhard, *Unter dem Rosenkreuz* (Stuttgart, 1925), p. 87.

37. Wilhelm E. Gierke, ed., *Friedrich Lienhard und Wir. Dem deutschen Dichter Friedrich Lienhard zum 50. Geburtstage*.

38. Adolf Bartels, *Die deutsche Dichtung der Gegenwart*, p. 48.

CHAPTER SEVEN

1. Karl Bleibtreu, *Revolution der Literatur*.

2. Bleibtreu, "Religion und Rasse," *Der Türmer*, 26 (October 1924), 19–26.

3. See Winthrop H. Root, *German Criticism of Zola, 1875–1893*, pp. 44ff., and Vernon L. Lidtke, "Naturalism and Socialism in Germany," *American Historical Review*, 79 (February 1974), 14–37.

4. Bleibtreu, *Grössenwahn. Pathologischer Roman*, 2nd ed., vol. 1, pp. i–ii; Lienhard, *Jugendjahre*, pp. 161ff.

5. Lienhard, "Reformation der Literatur," *Die Gesellschaft*, 4 (June 1888), 148.

6. Ibid., pp. 228ff. "Der Geist des Künstlers wiegt mehr als das Werk seiner Kunst."

7. Ibid., p. 152.

8. Ibid., p. 153.

9. Ibid., pp. 153–54.

10. Bülow, *Friedrich Lienhard*, p. 99.

11. Quoted in Bülow, *Friedrich Lienhard*, pp. 70–80.

12. Lienhard, *Jugendjahre*, p. 178; for a discussion of the opposition to Otto Brahm, see Soergel, *Dichtung und Dichter der Zeit*, p. 215.

13. Lienhard, *Neue Ideale*, pp. 51–52.

14. Ibid., pp. 54ff.

15. Ibid., pp. 56ff.

16. Lienhard, "Bedenken wider Ibsen," *Hochland*, 1 (November 1903), 160–66. Lienhard commemorated another literary anniversary in the same negative way in 1925. On the occasion of Thomas Mann's fiftieth birthday he accused Mann of infatuation with sickness and decline. See Langenbucher, *Friedrich Lienhard*, p. 50.

17. Lienhard, *Neue Ideale*, p. 149.

18. Langbehn, *Rembrandt als Erzieher*, 56–60th ed. (Leipzig, 1922), p. 264.

19. Lienhard, *Neue Ideale*, p. 155.

20. Ibid., pp. 150ff.

21. Ibid., pp. 170–71, 183ff.

22. Lienhard, *Wege nach Weimar*, vol. 1, p. 244; vol. 2, p. 241; vol. 4, p. 31.

23. Ibid., vol. 1, p. 18.

24. Lienhard, *Neue Ideale*, p. 229; *Wege nach Weimar*, vol. 2, pp. 10ff.

CHAPTER EIGHT

1. Stern, *Politics of Cultural Despair*, p. 311.

2. Lienhard, *Wege nach Weimar*, vol. 3, p. 191. For works using the Third Reich in their titles, see the novel by Johannes Schlaf, *Das Dritte Reich*, and Paul Friedrich, *Das Dritte Reich. Die Tragödie des Individualismus*, a play about Nietzsche, Wagner, and Heinrich von Stein. The term received a political coloration through the postwar book by Arthur Möller van den Bruck, *Das Dritte Reich* (Berlin, 1923). See also Jean F. Neurohr, *Der Mythos vom dritten Reich*.

3. Lienhard, *Wege nach Weimar*, vol. 3, p. 190.

4. Anchor, *Germany Confronts Modernization*, pp. 118ff.

5. Lienhard, *Wege nach Weimar*, vol. 2, p. 35.

6. Ibid., vol. 3, p. 50.

7. Ibid., vol. 6, pp. 27–28, 107.

8. For Chamberlain's *Goethe*, see Chapter 12; Möller van den Bruck, *Goethe* (Minden in Westfalen, 1907); Bartels, *Goethe der Deutsche*. For a provocative analysis of how the Goethe cult in Germany helped to obliterate distinctions between classes previously hostile to each other, see Bramstead, *Aristocracy and the Middle Classes in Germany*, pp. 279, 320.

9. "Höchstes Glück der Erdenkinder ist nur die Persönlichkeit."

10. Lienhard, *Neue Ideale*, p. 117.

11. Lienhard, *Wege nach Weimar*, vol. 3, p. 183.

12. For a suggestive discussion of authoritarian and elitist values in Wilhelmine Germany, see Walter Struve, *Elites Against Democracy*.

13. Lienhard, *Wege nach Weimar*, vol. 3, p. 177.

14. Ibid., vol. 2, p. 226.

15. Ibid., vol. 1, pp. 44–46; vol. 2, p. 226; vol. 5, pp. 8ff. For a persuasive analysis of Gobineau's racial doctrine as a reflection of chagrin at the erosion of aristocratic prerogatives, see Biddiss, *Father of Racist Ideology*, pp. 154ff.

16. Lienhard's relative moderation on race led Armin Mohler, *Die konservative Revolution*, p. 215, to conclude that Lienhard was not anti-Semitic. But this narrow definition of anti-Semitism excludes all but its racial forms. For a discussion of anti-Semitism in nineteenth-century German literature, see Bramstead, *Aristocracy and the Middle Classes in Germany*, pp. 132ff.

17. Lienhard, *Neue Ideale*, p. 43.

18. Lienhard, *Wege nach Weimar*, vol. 2, p. 83.

19. Lienhard, *Ahasver am Rhein, Trauerspiel aus der Gegenwart* (Stuttgart, 1914).

20. Lienhard, *Jugendjahre*, p. 18.

21. Lienhard, *Unter dem Rosenkreuz*, pp. 6–7.

22. Lienhard, *Wege nach Weimar*, vol. 4, pp. 5, 148.

23. Ibid., vol. 2, p. 158.

24. Lienhard, *Unter dem Rosenkreuz*, p. 13.

25. Lienhard, *Wege nach Weimar*, vol. 5, p. 244.

26. Ibid., vol. 2, p. 244.

27. Lienhard, *Der Meister der Menschheit*, vol. 3 (Stuttgart, 1921), p. 225.

CHAPTER NINE

1. In his *Die konservative Revolution*, Armin Mohler uses the term "conservative revolution" to distinguish the political thought of such *völkisch* idealists as Lienhard from the political opportunism of the Nazis, for whom considerations of power outweighed principle. Although Mohler's distinction helps to explain how barbarism could emerge from a refined cultural tradition, it tends to obscure the fateful contributions that *völkisch* idealists made to the triumph of Nazism in Germany. The term "conservative revolution" gained currency after it was used in an address by Hugo von Hofmannsthal, "Das Schrifttum als geistiger Raum der Nation" (Munich, 1927), to describe the quest for unity and wholeness. Hermann Rauschning used the phrase as the title of his book, *Die Konservative Revolution, Versuch und Bruch mit Hitler* (New York, 1941), translated as *The Conservative Revolution* (New York, 1941).

2. Lienhard, *Neue Ideale*, p. 108; *Unter dem Rosenkreuz*, p. 199.

3. Lienhard, *Wege nach Weimar*, vol. 6, p. 96.

4. Lienhard, *Der Spielmann, Roman aus der Gegenwart*, 10th ed. (Stuttgart, 1912), pp. 154, 179.

5. Ibid., pp. 16, 183, 199.

6. Ibid., p. 215.

7. Ibid., pp. 182, 187.

8. Lienhard, *Westmark, Roman aus dem gegenwärtigen Elsass*, 24th ed. (Stuttgart, 1919), p. 47.

9. Ibid., p. 188.

10. Ibid., p. 189.

11. Lienhard, *Meisters Vermächtnis, ein Roman vom heimlichen König*, 3rd ed. (Stuttgart, 1927), p. 39.

12. See Hans Kohn, *The Mind of Germany* (New York: Harper & Row, 1965), pp. 3–7.

13. Lienhard, *Meisters Vermächtnis*, p. 266.

14. Apparently a reference to the *Berliner Tageblatt*. Published by Rudolph Mosse, this liberal daily was a favorite target of *völkisch* authors.

15. *Der Türmer*, 24 (November 1921), 143.

16. *Der Türmer*, 26 (January 1924), 279.

17. Adolf Bartels, *Der völkische Gedanke. Ein Wegweiser*, p. 29.

18. Lienhard, *Meisters Vermächtnis*, p. 17.

19. Lienhard, *Unter dem Rosenkreuz*, p. 121. "Rembrandt-German" refers to Langbehn (see Chapter 6).

20. See George L. Mosse, *The Crisis of German Ideology*, p. 295.

21. Lienhard, *Unter dem Rosenkreuz*, pp. 61–62.

22. Lienhard, *Meisters Vermachtnis*, p. 41.

23. Lienhard, *Unter dem Rosenkreuz*, p. 117.

24. Hellmuth Langenbucher, *Friedrich Lienhard und sein Anteil am Kampf um die deutsche Erneuerung* (Hamburg, 1935), p. 157.

25. Ibid., pp. 152, 156.

CHAPTER TEN

1. *Kölnische Zeitung*, 4 November 1906, quoted in Lienhard, *Wege nach Weimar*, vol. 3, pp. 198–99.

2. Heinrich Class, *Wider den Strom*, pp. 87–88; Moeller van den Bruck, *Die Zeitgenossen* (Minden i. w., 1906), pp. 99–121; Robert Cecil, *The Myth of the Master Race* (New York, 1972), p. 12.

3. A selection of contemporary reviews, most of them favorable, of Chamberlain's works were published in Oscar Bulle et al., *Die Grundlagen des neunzehnten Jahrhunderts und Immanuel Kant, Kritische Urteile*, 3rd ed. (Munich, 1909). Chamberlain's interpretation of Dante's religious conceptions was disputed by Hermann Grauert, *Dante und Chamberlain*, 2nd ed. (Freiburg, 1904). Chamberlain's attacks on Judaism were countered by D. Baentsch, "Chamberlains Vorstellungen über die Religion der Semiten spez. der Israeliten," *Zeitschrift fur Philosophie und Pädagogik* 12 (1904–1905), 16–28, 124–39, 204–21, 291–306. Chamberlain's works were denounced by the French philosopher Ernest Seillière during World War I, *Houston Stewart Chamberlain*. D. R. H. Grützmacher criticized Chamberlain's religious doctrine from an orthodox Lutheran frame of reference in *Kritiker und Neuschöpfer der Religion im zwanzigsten Jahrhundert*. For an incisive critique of Chamberlain's racial theories, see Friedrich Hertz, *Race and Civilization*, trans. A. S. Levetus and W. Entz (1928; repr. KTAV Publ. House, 1970).

4. The phrase stems from the title of a book of selections from Chamberlain's works edited by Georg Schott, *Houston Stewart Chamberlain, der Seher des dritten Reiches*. Other works by the same author include *Das Lebenswerk Chamberlains in Umrissen*, and *Das Vermächtnis Houston Stewart Chamberlains*. The first of these two works is of interest for its use of Chamberlain's works to repudiate the pessimism of Oswald Spengler. Two works by Alfred Rosenberg, *Chamberlain als Verkünder und Begründer einer deutschen Zukunft*, and *Blut und Ehre. Ein Kampf für deutsche Wiedergeburt*, testify to the influence of Chamberlain on National Socialists. The most useful work from a *völkisch* frame of reference is Hugo Meyer's scholarly *Chamberlain als völkischer Denker*. A bibliography of Chamberlain's

works was assembled by Albert Vanselow, *Das Werk Chamberlains*. Of the large number of monographs and dissertations spawned during the Nazi period, the following were consulted in the preparation of this study: Wilhelm Vollrath, *Thomas Carlyle und Chamberlain. Zwei Freunde Deutschlands* and *Chamberlain und seine Theologie*; Martin Dippel, *Chamberlain*; Gerhard Stutzinger, *Die politischen Anschauungen Chamberlains*; Will Nielsen, *Der Lebens- und Gestaltbegriff bei Chamberlain*; Adolf Geprägs, *Germanentum und Christentum bei Chamberlain*; Waltraut Eckhart, *Chamberlains Naturanschauung;* and Rudolf Grabs, *Wegbereiter Deutschen Christentums, Paul de Lagarde und Chamberlain.*

5. For a critical discussion of Chamberlain's racial doctrine, see Jean Réal, "The Religious Conception of Race: Chamberlain and Germanic Christianity," in *The Third Reich*, pp. 243–86. See also Georg Lukács, *Die Zerstörung der Vernunft*, pp. 551–65; Max Rouché, "H. S. Chamberlain," *Études Germaniques* 17 (1962), 390–402; Heinrich Ritter von Srbik, *Geist und Geschichte vom deutschen Humanismus bis zur Gegenwart*, 2nd ed., vol. 2, pp. 355–57; Jean F. Neurohr, *Der Mythos vom dritten Reich*, pp. 147–49; William L. Shirer, *The Rise and Fall of the Third Reich*, pp. 104–9; George L. Mosse, *The Crisis of German Ideology*, pp. 93–98; Ernst Nolte, *Three Faces of Fascism*, trans. Leila Vennewitz, pp. 282–86; and Peter Viereck, *Metapolitics*, 2nd ed. (New York, 1961), pp. 147–50; Gerd-Klaus Kaltenbrunner, "Chamberlain—The Most Germanic of Germans," *Wiener Library Bulletin* 22 (Winter 1967–68), 6–12, and "Wahnfried und die Grundlagen: Houston Stewart Chamberlain," in *Propheten des Nationalismus*, ed. Karl Schwedhelm, pp. 105–23. Kaltenbrunner argues that Chamberlain's racial doctrine may, like Hitler's, have originated in his experience of racial tensions in Vienna, a suggestion reiterated by William M. Johnston, *The Austrian Mind*, pp. 328–32. E. J. Young, *Gobineau und der Rassismus,* emphasizes the derivative nature of Chamberlain's racial doctrine. Chamberlain's *Grundlagen* are analyzed by Winfried Schüler, *Der Bayreuther Kreis*, pp. 112–27 and 252–67. George L. Mosse has written a critical introduction to the latest edition in English of *The Foundations of the Nineteenth Century*, 2 vols., trans. John Lees (1910; repr. New York, 1968).

6. On the "identity crisis," see Erik H. Erikson, *Childhood and Society*, 2nd ed., pp. 247–74, 326–58. The best published source for biographic information are Chamberlain's own memoirs, *Lebenswege meines Denkens* (Munich, 1919), as well as three volumes of letters, *Briefe 1882–1924 und Briefwechsel mit Kaiser Wilhelm II*, 2 vols., and *Cosima Wagner und Chamberlain im Briefwechsel, 1888–1908*, ed. Paul Pretzsch. An excellent source of information on Chamberlain's personal life is a plainly written but moving volume of memoirs by his first wife Anna Chamberlain, *Meine Erinnerungen an Houston Stewart Chamberlain* (Munich, 1918); memoirs by Hermann von Keyserling, *Reise durch die Zeit* (Innsbruck, 1948), esp. pp. 115–46, and Rudolf Kassner, *Buch der Erinnerung* (Leipzig, 1938); and a brief biographical sketch by Otto Graf zu Stolberg-Wernigerode in *Neue deutsche Biographie*, vol. 3 (Berlin, 1957), pp. 187–89. A thorough description of Chamberlain's life up to 1914 is contained in Field, "Houston Stewart Chamberlain."

7. Chamberlain to Hans v. Wolzogen, 15 November 1897, *Briefe*, vol. 1, p. 60.

8. Chamberlain, *Lebenswege*, pp. 34ff.

9. Ibid., p. 37.

10. Chamberlain to Oberbürgermeister Casselmann, 30 August 1914, *Briefe*, vol. 1, p. 241.

11. Chamberlain, *Lebenswege*, p. 53; "Erinnerungen aus dem Jahre 1870," *Deutsches Wesen* (Munich, 1916). This was the meeting at which the French ambassador presented the demands of his government, which, transmitted to Bismarck in the celebrated Ems Telegram, became the pretext for war between Prussia and France. The fact that Chamberlain first publicized this account in 1915 suggests that he may well have concocted it for wartime purposes.

12. Chamberlain, *Lebenswege*, p. 60.

13. Anna Chamberlain, *Meine Erinnerungen*, pp. 1ff.

14. Chamberlain, *Lebenswege*, pp. 77, 82; Anna Chamberlain, *Meine Erinnerungen*, pp. 46, 108, 113. Chamberlain published his doctoral dissertation under the title, *Recherches sur la sève ascendante* (Neuchâtel, 1897).

15. Chamberlain, *Lebenswege*, p. 161.

16. Ibid., pp. 119, 162.

17. Ibid., pp. 159, 181.

18. Ibid., p. 218.

19. Ibid., p. 235. For a striking description of this premiere, see Malvida von Meysenbug, *Memoiren einer Idealistin*, p. 344, who cites Daniela von Bülow's reaction to *Parsifal*: "I wish I had a deadly enemy so that at this moment I could forgive him."

20. Cosima Wagner to Chamberlain, 17 September 1888, in Pretzsch, *Briefwechsel*, p. 22.

21. Cosima Wagner to Eva Wagner, 1888, ibid., p. 8.

22. Chamberlain to Siegfried Wagner, July 1896, *Briefe*, vol. 1, p. 43.

23. "Le Wagnérisme en 1888" and "Notes chronologiques sur l'anneau du Nibelung," *Revue wagnérienne* 3 (1888), 263–76, 281–92. For a discussion of the Wagnerian movement in France, see Leon Poliakov, *The Aryan Myth*, trans. Edmund Howard, pp. 311–12.

24. "Die Sprache in Tristan und Isolde und ihr Verhältnis zur Musik," *Allgemeine Musik-Zeitung* 15 (1888), 283–87, 306–8.

25. "The Personal Side of Richard Wagner" and "How Richard Wagner Wrote his Operas," *The Ladies' Home Journal* 15 (October, 1898), 11–12; (November 1898), 11–12.

26. Chamberlain to Hans Wolzogen, 15 November 1897, *Briefe*, vol. 1, p. 57.

27. Chamberlain, *Lebenswege*, pp. 1, 124.

28. Chamberlain to Cosima Wagner, 17 October 1888, in Pretzsch, *Briefwechsel*, p. 26.

29. Chamberlain, *Das Drama Richard Wagner's*, 4th ed. (Leipzig, 1910), pp. 143ff.

30. Ibid., p. 24.

31. Ibid., pp. 13–14, 67ff.

32. See Chapter 1.

33. Chamberlain to Ehrenfels, 7 November 1894, *Briefe*, vol. 1, p. 16.

34. Ibid., p. 20.

35. Chamberlain, *Die Grundlagen des neunzehnten Jahrhunderts*, 2 vols., 10th ed. (Munich, 1912), vol. 2, p. 985.

36. Chamberlain to Ehrenfels, 7 November 1894, *Briefe*, vol. 1, p. 19.

37. Chamberlain, "Büchners Sturz," *Neue Deutsche Rundschau* 6 (1895), 573.

38. Ibid., p. 574.

39. *Lebenswege*, p. 120.

40. Ibid., p. 6.

41. Keyserling, *Reise durch die Zeit*, p. 142; Chamberlain to Sidonie Peter, 23 December 1914, *Briefe*, vol. 1, p. 272.

42. *Kritische Urteile*, pp. 51, 69.

43. Circulation figures from Shirer, *Rise and Fall*, p. 107.

44. Carl Becker, "The Foundations of the Nineteenth Century," *The Dial* 50 (1911), 391. See also Colin Holmes, "Houston Stewart Chamberlain in Great Britain," *Wiener Library Bulletin* 24 (1970), 31–36.

45. Chamberlain to Hugo Bruckmann, 11 February 1915, *Briefe*, vol. 1, p. 279.

46. Reinhold Conrad Muschler, *Philipp zu Eulenburg* (Leipzig, 1930), p. 527; Anna Chamberlain, *Meine Erinnerungen*, p. 135.

47. *Die Fackel* 4 (January 1903), 18–20; (February 1903), 17–19.

48. Chamberlain, "Katholische Universitäten," *Die Fackel* 3 (January 1902), 1–32. For Schönerer, see Andrew G. Whiteside, *The Socialism of Fools*.

49. Chamberlain to Studiosus Gokel, 26 March 1915, *Briefe*, vol. 1, p. 302.

50. Chamberlain, "Der voraussetzungslose Mommsen," *Die Fackel* 3 (November 1901), 2.

51. Ibid., 4–5.

52. Chamberlain to Anna Chamberlain, 29 January 1905, in Anna Chamberlain, *Meine Erinnerungen*, p. 159.

53. Keyserling, *Reise durch die Zeit*, p. 125.

54. Chamberlain to William II, 11 December 1908, *Briefe*, vol. 2, p. 231.

55. Keyserling, *Reise durch die Zeit*, p. 130.

56. The diagnosis of syphilis is based on the findings of Philip Wults, who is preparing a book on the Wagner family. On the other hand, Keyserling, *Reise durch die Zeit*, p. 131, claims that Chamberlain suffered from multiple sclerosis, while Stolberg-Wernigerode, *Neue deutsche Biographie*, vol. 3, p. 187, speaks of mercury poisoning.

57. William II to Chamberlain, 21 November 1921, *Briefe*, vol. 2, p. 260.

58. Schweitzer to Chamberlain, 23 July 1922, in Donald E. Thomas, Jr., "Idealism, Romanticism, and Race: The Weltanschauung of Houston Stewart Chamberlain" (Ph.D. diss., U. of Chicago, 1971), p. 178.

59. Ibid., p. 176.

60. Chamberlain, *Hammer oder Amboss* (Munich, 1916), pp. 29ff., 49ff.; Chamberlain to Max von Baden, 16 May 1916, *Briefe*, vol. 2, p. 16.

61. Chamberlain to Hitler, 7 October 1923, *Briefe*, vol. 2, p. 125.

62. Joseph Stolzing-Cerny to Eva Chamberlain, 19 October 1923, in Donald E. Thomas, Jr., "Idealism, Romanticism, and Race," p. 258.

63. Chamberlain contributed to a pamphlet entitled, *Was denkt der deutsche Denker, der deutsche Soldat, der deutsche Arbeiter über Adolf Hitler, den Herold des völkischen Gross-deutschland?* (Munich, n.d.).

CHAPTER ELEVEN

1. Chamberlain, *Wehr und Gegenwehr* (Munich, 1912).

2. Chamberlain, *Die Grundlagen*, vol. 2, pp. 1122–123; English version, *The Foundations of the Nineteenth Century*, vol. 2, p. 490.

3. *Die Grundlagen*, vol. 1, pp. 221ff.

4. Ibid., vol. 1, pp. 239ff.

5. Ibid., vol. 1, pp. 566ff.; vol. 2, pp. 641ff. Shaw is cited in Chamberlain, *Briefe*, vol. 1, p. 334.

6. *Die Grundlagen*, vol. 2, pp. 777ff., 1089ff.

7. Chamberlain, *Neue Kriegsaufsätze* (Munich, 1915), p. 48.

8. *Die Grundlagen*, vol. 1, p. 378.

9. Chamberlain, *Immanuel Kant* (Munich, 1905), p. 695.

10. The racial anthropologist Ludwig Woltmann (1871–1907) supported Chamberlain's contentions in *Die Germanen und die Renaissance in Italien* (Leipzig, 1905).

11. *Die Grundlagen*, vol. 1, pp. 592ff., 618ff.; vol. 2, 737ff., 828ff., 895ff., 927ff., 1039ff.

12. Ibid., vol. 2, p. 1101.

13. Ibid., vol. 1, pp. 19, 632.

14. Ibid., vol. 1, p. 322.

15. Ibid., vol. 1, p. 536.

16. Ibid., vol. 1, pp. 162–263, 480ff.

17. See Leo Kuper, eds., *Race, Science and Society* (New York, 1974), and Raphael Patai and Jennifer Patai Wing, *The Myth of the Jewish Race*.

18. *Die Grundlagen*, vol. 1, pp. 317–18.
19. Ibid., vol. 1, p. 322; *Wehr und Gegenwehr*, pp. 39ff.
20. *Kritische Urteile*, pp. 31ff.
21. Chamberlain to Ludwig Stein, 19 September 1904, *Briefe*, vol. 1, p. 149.
22. "Die Rassenfrage," *Rasse und Persönlichkeit* (Munich, 1925), p. 74.
23. *Die Grundlagen*, vol. 1, pp. 320, 322.
24. Moeller van den Bruck, *Die Zeitgenossen*, p. 109.
25. *Die Grundlagen*, vol. 1, pp. 314, 343.
26. *Wehr und Gegenwehr*, p. 43.
27. Chamberlain to Ludwig Stein, 19 September 1904, *Briefe*, vol. 1, p. 149.
28. *Die Grundlagen*, vol. 1, pp. 255–56.
29. Ibid., vol. 1, p. 591.
30. Ibid., vol. 1, p. 599.
31. Ibid., vol. 1, pp. 266ff., 544, 574.
32. Chamberlain to William II, 20 February 1902, *Briefe*, vol. 2, p. 151.
33. *Die Grundlagen*, vol. 1, p. 339.
34. *Kritische Urteile*, p. 80.
35. Chamberlain to Ernst v. Wolzogen, 5 February 1900, *Briefe*, vol. 1, p. 83.
36. See George G. Iggers, *The German Conception of History*, p. 5.
37. *Wehr und Gegenwehr*, pp. 21ff.
38. *Die Grundlagen*, vol. 1, p. 536.
39. Chamberlain to J. v. Uexküll, 8 January 1919, *Briefe*, vol. 2, p. 72.
40. Chamberlain to William II, 20 February 1902, *Briefe*, vol. 2, p. 150.
41. *Mensch und Gott* (Munich, 1921), p. 296.
42. Chamberlain to Postrat Pretsch, 30 August 1911, *Briefe*, vol. 1, p. 198.
43. Cited in *Kritische Urteile*, p. 53.
44. Chamberlain to Vult von Steyern, 6 September 1898, *Briefe*, vol. 1, p. 65.
45. *Die Grundlagen*, vol. 1, p. 584.

CHAPTER TWELVE

1. *Immanuel Kant*, p. 7. Hereafter *Kant*, with page references in text.
2. Chamberlain to Bruckmann, 29 March 1912, *Briefe*, vol. 1, p. 202.
3. Wolfgang Leppmann, *The German Image of Goethe*, p. 176; see also Heinz Kindermann, *Das Goethebild des zwanzigsten Jahrhunderts*, pp. 68–77.
4. (Mathias Matzek), "Goethes Begriff von der Persönlichkeit," Goethe Prize Essay, Carl Schurz Memorial Foundation, 1933. There is no indication when the plagiarism was detected.
5. Chamberlain to William II, 31 December 1905, *Briefe*, vol. 2, p. 219.
6. "Die grösste Angelegenheit des Menschen ist zu wissen, was man sein muss, um ein Mensch zu sein."
7. Chamberlain, *Goethe*, 5th ed. (Munich, 1932), pp. 337ff.
8. *Kant*, pp. 63–66, 107, 118, 123–25, 142, 153–69, 209.
9. *Kant*, pp. 507ff. An unfinished manuscript of Chamberlain's doctrine of *Gestalt*, first formulated in the late 1890s, was published posthumously under the editorship of the biologist J. von Uexküll, *Natur und Leben* (Munich, 1928). Chamberlain may have been influenced by his friend Christian von Ehrenfels, whose pioneering article, "Über Gestaltqualitäten," appeared in 1890.

10. See Arthur Koestler, *The Act of Creation*, p. 120 (on the polarity of logic and intuition) and p. 146 (on creativity in scientific discovery).
11. Chamberlain, *Politische Ideale*, 2nd ed. (Munich, 1915), p. 100.
12. *Goethe*, pp. 740ff.
13. See Lukács, *Die Zerstörung der Vernunft*, p. 556.

<h2 style="text-align:center">CHAPTER THIRTEEN</h2>

1. Chamberlain to Max von Baden, 19 March 1915, *Briefe*, vol. 2, p. 299.
2. See Fritz Stern, "The Political Consequences of the Unpolitical German," *History*, 3 (September 1960), 104–34.
3. *Politische Ideale*, p. 92.
4. Chamberlain, *Die Zuversicht* (Munich, 1915), p. 15.
5. Chamberlain, *Ideal und Macht* (Munich, 1916), p. 35.
6. *Die Zuversicht*, p. 11.
7. Chamberlain, *Neue Kriegsaufsätze* (Munich, 1915), p. 89.
8. Chamberlain to William II, 20 February 1902, *Briefe*, vol. 2, pp. 158, 160; *Politische Ideale*, pp. 84–85.
9. Examples of *völkisch* attacks on Wilhelmine policies include Daniel Fryman (pseudonym of Heinrich Class), *Wenn ich der Kaiser wär'*, and Adolf Bartels, *Der völkische Gedanke*. Because of Chamberlain's later opposition to monarchism, Gerd-Klaus Kaltenbrunner, "Wahnfried und die Grundlagen," in *Propheten des Nationalismus*, p. 106, described him as a foe of the establishment, opposed to the traditional conservatism of throne and altar. But Chamberlain criticized traditional institutions in Germany only because they no longer seemed to provide a secure bulwark against the left.
10. Chamberlain to William II, 4 February 1903, *Briefe*, vol. 2, p. 168. His protestations notwithstanding, Chamberlain enjoyed his status as an Englishman abroad and complained about the ease with which British passports (as well as peerages) could be obtained.
11. Ibid., p. 171.
12. William II to Chamberlain, 16 February 1903, ibid., pp. 188–89.
13. Chamberlain to Graf Pückler, 18 September 1914, *Briefe*, vol. 1, p. 245.
14. Chamberlain, *Kriegsaufsätze* (Munich, 1915), pp. 19, 47; *Politische Ideale*, p. 82.
15. Chamberlain to Basil Hall Chamberlain, 30 October 1914, *Briefe*, vol. 1, p. 262. Basil Hall Chamberlain became a well-known orientalist who published numerous volumes on Japanese language and culture.
16. *Politische Ideale*, pp. 74, 76.
17. Ibid., pp. 37, 72.
18. *Ideal und Macht*, pp. 23–24.
19. Chamberlain to William II, 4 February 1903, *Briefe*, vol. 2, p. 169.
20. Ibid., p. 160.
21. Chamberlain to Max von Baden, 22 September 1914, ibid., p. 249.
22. *Politische Ideale*, p. 60.
23. Ibid., p. 62.
24. Ibid., p. 54.
25. Ibid., p. 30.
26. *Kriegsaufsätze*, pp. 20, 22.
27. *Politische Ideale*, pp. 39–40.
28. *Die Zuversicht*, pp. 20–21.
29. *Politische Ideale*, pp. 26, 72.

30. Chamberlain to J. F. Lehmann, 26 August 1916, *Briefe*, vol. 2, p. 35.
31. *Politische Ideale*, pp. 101, 112.
32. Ibid., p. 70.
33. Chamberlain to Alicehié, 5 November 1895, *Briefe*, vol. 1, p. 32.
34. *Mensch und Gott*, p. 136.
35. Chamberlain to Generalmajor Hagen, 30 December 1914, *Briefe*, vol. 1, p. 274.
36. Chamberlain to Lehmann, 22 April 1916, *Briefe*, vol. 2, p. 14.
37. Chamberlain to Freiherr von Seckendorff, 24 December 1918, ibid., p. 62.
38. Chamberlain, *Drei Vorworte* (Munich, 1923), p. 19.
39. Chamberlain to Dr. Wildgrube, 3 January 1919, *Briefe*, vol. 2, p. 65.
40. *Drei Vorworte*, p. 12.
41. Chamberlain to J. v. Uexküll, 8 January 1919, *Briefe*, vol. 2, pp. 71–72.
42. *Mensch und Gott*, p. 18.
43. Chamberlain to Hitler, 7 October 1923, *Briefe*, vol. 2, p. 125.

CHAPTER FOURTEEN

1. Mohler, *Die konservative Revolution*, pp. 38–57, and Martin Greiffenhagen, *Das Dilemma des Konservatismus in Deutschland*, pp. 241–56.
2. This is the title of a book by Edgar Julius Jung, *Die Herrschaft der Minderwärtigen. Ihr Zerfall und ihre Ablösung durch ein neues Reich*.
3. For a description of the *Mittelstand* and its ideology, see Robert Gellately, *The Politics of Economic Despair*, pp. 1–11; Volkov, *The Rise of Popular Antimodernism*, pp. 123–46; Herman Lebovics, *Social Conservatism and the Middle Classes in Germany, 1914–1944*, pp. 3–48; Heinrich August Winkler, "From Social Protectionism to National Socialism: The German Small–Business Movement in Comparative Perspective," *Journal of Modern History* 48 (March, 1976), 1–18, and *Mittelstand, Demokratie, und Nationalsozialismus*, pp. 100–20 and 157–82.
4. Greiffenhagen, *Das Dilemma des Konservatismus*, pp. 291–301. An interesting document of conservative hostility to Nazism is Friedrich Reck-Malleczewen, *The Diary of a Man in Despair*. See also Hermann Rauschning, *The Revolution of Nihilism*.
5. Reinhard Kühnl, *Die nationalsozialistische Linke 1925–1930*, pp. 245–61.
6. See George K. Romoser, "The Politics of Uncertainty: The German Resistance Movement," *Social Research* 31 (Spring, 1964), 73–93.

BIBLIOGRAPHY

I. Works by and on Heinrich von Stein

Stein's Major Works (by date of publication)

Über Wahrnehmung. Dissertation. Berlin: Duncker, 1877.
Die Ideale des Materialismus. Lyrische Philosophie von Armand Pensier. 1878.
Vol. 1 of *Gesammelte Dichtungen.* Edited by Friedrich Poske. Leipzig: Insel
Verlag, n.d. [1917].
*Über die Bedeutung des dichterischen Elementes in der Philosophie des Giordano
Bruno.* Habilitationsschrift. Halle, 1881.
Helden und Welt. Dramatische Bilder. 1883. Vol. 2 of *Gesammelte Dichtungen.*
Edited by Friedrich Poske. Leipzig: Insel Verlag, n.d. [1917].
(with Glasenapp, Carl Friedrich.) *Wagner-Lexikon. Hauptbegriffe der Kunst-und
Weltanschauung Richard Wagners.* Stuttgart: J. G. Cotta, 1883.
Die Entstehung der neueren Ästhetik. 1886. Repr. Hildesheim: Georg Olms, 1964.
Goethe und Schiller. Beiträge zur Ästhetik der deutschen Klassiker. 1887. Leipzig:
Reclam, n.d.
Aus dem Nachlass. Dramatische Bilder und Erzählungen. 1888. Vol. 3 of *Gesam-
melte Dichtungen.* Edited by Friedrich Poske. Leipzig: Insel Verlag, n.d.
[1917].
Vorlesungen über Aesthetik. Nach vorhandenen Aufzeichnungen bearbeitet. Stutt-
gart: J. G. Cotta, 1897.
"*Weltpolitik* von C. Frantz." *Schmeitzners Internationale Monatsschrift,* 1 (1882).
Zur Kultur der Seele. Gesammelte Aufsätze. Edited be Friedrich Poske. Stuttgart:
J. G. Cotta, 1906.

Letters

Förster-Nietzsche, Elisabeth. "Friedrich Nietzsche und Heinrich von Stein." *Neue
Deutsche Rundschau (Freie Bühne)* 11 (1900): 747–62.
Wolzogen, Hans von, ed. *Heinrich von Steins Briefwechsel mit Hans von Wolzo-
gen. Ein Beitrag zur Geschichte des Bayreuther Gedankens.* Berlin: B. Behr's
Verlag, 1914.

Anthology

Ralfs, Günter, ed. *Heinrich von Stein, Idee und Welt. Das Werk des Philosophen
und Dichters.* Stuttgart: Alfred Kröner, 1940.

Books and Articles on Stein

Chamberlain, Houston Stewart. "Un Philosophe wagnérien: Heinrich von Stein."
Revue des deux Mondes 159 (1900): 831–58.

————, and Poske, Friedrich. *Heinrich von Stein und seine Weltanschauung.* Leipzig: Georg Heinrich Meyer, 1903.

Ettlinger, Max. "Heinrich von Steins ästhetische Weltanschauung." *Hochland* 1 (1903-04): 610-15.

Glockner, Hermann. *Heinrich von Stein. Schicksal einer deutschen Jugend.* Tübingen: J. C. B. Mohr, 1934.

Schmidt, Ferdinand Jakob. "Stein." In *Allgemeine Deutsche Biographie.* Vol. 54, pp. 456-59. Leipzig: Duncker & Humblot, 1908.

Stackelberg, Roderick. "The Role of Heinrich von Stein in Nietzsche's Emergence as a Critic of Wagnerian Idealism and Cultural Nationalism." *Nietzsche-Studien* 5 (1976): 178-93.

Wahnes, G. H. *Heinrich von Stein und sein Verhältnis zu Richard Wagner und Friedrich Nietzsche.* Dissertation. Jena, 1926.

II. Works by and on Friedrich Lienhard

Lienhard's Major Works
(by date of publication)

Naphtali. 1888, n.p.

"Reformation der Literatur." *Die Gesellschaft. Monatsschrift für Literatur und Kunst* 4 (1888): 145-58, 224-38.

Weltrevolution. 1889, n.p.

Die weisse Frau. 1889, n.p.

Lieder eines Elsässers. 1895, n.p.

Wasgaufahrten. 1896. 23rd ed. Stuttgart: Greiner & Pfeiffer, n.d.

Gottfried von Strassburg. Dramatische Dichtung in fünf Aufzügen. 1897. 2nd ed. Stuttgart: Greiner & Pfeiffer, 1902.

Odilia. Legende. Strassburg: Schlesier & Sctiweiktiardt, 1898.

König Arthur. 1900. 3rd ed. Stuttgart: Greiner & Pfeiffer, 1908.

Münchhausen. Lustspiel. Leipzig: G. H. Meyer, 1900.

Helden, Bilder und Gestalten. Leipzig: G. H. Meyer, 1900.

Die Schildbürger. Frühlingsdichtung in 10 Gesängen. 1900. 2nd ed. Stuttgart: Greiner & Pfeiffer, 1906.

Neue Ideale nebst Vorherrschaft Berlins. Gesammelte Aufsätze. 1900-1901. 4th ed. Stuttgart: Greiner & Pfeiffer, 1920.

Till Eulenspiegel. Dramatische Dichtung in drei Teilen. 1901. 4th ed. Stuttgart: Greiner & Pfeiffer, 1911.

Gedichte. 1902. 2nd ed. Stuttgart: Greiner & Pfeiffer, 1906.

Thüringer Tagebuch. 1903. Stuttgart: Greiner & Pfeiffer, 1910.

"Bedenken wider Ibsen." *Hochland* 1 (1903): 160-66.

Wieland der Schmied. Dramatische Dichtung. 1905. 3rd ed. Stuttgart: Greiner & Pfeiffer, 1913.

Wartburg. Dramatische Dichtung in drei Teilen. 1903-1906. Stuttgart: Greiner & Pfeiffer, n.d.

Wege nach Weimar. Beiträge zur Erneuerung des Idealismus. 6 vols. 1905-1908. 2nd ed. Stuttgart: Greiner & Pfeiffer, 1911.

(ed.) *Friedrich der Grosse. Auswahl aus seinen Schriften und Briefen.* Stuttgart: Greiner & Pfeiffer, n.d.

Das klassische Weimar. 1908. 5th ed. Leipzig: Quelle & Meyer, 1926.

Oberlin. Roman aus der Revolutionszeit im Elsass. 1910. 13th ed. Stuttgart: Greiner & Pfeiffer, n.d.

Odysseus auf Ithaka. Dramatische Dichtung. Stuttgart: Greiner & Pfeiffer, 1911.

Der Spielmann. Roman aus der Gegenwart. 1913. 10th ed. Stuttgart: Greiner & Pfeiffer, n.d.

Ahasver am Rhein. Trauerspiel aus der Gegenwart in drei Aufzügen. Stuttgart: Greiner & Pfeiffer, 1914.

Parsifal und Zarathustra. Vortrag. Stuttgart: Greiner & Pfeiffer, 1914.

Der deutsche Elsass. Vol. 17 of *Der deutsche Krieg*, edited by Ernst Jäckh. Stuttgart: Deutsche Verlagsanstalt, 1914.

Deutschlands europäische Sendung. Kriegsgedanken. Stuttgart: Greiner & Pfeiffer, 1914.

Wohin gehört Elsass-Lothringen? Zürich: Rascher & Cie., 1915.

(with Kannengiesser, Paul, eds.) *Schicksale einer Verschleppten in Frankreich von ihr selbst erzählt.* Strassburg: Strassburger Druckerei, 1915.

Der Einsiedler und sein Volk. Novellen. Stuttgart: Greiner & Pfeiffer, 1915.

Lebensfrucht. Gesammelte Gedichte. Stuttgart: Greiner & Pfeiffer, 1915.

Phidias. Stuttgart: Greiner & Pfeiffer, 1916.

Deutsche Dichtung in ihren geschichtlichen Grundzügen. 1916. 2nd ed. Leipzig: Quelle & Meyer, 1919.

Jugendjahre. Erinnerungen. 10th ed. Stuttgart: Greiner & Pfeiffer, 1918.

Westmark. Roman aus dem gegenwärtigen Elsass. 24th ed. Stuttgart: Greiner & Pfeiffer, 1919.

Der Meister der Menschheit. 3 vols. Stuttgart: Greiner & Pfeiffer, 1919–1921.

Was wir verloren haben—Entrissenes doch nie vergessenes deutsches Land. Berlin: F. Zillessen, 1920.

Wer zuletzt lacht. Ein Schlossidyll. Stuttgart: Greiner & Pfeiffer, 1921.

Unter dem Rosenkreuz. Ein Hausbuch aus dem Herzen Deutschlands. Stuttgart: Greiner & Pfeiffer, 1925.

Meisters Vermächtnis. Ein Roman vom heimlichen König. 3rd ed. Stuttgart: Greiner & Pfeiffer, 1927.

Das Landhaus bei Eisenach. Ein Burschenschaftsroman aus dem 19. Jahrhundert. Leipzig: A. Deichertsche Verlagsbuchhandlung, 1928.

ANTHOLOGY

Bülow, Paul, ed. *Von Weibes Wonne und Wert. Worte und Gedanken von Friedrich Lienhard.* Leipzig: Max Koch, 1921.

BOOKS AND ARTICLES ON LIENHARD

Bartels, Adolf. *Die deutsche Dichtung der Gegenwart. Die Jüngsten.* Leipzig: H. Haessel Verlag, 1921.

Bergmann, Klaus. *Agrarromantik und Grossstadtfeindschaft.* Meisenheim am Glan: Anton Hain, 1970.

Bülow, Paul. *Friedrich Lienhard. Der Mensch und das Werk.* Leipzig: Max Koch, 1923.

Gaude, Paul. *Das Odysseusthema in der neueren deutschen Literatur, besonders bei Hauptmann und Lienhard.* Dissertation. Halle: Erhardt Karras, 1916.

Gierke, Wilhelm Edward, ed. *Friedrich Lienhard und Wir. Dem deutschen Dichter Friedrich Lienhard zum 50. Geburtstage.* Stuttgart: Greiner & Pfeiffer, 1915.

Gruber, Karl. "Dichter-Erzieher. Anlässlich eines *Thüringer Tagebuchs* von Fritz Lienhard." *Hochland* 2 (1905): 572–86.

Hamann, Richard, and Hermand, Jost. *Epochen deutscher Kultur von 1870 bis zur Gegenwart.* 4 vols. East Berlin: Akademie-Verlag, 1967.

Hanstein, Adalbert von. *Das jüngste Deutschland. Zwei Jahrzehnte miterlebter Literaturgeschichte.* Leipzig: R. Voigtländer, 1900.

Hermand, Jost. "Gralsmotive um die Jahrhundertwende." In *Von Mainz nach Weimar 1793–1919. Studien zur deutschen Literatur.* Stuttgart: J. B. Metzlersche Verlagsbuchhandlung, 1969.

Kratzsch, Gerhard. *Kunstwart und Dürerbund. Ein Beitrag zur Geschichte der Gebildeten im Zeitalter des Imperialismus.* Göttingen: Vandenhoeck & Ruprecht, 1969.

Langenbucher, Hellmuth. *Friedrich Lienhard und sein Anteil am Kampf um die deutsche Erneuerung.* Hamburg: Agentur des Rauhen Hauses, 1935.

Laubenthal, Wilhelm. *Der Gedanke einer geistigen Erneuerung Deutschlands im deutschen Schrifttum von 1871 bis zum Weltkrieg.* Frankfurt/Main: Moritz Diesterweg, 1938.

Muth, Karl. "Oberflächen-Kultur." *Hochland* 1 (1903): 233–37.

Pross, Harry. *Literatur und Politik. Geschichte und Programme der politisch-literarischen Zeitschriften im deutschen Sprachgebiet seit 1870.* Olten and Freiburg: Walter-Verlag, 1963.

Rossbacher, Karlheinz. *Heimatkunstbewegung und Heimatroman. Zu einer Literatursoziologie der Jahrhundertwende.* Stuttgart: Klett, 1975.

Soergel, Albert. *Dichtung und Dichter der Zeit. Eine Schilderung der deutschen Literatur der letzten Jahrzehnte.* 2 vols. 21st ed. Leipzig: R. Voigtländer, 1928.

Stackelberg, Roderick. "*Völkisch* Idealism and National Socialism: The Case of Freidrich Lienhard." *The Wiener Library Bulletin* 29 (1976): 34–41.

III. Works by and on Houston Stewart Chamberlain

Chamberlain's Major Works (by date of publication)

"Notes chronologiques sur l'anneau du Nibelung." *Revue wagnérienne* (1888): 263–76.

"Le Wagnerisme en 1888." *Revue wagnérienne* (1888): 281–92.

"Die Sprache in Tristan und Isolde und ihr Verhältnis zur Musik." *Allgemeine Musik-Zeitung* 15 (1888): 283–87, 306–8.

Das Drama Richard Wagner's. Eine Anregung. 1892. 4th ed. Leipzig: Breitkopf & Härtel, 1910.

The Wagnerian Drama: An Attempt to Inspire a Better Appreciation of Wagner as a Dramatic Poet. London: John Lane, 1915.

"Büchners Sturz." *Neue Deutsche Rundschau (Freie Bühne)* 6 (1895): 572–84.

Richard Wagner. 1896. 5th ed. Munich: F. Bruckmann, 1910.

Recherches sur la sève ascendante. Neuchâtel: Attinger frères, 1897.

"The Personal Side of Richard Wagner." *The Ladies' Home Journal* 15 (October 1898): 11–12.

"How Richard Wagner Wrote His Operas." *The Ladies' Home Journal* 15 (November 1898): 11–12.

Die Grundlagen des neunzehnten Jahrhunderts. 2 vols. 1899. 10th ed. Munich: F. Bruckmann, 1912.

The Foundations of the Nineteenth Century. 2 vols. Translated by John Lees, with Introduction by George L. Mosse. 1912. Repr. New York: Howard Fertig, 1968.

Parsifal-Märchen. Munich: F. Bruckmann, 1900.

"Der voraussetzungslose Mommsen." *Die Fackel* 3 (November 1901): 1–13.

"Katholische Universitäten." *Die Fackel* 3 (January 1902): 1–32.

Worte Christi. 1902. 2nd ed. Munich: F. Bruckmann, 1902.

Drei Bühnendichtungen. Munich: F. Bruckmann, 1902.

Immanuel Kant. Die Persönlichkeit als Einführung in das Werk. Munich: F. Bruckmann, 1905.

Immanuel Kant: A Study and a Comparison with Goethe, Leonardo Da Vinci, Bruno, Plato and Descartes. 2 vols. Translated by Lord Redesdale. London: John Lane, 1914.

Arische Weltanschauung. 1906. 2nd ed. Munich: F. Bruckmann, 1912.

Wehr und Gegenwehr: Vorworte zur dritten und zur vierten Auflage der Grundlagen des neunzehnten Jahrhunderts. Munich: F. Bruckmann, 1912.

Goethe. Munich: F. Bruckmann, 1912.

Kriegsaufsätze. 11th ed. Munich: F. Bruckmann, 1915.

Neue Kriegsaufsätze. Munich: F. Bruckmann, 1915.

Die Zuversicht. Munich: F. Bruckmann, 1915.

Politische Ideale. 2nd ed. Munich: F. Bruckmann, 1915.

Ideal und Macht. Munich: F. Bruckmann, 1916.

Deutsches Wesen (Ausgewählte Aufsätze). Munich: F. Bruckmann, 1916.

Hammer oder Amboss. Dritte Reihe der Kriegsaufsätze. Munich: F. Bruckmann, 1916.

Lebenswege meines Denkens. Munich: F. Bruckmann, 1919.

Mensch und Gott. Betrachtungen über Religion und Christentum. Munich: F. Bruckmann, 1921.

Herrn Hinkebein's Schädel. Gedankenhumoreske. Munich: F. Bruckmann, 1922.

Drei Vorworte. Munich: F. Bruckmann, 1923.

Rasse und Persönlichkeit. Aufsätze. Munich: F. Bruckmann, 1925.

Natur und Leben. Edited by J. von Uexküll. Munich: F. Bruckmann, 1928.

LETTERS

Chamberlain, Houston Stewart. *Briefe 1882–1924 und Briefwechsel mit Kaiser Wilhelm II.* 2 vols. Munich: F. Bruckmann, 1928.
Pretzsch, Paul, ed. *Cosima Wagner und Houston Stewart Chamberlain im Briefwechsel 1888–1908.* Leipzig: Reclam, 1934.

ANTHOLOGIES

Döring, Oskar, ed. *Ein Deutscher namens Chamberlain.* Berlin: Julius Beltz, 1937.
Schmidt, Hardy L. *Chamberlain. Auswahl aus seinen Werken.* Breslau: Ferdinand Hirt, 1934.
Schott, Georg. *Houston Stewart Chamberlain, der Seher des Dritten Reiches. Das Vermächtnis Houston Stewart Chamberlains an das deutsche Volk in einer Auslese aus seinen Werken.* Munich: F. Bruckmann, 1934.

BOOKS AND ARTICLES ON CHAMBERLAIN

Baentsch, D. "Houston Stewart Chamberlains Vorstellungen über die Religion der Semiten spez. der Israeliten." *Zeitschrift für Philosophie und Pädagogik* 12 (1904–05): 16–28, 124–39, 204–21, 291–306.
Baylen, Joseph O., and Munster, Rolf F. "Adolph Hitler as Seen by Houston Stewart Chamberlain: A Forgotten Letter." *Duquesne Review* 12, No. 2 (Fall 1967): 81–88.
Becker, Carl. "The Foundations of the Nineteenth Century." *The Dial* 50 (1911): 389–92.
Bulle, Oscar, et. al. *Die Grundlagen des neunzehnten Jahrhunderts und Immanuel Kant. Kritische Urteile.* 3rd ed. Munich: F. Bruckmann, 1909.
Chamberlain, Anna. *Meine Erinnerungen an Houston Stewart Chamberlain.* Munich: Oskar Beck, n.d.
Dippel, Martin. *Houston Stewart Chamberlain.* Munich: Deutscher Volksverlag, 1938.
Eckhart, Waltraut. *Houston Stewart Chamberlains Naturanschauung.* Leipzig: Armanen-Verlag, 1941.
Field, Geoffrey G. "Houston Stewart Chamberlain: Prophet of Bayreuth." Ph.D. dissertation, Columbia University, 1972.
Geprägs, Adolf. *Germanentum und Christentum bei Houston Stewart Chamberlain.* Göttingen: Vandenhoeck & Ruprecht, 1938.
Grabs, Rudolf. *Wegbereiter Deutschen Christentums. Paul de Lagarde und Houston Stewart Chamberlain.* Weimar: Verlag Deutsche Christen, n.d.
Grauert, Hermann. *Dante und Houston Stewart Chamberlain.* 2nd ed. Freiburg: Herdersche Verlagsbuchhandlung, 1904.
Grützmacher, D. R. H. *Kritiker und Neuschöpfer der Religion im zwanzigsten Jahrhundert. Keyserling—L. Ziegler—Blüher—Chamberlain—Steiner—Scholz—Scheler—Hauck.* Leipzig: A. Deichertsche Verlagsbuchhandlung, 1921.

Hertz, Friedrich. *Race and Civilization*. Translated by A. S. Levetus and W. Entz. 1915, 1928. Repr. KTAV Publishing House, 1970.

Holmes, Colin. "Houston Stewart Chamberlain in Great Britain." *The Wiener Library Bulletin* 24 (1970): 31–36.

Kaltenbrunner, Gerd-Klaus. "Houston Stewart Chamberlain—The Most Germanic of Germans." *The Wiener Library Bulletin* 22 (Winter 1967–68): 6–12.

———. "Wahnfried und die Grundlagen: Houston Stewart Chamberlain." In *Propheten des Nationalismus*, edited by Karl Schwedhelm, pp. 105–23. Munich: List Verlag, 1969.

Meyer, Hugo. *Houston Stewart Chamberlain als völkischer Denker*. Munich: F. Bruckmann, 1939.

Nielsen, Will. *Der Lebens- und Gestaltbegriff bei Houston Stewart Chamberlain. Eine Untersuchung seiner Lebenslehre*. Kiel: Schmidt & Klaunig, 1938.

Réal, Jean. "The Religious Conception of Race: Houston Stewart Chamberlain and Germanic Christianity." In *The Third Reich*, with Introduction by Jacques Rueff, pp. 243–86. London: Weidenfeld & Nicolson, 1955.

Rosenberg, Alfred. *Blut und Ehre. Ein Kampf für deutsche Wiedergeburt*. Munich: Franz Eher Verlag, 1934.

———. *Houston Stewart Chamberlain als Verkünder und Begründer einer deutschen Zukunft*. Munich: F. Bruckmann, 1927.

Rouché, Max. "Houston Stewart Chamberlain (1855–1927)." *Études Germaniques* 17 (1962): 390–402.

Schott, Georg. *Das Lebenswerk Chamberlains in Umrissen*. Munich: J. F. Lehmann, 1927.

———. *Das Vermächtnis Houston Stewart Chamberlains*. Stuttgart: Tazzelwurm Verlag, 1940.

Schroeder, Leopold von. *Houston Stewart Chamberlain. Ein Abriss seines Lebens auf Grund eigener Mitteilungen*. Munich: J. F. Lehmann, 1918.

Schüler, Winfried. *Der Bayreuther Kreis von seiner Entstehung bis zum Ausgang der wilhelminischen Ära. Wagnerkult und Kulturreform im Geiste völkischer Weltanschauung*. Münster: Aschendorff, 1971.

Seillière, Ernest. *Houston Stewart Chamberlain. Le plus récent philosophe du pangermanisme mystique*. Paris, 1917.

Stackelberg, Roderick. "Houston S. Chamberlain: From Monarchism to National Socialism." *The Wiener Library Bulletin* 31 (1978): 118–25.

Stolberg-Wernigerode, Otto Graf zu. "Chamberlain." In *Neue deutsche Biographie*. Vol. 3, pp. 187–89. Berlin: Duncker & Humblot, 1957.

Stutzinger, Gerhard. *Die politischen Anschauungen Houston Stewart Chamberlains*. Bottrop: Wilhelm Postberg, 1938.

Thomas, Donald E., Jr. "Idealism, Romanticism, and Race: The Weltanschauung of Houston Stewart Chamberlain." Ph.D. dissertation, University of Chicago, 1971.

Vanselow, Albert. *Das Werk Houston Stewart Chamberlains. Eine Bibliographie*. Munich, 1927.

Vollrath, Wilhelm. *Houston Stewart Chamberlain und seine Theologie*. Erlangen: Palm & Enke, 1937.

————. *Thomas Carlyle und Houston Stewart Chamberlain. Zwei Freunde Deutschlands.* Munich: J. F. Lehmann, 1935.

IV. OTHER WORKS CITED OR CONSULTED

Anchor, Robert. *Germany Confronts Modernization: German Culture and Society, 1790–1890.* Lexington, Mass.: D. C. Heath, 1972.

Arent, Wilhelm; Conradi, Hermann; and Henckell, Karl, eds. *Moderne Dichter-Charaktere.* Leipzig, 1884.

Bahr, Hermann. *Selbstbildnis.* Berlin: S. Fischer, 1923.

Barraclough, Geoffrey. "A New View of German History." *New York Review of Books* (16 November 1972): 25–31.

Bartels, Adolf. *Goethe der Deutsche.* Frankfurt/Main: M. Disterweg, 1932.

————. *Rasse und Volkstum. Gesammelte Aufsätze zur nationalen Weltanschauung.* 2nd ed. Weimar: Alexander Duncker, 1920.

————. *Der völkische Gedanke. Ein Wegweiser.* Weimar: Fritz Fink Verlag, 1923.

Barzum, Jacques. *Darwin, Marx, Wagner: Critique of a Heritage.* 1941. Rev. 2nd ed. Garden City, N.Y.: Doubleday Anchor, 1958.

Biddiss, Michael D. *Father of Racist Ideology: The Social and Political Thought of Count Gobineau.* New York: Weybright & Talley, 1970.

————. *The Age of the Masses: Ideas and Society in Europe Since 1870.* New York: Harper & Row, 1977.

Binion, Rudolph. *Frau Lou: Nietzsche's Wayward Disciple.* Princeton, N.J.: Princeton University Press, 1968.

Bleibtreu, Karl. *Grössenwahn. Pathologischer Roman.* 2 vols. 2nd ed. Jena: Hermann Costenoble, 1889.

————. "Religion und Rasse." *Der Türmer* 26 (October 1924): 19–26.

————. *Revolution der Literatur.* Leipzig: Wilhelm Friedrich, 1886.

Boas, Franz. *Race, Language and Culture.* New York: Macmillan, 1940.

Böhme, Helmut. *Deutschlands Weg zur Grossmacht. Studien zum Verhältnis von Wirtschaft und Staat während der Reichsgründungs-Zeit 1848–1881.* Cologne: Kiepenheuer & Witsch, 1966.

Bowen, Ralph H. *German Theories of the Corporative State with Special Reference to the Period 1870–1919.* New York: McGraw-Hill, 1947.

Bracher, Karl Dietrich. *The German Dictatorship: The Origins, Structure and Effects of National Socialism.* Translated by Jean Steinberg. New York: Praeger, 1970.

Bramstead, Ernest K. *Aristocracy and the Middle Classes in Germany: Social Types in German Literature, 1830–1900.* 1937. Repr. Chicago: University of Chicago Press, 1964.

Butler, Rohan d'O. *The Roots of National Socialism, 1783–1933.* London: Faber & Faber, 1942.

Caralli-Sforza, L. L., and Bodmer, Walter F. *The Genetics of Human Populations.* San Francisco: W. H. Freeman, 1971.

Cecil, Robert. *The Myth of the Master Race: Alfred Rosenberg and Nazi Ideology.* London: B. T. Batsford, 1972.

Class, Heinrich. *Wider den Strom. Vom Werden und Wachsen der nationalen Opposition im alten Reich.* Leipzig: K. F. Koehler, 1932.

———. [Daniel Frymann]. *Wenn ich der Kaiser wär'. Politische Wahrheiten und Notwendigkeiten.* Leipzig: Dieterich'schen Verlagsbuchhandlung, 1912.

Coates, Wilson H., and White, Hayden V. *The Ordeal of Liberal Humanism: An Intellectual History of Western Europe.* Vol. 2. New York: McGraw-Hill, 1970.

Count, Earl W., ed. *This is Race.* New York: Schuman, 1950.

Dehio, Ludwig. *Germany and World Politics in the Twentieth Century.* New York: Alfred A. Knopf, 1960.

Dewey, John. *German Philosophy and Politics.* New York: Henry Holt, 1915.

Dühring, Eugen. *Der Ersatz der Religion durch Vollkommeneres und die Ausscheidung alles Judenthums durch den modernen Völkergeist.* Karlsruhe: H. Reuther, 1883.

———. *Die Grössen der modernen Literatur popular und kritisch nach neuen Gesichtspunkten dargestellt.* 2 vols. 2nd ed. Leipzig: C. G. Naumann, 1904, 1910.

———. *Die Judenfrage als Frage der Rassenschädlichkeit für Existenz, Sitte und Kultur der Völker.* 1880. 3rd ed. Karlsruhe: H. Reuther, 1886.

———. *Kritische Geschichte der Nationalökonomie und des Sozialismus.* 2nd ed. Berlin: Theobald Grieben, 1875.

———. *Leben, Sache und Feinde. Als Hauptwerk und Schlüssel zu seinen sämtlichen Schriften.* Karlsruhe: H. Reuther, 1882.

———. *Der Werth des Lebens.* 3rd ed. Leipzig: Fues's Verlag, 1881.

———. *Wirklichkeitsphilosophie. Phantasmenfreie Naturergründung und gerecht freiheitliche Lebensordnung.* Leipzig: O. R. Reisland, 1895.

Dunn, L. C., and Dobzhansky, Theodosius. *Heredity, Race, and Society.* New York: New American Library, 1952.

Engels, Friedrich. *Herrn Eugen Dührings Umwälzung der Wissenschaft (Anti-Dühring).* 1878. Repr. East Berlin, 1960.

Ergang, R. R. *Herder and the Foundations of German Nationalism.* 1931. Repr. New York: Octagon, 1966.

Erikson, Erik H. *Childhood and Society.* New York: Norton, 1963.

———. *Identity, Youth and Crisis.* New York: Norton, 1968.

———. *Young Man Luther: A Study in Psychoanalysis and History.* New York: Norton, 1958.

Ernst, Paul. *Der Zusammenbruch des deutschen Idealismus. An die Jugend.* Munich: Georg Müller, 1918.

Eucken, Rudolf. *Life's Basis and Life's Ideal: The Fundamentals of a New Philosophy of Life.* Translated by Alban G. Widgery. London: A. & C. Black, 1911.

Fichte, J. G. *Addresses to the German Nation.* Translated by R. F. Jones and G. M. Turnbull. London: Open Court, 1922.

Fischer, Fritz. *Germany's Aims in the First World War.* New York: Norton, 1967.

Förster-Nietzsche, Elisabeth. *Das Leben Friedrich Nietzsche's.* 2 vols. Leipzig: C. G. Naumann, 1904.

Friedrich, Paul. *Das Dritte Reich. Die Tragödie des Individualismus.* Leipzig: Xenien Verlag, 1910.

_____. *Nationalismus oder Weltbürgertum.* Berlin: Reform Verlag Futurig, 1920.

_____. *Schiller und der Neuidealismus.* Leipzig: Xenien Verlag, 1910.

Gasman, Daniel. *The Scientific Origins of National Socialism: Social Darwinism in Ernst Haeckel and the German Monist League.* London: Macdonald, 1971.

Gay, Peter. *The Dilemma of Democratic Socialism.* New York: Columbia University Press, 1952.

_____. *Freud, Jews and Other Germans: Masters and Victims in Modernist Culture.* New York: Oxford University Press, 1978.

Gellately, Robert. *The Politics of Economic Despair: Shopkeepers and German Politics, 1890–1914.* London: Sage, 1974.

Gerstenberger, Heide. *Der revolutionäre Konservatismus. Ein Beitrag zur Analyse des Liberalismus.* Berlin: Duncker & Humblot, 1969.

Glockner, Hermann. *Vom Wesen der deutschen Philosophie.* Stuttgart: W. Kohlhammer, 1941.

Gobineau, Artur Comte de. *Essai sur l'inégalité des races humaines.* 4 vols. 1853–1855. 4th ed. Paris: Firmin-Didot, n.d.

Greiffenhagen, Martin. *Das Dilemma des Konservatismus in Deutschland.* Munich: R. Piper, 1971.

Günther, Hans F. K. *Rassenkunde des deutschen Volkes.* Munich: J. F. Lehmann, 1923.

Haeckel, Ernst. *Die Welträtsel. Gemeinverständliche Studien über monistische Philosophie.* Leipzig: Alfred Kroner, 1918.

Hitler, Adolf. *Mein Kampf.* Translated by Ralph Manheim. Boston: Houghton Mifflin, 1943.

Hofmannsthal, Hugo von. *Das Schrifttum als geistiger Raum der Nation.* Munich: Bremer Presse, 1927.

Holborn, Hajo. "German Idealism in the Light of Social History." In *Germany and Europe: Historical Essays.* Garden City, N.Y.: Doubleday, 1970.

Huch, Rudolf. *Mehr Goethe.* Leipzig: G. H. Meyer, 1899.

Hughes, H. Stuart. *Consciousness and Society: The Reconstruction of European Social Thought, 1890–1930.* New York: Random House, 1958.

_____. *The Sea Change: The Migration of Social Thought, 1930–1965.* New York: Harper & Row, 1975.

Iggers, George G. *The German Conception of History: The National Tradition of Historical Thought from Herder to the Present.* Middletown, Conn.: Wesleyan University Press, 1968.

Joel, Karl. *Wandlungen der Weltanschauungen. Eine Philosophie-geschichte als Geschichtsphilosophie.* 2 vols. Tübingen: J. C. B. Mohr, 1934.

Johnston, William M. *The Austrian Mind: An Intellectual and Social History, 1848–1938.* Berkeley: University of California Press, 1972.

Jung, Edgar Julius. *Die Herrschaft der Minderwertigen. Ihr Zerfall und ihre Ablösung durch ein neues Reich.* Berlin: Verlag Deutsche Rundschau, 1927.

Kaltenbrunner, Gerd-Klaus. "Vom Konkurrenten des Karl Marx zum Vorläufer

Hitlers: Eugen Dühring." In *Propheten des Nationalismus*, edited by Karl Schwedhelm. Munich: List Verlag, 1969.

Kassner, Rudolf. *Buch der Erinnerung*. Leipzig: Insel Verlag, 1938.

Kaufmann, Walter A. *Nietzsche: Philosopher, Psychologist, Anti-Christ*. Princeton, N.J.: Princeton University Press, 1950.

Kehr, Eckart. *Der Primat der Innenpolitik. Gesammelte Aufsätze zur preussisch-deutschen Sozialgeschichte des 19, und 20. Jahrhundert*, edited by Hans-Ulrich Wehler. Berlin: Walter de Gruyter, 1965.

Keyserling, Hermann. *Reise durch die Zeit. Ursprünge und Entfaltungen*. Innsbruck: Verlag der Palme, 1948.

Kindermann, Heinz. *Das Goethebild des zwanzigsten Jahrhunderts*. Vienna: Humboldt Verlag, 1952.

Klemperer, Klemens von. *Germany's New Conservatism: Its History and Dilemma in the Twentieth Century*. Princeton, N.J.: Princeton University Press, 1957.

Koestler, Arthur. *The Act of Creation*. New York: Macmillan, 1964.

Kohn, Hans. *The Mind of Germany: The Education of a Nation*. New York: Charles Scribner's, 1960.

Kosch, Wilhelm, ed. *Deutsches Literatur-Lexikon*. 4 vols. 2nd ed. Bern: Francke, 1958.

Kruck, Alfred. *Geschichte des Alldeutschen Verbandes 1890-1939*. Wiesbaden: Franz Steiner Verlag, 1954.

Kühnl, Reinhard. *Die nationalsozialistische Linke 1925-1930*. Meisenheim am Glan: Verlag Anton Hain, 1966.

Lagarde, Paul de. *Deutsche Schriften*. 5th ed. Göttingen: Dieterich'sche Universitäts-Buchhandlung, 1920.

Langbehn, Julius. *Rembrandt als Erzieher. Von einem Deutschen*. Leipzig: C. L. Hirschfeld, 1890.

Laqueur, Walter Z. *Young Germany: A History of the German Youth Movement*. New York: Basic Books, 1962.

Lebovics, Herman. *Social Conservatism and the Middle Classes in Germany, 1914-1933*. Princeton, N.J.: Princeton University Press, 1969.

Leppmann, Wolfgang. *The German Image of Goethe*. Oxford: Clarendon Press, 1961.

Levy, Richard S. *The Downfall of the Anti-Semitic Political Parties in Imperial Germany*. New Haven: Yale University Press, 1975.

Lidtke, Vernon L. "Naturalism and Socialism in Germany." *American Historical Review* 79 (February 1974): 14–37.

Loeb, Jacques. *The Mechanistic Conception of Life*. Edited by Donald Fleming. 1912. Cambridge, Mass.: Harvard University Press, 1964.

Lütgert, D. Wilhelm. *Die Religion des deutschen Idealismus und ihr Ende*. Vol. 4, *Das Ende des Idealismus im Zeitalter Bismarcks*. Gütersloh: C. Bertelsmann, 1930.

Lukács, Georg. *Die Zertsörung der Vernunft*. East Berlin: Aufbau Verlag, 1954.

Lunn, Eugene. *Prophet of Community: The Romantic Socialism of Gustav Landauer*. Berkeley: University of California Press, 1973.

Lutz, Rolland. " 'Father' Jahn and his Teacher-Revolutionaries from the German Student Movement." On-demand supplement to *The Journal of Modern History* 48 (June 1976).

McGovern, William M. *From Luther to Hitler: The History of Fascist-Nazi Political Philosophy.* Boston: Houghton Mifflin, 1941.

McGrath, William J. *Dionysian Art and Populist Politics in Austria.* New Haven: Yale University Press, 1974.

Masur, Gerhard. *Prophets of Yesterday: Studies in European Culture, 1890-1914.* New York: Macmillan, 1961.

Mayer, Arno J. *Dynamics of Counterrevolution in Europe, 1870-1956: An Analytic Framework.* New York: Harper Torchbooks, 1971.

Meysenbug, Malvida von. *Memoiren einer Idealistin.* 2 vols. 1898. Stuttgart: Deutsche Verlags-Anstalt, 1922.

Moeller van den Bruck, Arthur. *Das Dritte Reich.* Berlin: Der Ring, 1923.

————. *Die Deutschen. Unsere Menschengeschichte.* Vol. 6, *Goethe.* Minden in Westfalen: J. C. C. Bruns, 1907.

————. *Die Zeitgenossen. Die Geister—die Menschen.* Minden i. W.: J. C. C. Bruns, 1906.

Mohler, Armin. *Die konservative Revolution in Deutschland 1918-1932. Ein Handbuch.* 2nd rev. ed. Darmstadt: Wissenschaftliche Buchgesellschaft, 1972.

Mosse, George L. *The Crisis of German Ideology: Intellectual Origins of the Third Reich.* New York: Universal Library, 1964.

————. *The Culture of Western Europe.* 2nd ed. Chicago: Rand McNally, 1974.

————. *Germans and Jews: The Right, the Left, and the Search for a "Third Force" in Pre-Nazi Germany.* New York: Grosset & Dunlap, 1970.

————. *The Nationalization of the Masses: Political Symbolism and Mass Movements in Germany from the Napoleonic Wars Through the Third Reich.* New York: Howard Fertig, 1975.

————. *Toward the Final Solution: A History of European Racism.* New York: Howard Fertig, 1978.

Müller, Jakob. *Die Jugendbewegung als deutsche Hauptrichtung neukonservativer Reform.* Zürich: Europa-Verlag, 1971.

Müller, Johannes. *Vom Geheimnis des Lebens. Erinnerungen.* Stuttgart: Deutsche Verlagsanstalt, 1922.

Muschler, Reinhold Conrad. *Philipp zu Eulenburg. Sein Leben und seine Zeit.* Leipzig: Fr. Wilh. Grunow, 1930.

Neurohr, Jean F. *Der Mythos vom dritten Reich. Zur Geistesgeschichte des Nationalsozialismus.* Stuttgart: J. G. Cotta'sche Buchhandlung, 1957.

Nietzsche, Friedrich. *Friedrich Nietzsche: Werke in drei Bänden.* Edited by Karl Schlechta. 3 vols. Munich: Carl Hanser, 1956.

Nolte, Ernst. *Three Faces of Fascism.* Translated by Leila Vennewitz. New York: Holt, Rinehart & Winston, 1966.

Orlow, Dietrich. *The History of the Nazi Party, 1919-1933.* Pittsburgh: University of Pittsburgh Press, 1969.

Pascal, Roy. *From Naturalism to Expressionism: German Literature and Society, 1880–1918.* London: Weidenfeld & Nicolson, 1973.

Patai, Raphael, and Wing, Jennifer Patai. *The Myth of the Jewish Race.* New York: Charles Scribner's, 1975.

Peck, Abraham J. *Radicals and Reactionaries: The Crisis of Conservatism in Wilhelmine Germany.* Washington: University Press of America, 1978.

Pfeiffer, Ernst, ed. *Friedrich Nietzsche, Paul Rée, Lou von Salomé: Die Dokumente ihrer Begegnung.* Frankfurt/Main: Insel Verlag, 1970.

Pflanze, Otto. *Bismarck and the Development of Germany: The Period of Unification, 1815–1871.* Princeton, N.J.: Princeton University Press, 1963.

Plessner, Hellmuth. *Die verspätete Nation. Über die politische Verführbarkeit bürgerlichen Geistes.* Stuttgart: W. Kohlhammer, 1959.

Poliakov, Léon. *The Aryan Myth: A History of Racist and Nationalist Ideas in Europe.* Translated by Edmund Howard. New York: Basic Books, 1974.

———. *The History of Anti-Semitism.* Vol. 3, *From Voltaire to Wagner.* Translated by Miriam Kochan. New York: Vanguard, 1975.

Puhle, Hans Jürgen. *Agrarische Interessenpolitik und preussischer Konservatismus.* Hanover: Verlag für Literatur und Zeitgeschehen, 1966.

———. *Von der Agrarkrise zum Präfaschismus. Thesen zum Stellenwert der agrarischen Interessenverbände in der deutschen Politik am Ende des neunzehnten Jahrhunderts.* Wiesbaden: Steiner, 1972.

Pulzer, Peter G. J. *The Rise of Political Anti-Semitism in Germany and Austria.* New York: John Wiley, 1964.

———. "From Bismarck to the Present." In *Germany: A Companion to German Studies.* Edited by Malcolm Pasley. London: Methuen, 1972.

Rauschning, Hermann. *The Conservative Revolution.* New York: G. P. Putnam's, 1941.

———. *The Revolution of Nihilism: Warning to the West.* New York: Longmans, Green & Co., 1939.

Reck-Malleczewen, Friedrich. *The Diary of a Man in Despair.* Translated by Paul Rubens. New York: Macmillan, 1970.

Richards, Donald Ray. *The German Bestseller in the Twentieth Century: A Complete Bibliography and Analysis, 1915–1940.* Berne: Herbert Lang, 1968.

Ringer, Fritz K. *The Decline of the German Mandarins: The German Academic Community, 1890–1933.* Cambridge, Mass.: Harvard University Press, 1969.

Ritter, Gerhard A., and Kocka, Jürgen, eds. *Deutsche Sozialgeschichte, Dokumente und Skizzen.* 2 vols. Vol. 2, *1870–1914.* Munich: C. H. Beck, 1974.

Röhl, J. C. G. *Germany Without Bismarck: The Crisis of Government in the Second Reich, 1890–1900.* Berkeley: University of California Press, 1967.

Romein, Jan. *The Watershed of Two Eras.* Middletown, Conn.: Wesleyan University Press, 1968.

Romoser, George K. "The Politics of Uncertainty: The German Resistance Movement." *Social Research* 31 (Spring 1964): 73–93.

Root, Winthrop H. *German Criticism of Zola, 1875–1893.* 1931. Repr. New York: AMS Press, 1966.

Rosenberg, Alfred. *Der Mythus des 20. Jahrhunderts. Eine Wertung der seelisch-geistigen Gestaltungskämpfe unserer Zeit.* 111th ed. Munich: Hoheneichen, 1937.

Rosenberg, Hans. *Grosse Depression und Bismarckzeit. Wirtschaftsablauf, Gesellschaft und Politik in Mitteleuropa.* Berlin: de Gruyter, 1967.

————. "Political and Social Consequences of the Great Depression of 1873–1896 in Central Europe." In *Imperial Germany.* Edited by James J. Sheehan. New York: New Viewpoints, 1976.

Ruprecht, Erich, and Bänsch, Dieter, eds. *Literarische Manifeste der Jahrhundertwende 1890–1910.* Stuttgart: J. B. Metzlersche Verlagsbuchhandlung, 1970.

Santayana, George. *The German Mind: A Philosophical Diagnosis.* 1916. Repr. New York: Crowell, 1968.

Schemann, Ludwig. *Die Rasse in den Geisteswissenschaften: Studien zur Geschichte des Rassengedankens.* 3 vols. Munich: J. F. Lehmann, 1930.

Schlaf, Johannes. *Das Dritte Reich.* Berlin: E. Fleischel, 1903.

Schorske, Carl E. "Politics in a New Key: An Austrian Triptych." *Journal of Modern History* 39 (December 1967): 343–86.

————. "The Quest for the Grail: Wagner and Morris." In *The Critical Spirit.* Edited by Kurt H. Wolff and Barrington Moore, Jr. Boston: Beacon, 1967.

Shirer, William L. *The Rise and Fall of the Third Reich: A History of Nazi Germany.* New York: Simon & Schuster, 1960.

Snyder, Louis L. *Roots of German Nationalism.* Bloomington: Indiana University Press, 1978.

Spengler, Oswald. *Der Untergang des Abendlandes. Umrisse einer Morphologie der Weltgeschichte.* 2 vols. Munich: Beck, 1922–1923.

Srbik, Heinrich Ritter von. *Geist und Geschichte vom deutschen Humanismus bis zur Gegenwart.* 2 vols. Vol. 2, 1951. 2nd ed. Salzburg: Otto Müller Verlag, 1964.

Stegmann, Dirk. *Die Erben Bismarcks. Parteien und Verbände in der Spätphase des Wilhelminischen Deutschlands. Sammlungspolitik 1897–1918.* Cologne: Kiepenheuer & Wietsch, 1970.

Stern, Fritz. *The Failure of Illiberalism: Essays on the Political Culture of Modern Germany.* New York: Alfred A. Knopf, 1972.

————. "The Political Consequences of the Unpolitical German." *History* 3 (September 1960): 104–34.

————. *The Politics of Cultural Despair: A Study in the Rise of the Germanic Ideology.* Garden City, N.Y.: Doubleday Anchor, 1965.

Stürmer, Michael, ed. *Das kaiserliche Deutschland. Politik und Gesellschaft 1870–1918.* Düsseldorf: Droste, 1970.

Struve, Walter. *Elites Against Democracy: Leadership Ideals in Bourgeois Political Thought in Germany, 1890–1933.* Princeton, N.J.: Princeton University Press, 1973.

Tal, Uriel. *Christians and Jews in Germany: Religion, Politics, and Ideology in the Second Reich, 1870–1914.* Translated by Noah Jonathan Jacobs. Ithaca, N.Y.: Cornell University Press, 1975.

Treitschke, Heinrich von. *Politics*. 2 vols. Translated by Blanche Dugdale and Torben de Bille. London: Constable, 1916.

Troeltsch, Ernst. "Die Ideen von 1914." In *Deutscher Geist und Westeuropa. Gesammelte kulturphilosophische Aufsätze und Reden*. Tübingen: I. C. B. Mohr, 1925.

Turner, Henry A., Jr. "Fascism and Modernization." *World Politics* 24 (1972): 547–64.

Ullmann, Hermann. *Das neunzehnte Jahrhundert. Volk gegen Masse um die Gestalt Europas*. Jena: Eugen Diederichs, 1930.

Vermeil, Edmond. *Doctrinaires de la Révolution Allemande*. Paris: Fernand Sorlot, 1938.

―――. "The Origin, Nature and Development of German Nationalist Ideology in the 19th and 20th Centuries." In *The Third Reich*. Edited by Jacques Rueff. London: Weidenfeld & Nicolson, 1955.

Viereck, Peter. *Meta-Politics: From the Romantics to Hitler*. New York: Knopf, 1941. Repr. New York: Capricorn Books, 1941.

Volkov, Shulamit. *The Rise of Popular Antimodernism in Germany: The Urban Master Artisans, 1873–1896*. Princeton, N.J.: Princeton University Press, 1978.

Wagner, Richard. *Gesammelte Schriften und Dichtungen*. 10 vols. Leipzig: Fritzsch, 1871–1883.

Wallace, Anthony F. C. *Religion: An Anthropological View*. New York: Random House, 1966.

Wehler, Hans-Ulrich. *Bismarck und der Imperialismus*. Cologne: Kiepenheuer & Witsch, 1969.

―――. *Krisenherde des Kaiserreichs, 1871–1918. Studien zur deutschen Sozial- und Verfassungsgeschichte*. Göttingen: Vandenhoeck & Ruprecht, 1970.

Weiss, John, ed. *The Origins of Modern Consciousness*. Detroit: Wayne State University Press, 1965.

Wernecke, Klaus. *Der Wille zur Weltgeltung. Aussenpolitik und Öffentlichkeit im Kaiserreich am Vorabend des 1. Weltkrieges*. Düsseldorf: Droste, 1970.

Westphal, Otto. *Feinde Bismarcks. Geistige Grundlagen der deutschen Opposition 1848–1918*. Munich: R. Oldenbourg, 1930.

Whiteside, Andrew G. *The Socialism of Fools: Georg Ritter von Schönerer and Austrian Pan-Germanism*. Berkeley: University of California Press, 1975.

Wiesner, J. v. *Erschaffung, Entstehung, Entwicklung und über die Grenzen der Berechtigung des Entwicklungsgedankens*. Berlin: Gebrüder Paetel, 1916.

Windell, George G. "Hitler, National Socialism, and Richard Wagner." *Journal of Central European Affairs* 22 (January 1963): 479–97.

Winkler, Heinrich August. "From Social Protectionism to National Socialism: The German Small-Business Movement in Comparative Perspective." *The Journal of Modern History* 48 (March 1976): 1–18.

―――. *Mittelstand, Demokratie und Nationalsozialismus. Die politische Entwicklung vom Handwerk und Kleinhandel in der Weimarer Republik*. Cologne: Kiepenheuer & Witsch, 1972.

Woltmann, Ludwig. *Die Germanen und die Renaissance in Italien*. Leipzig: Thüringische Verlagsanstalt, 1905.

Young, E. J. *Gobineau und der Rassismus. Eine Kritik der anthropologischen Geschichtstheorie.* Meisenheim am Glan: Verlag Anton Hain, 1968.

Ziegler, Theobald. *Die Geistigen und sozialen Strömungen Deutschlands im 19. und 20. Jahrhundert bis zum Beginn des Weltkrieges.* Berlin: Georg Bondi, 1921.

INDEX